Embedded C

Embedded C

Michael J. Pont

PEARSON

ISBN 978-81-317-1589-5

First Impression, 2008
Nineteenth Impression, 2013
Twentieth Impression

Published by Dorling Kindersley (India) Pvt. Ltd., licensees of Pearson Education in South Asia.

Head Office: 7th Floor, Knowledge Boulevard, A-8(A), Sector-62, Noida 201309, UP, India.
Registered Office: 11 Community Centre, Panchsheel Park, New Delhi 110 017, India.

Printed in India by Saurabh Printers Pvt. Ltd.

This book is dedicated to Sarah

About the author

Michael J. Pont is an experienced software engineer who began his first embedded project in 1986. Since then he has lectured and carried out research at the University of Sheffield and the University of Leicester, and has provided consultancy and training services to a range of international companies. Michael is the author of two previous books *Patterns for Time-Triggered Embedded Systems* and *Software Engineering with C++ and CASE tools*.

Contents

Preface

This book provides a 'hardware-free' introduction to embedded software for people who:

- Already know how to write software for 'desktop' computer systems.
- Are familiar with a C-based language (Java, C++ or C).
- Want to learn how C is used in practical embedded systems.

The remainder of this preface attempts to answer some questions which prospective readers may have about the contents.

I What is an embedded system?

As far as this book is concerned:

> An embedded system is an application that contains at least one programmable computer (typically in the form of a microcontroller, a microprocessor or digital signal processor chip) and which is used by individuals who are, in the main, unaware that the system is computer-based.

This type of embedded system is all around us. Use of embedded processors in passenger cars, mobile phones, medical equipment, aerospace systems and defence systems is widespread, and even everyday domestic appliances such as dishwashers, televisions, washing machines and video recorders now include at least one such device.

II What type of processor is discussed?

This book focuses on the embedded systems based on the 8051 family of microcontrollers. Prices for 8051 devices start at less than $1.00 (US). At this price, you get a performance of around 1 million instructions per second, and 256 **bytes** (not megabytes!) of on-chip RAM. The 8051's profile (price, performance, available memory) matches the needs of many embedded systems very well. As a result, the

8051 architecture – originally developed by Intel – is now implemented in more tha 400 chips; these are produced by a diverse range of companies including Philip Infineon, Atmel and Dallas. Together, sales of this vast family are generally estimate to account for more than 50% of the 8-bit microcontroller market, and to have a larg share (around 30%) of the microcontroller market as a whole. Versions of the 805 are currently used in a long list of embedded products, from automotive systems children's toys.

The low cost, huge range, easy availability and widespread use of the 805 family makes it an excellent platform for developing embedded systems: the same factors also make it an ideal platform for *learning* about embedded system Whether you will subsequently use 8-, 16- or 32-bit embedded processors, learnir to work within the performance and memory limits of devices such as the 8051 a crucial requirement in the cost-conscious embedded market. You simply cann acquire these skills by developing code for a Pentium (or similar) processor.

III Which operating system is used?

The 256 bytes of memory in the 8051 are – of course – insufficient to support any ve sion of Windows, Linux or similar desktop operating systems. Instead, we will describ how to create your own simple 'embedded operating system' (see Chapter 7). This 'd it-yourself' approach is typical in small embedded applications, where the memo requirements and expense of a desktop operating system (like Windows or Linux) or a so-called 'real-time operating system' simply cannot be justified. However, th approach is also in widespread use in large embedded systems (for example, aerospac applications or X-by-wire systems in the automotive industry), where convention operating systems are generally considered to be too unpredictable.

Learning to work on a 'naked' processor and create your own operating system a key requirements for software developers wishing to work with embedded systems.

IV What type of system is discussed?

This book presents a number of examples adapted from working embedded sy tems. These include:

- A remotely-controlled robot.
- A traffic-light sequencer.
- A system for monitoring liquid flow rates.
- A controller for a domestic washing machine.

- An animatronic dinosaur.
- A general-purpose data acquisition system.

These and other examples are used to illustrate key software architectures that are in widespread use in embedded designs; the examples may be adapted and extended to match the needs of your own applications.

The book concludes with a final case study: this brings together all of the features discussed in earlier chapters in order to create an intruder alarm system. This case study includes the following key components:

- A suitable embedded operating system.
- A multi-state system framework.
- Software to process the inputs from door and window sensors.
- A simple 'keypad' library to process passwords entered by the user.
- Software to control external port pins (to activate the external bell).
- An 'RS-232' library to assist with debugging.

V Do I need a degree in electronics in order to use this book?

Please consider the following statement:

> *'I'd like to learn about embedded software, but I don't know enough about electronics.'*

This is a concern which is commonly expressed by desktop programmers who – if they ever learned anything about electronics at school, college or university – have probably forgotten it.

If you don't know the difference between a MOSFET and a BJT, or even the difference between a resistor and a capacitor, please relax. **You don't need to have any knowledge of electronics in order to make full use of this book**. Neither will you need a soldering iron, breadboard or any electronic components. In short, this book is (99%) hardware free.

To write software for the 8051 devices considered in this book, we will use an industry-standard (Keil) compiler. To test this software, we will use a hardware simulator. Copies of both compiler tools and the simulator are included on the enclosed CD. Using these tools, all of the examples in the book may be run, modified and recompiled and tested, using a standard Windows PC.

This approach allows experienced desktop programmers to quickly understand the key features of embedded systems before they need to 'get their hands dirty' and build some hardware.

VI What's on the CD?

In addition to the Keil compiler and hardware simulator (discussed in the previous section), the CD also includes source code files for all the examples and the case study: this code is in the 'C' programming language and is compatible with the Keil compiler.

The CD also contains useful information about the 8051 microcontroller family, including a large number of relevant data sheets and application notes.

VII What's the link between this book and your other 8051 book (*Patterns for Time-Triggered Embedded Systems*)?

Embedded C provides an introduction to the use of C in embedded projects. If you want to learn more about embedded systems after you finish this book, then *Patterns for Time-Triggered Embedded Systems* (PTTES) may be of interest.[1]

PTTES is a large (1000-page) book which includes a comprehensive set of 'design patterns' to support the development of embedded systems based on the 8051 family of microcontrollers. In total, details of more than 70 useful patterns are provided, complete with guidelines to help you apply these techniques in your own projects: full source code for all of the patterns is included on the PTTES CD.

The book includes: patterns for embedded operating systems (for both single-processor and multi-processor applications); patterns for user-interface designs using switches, keypads, LED and liquid crystal displays; patterns for PID control; patterns for PWM; patterns for analogue-to-digital and digital-to-analogue conversion; patterns for RS-232, RS-485, CAN, SPI and I^2C serial networks; hardware patterns describing reset, oscillator and memory circuits.

VIII Is the code 'free ware'?

The code included in this book took many years to produce. It is not 'free ware', and is subject to some simple copyright restrictions. These are as follows:

- If you have purchased a copy of this book, you are entitled to use the code listed in the text (and included on the CD) in your projects, should you choose to do so. If you use the code in this way, then no run-time royalties are due.

1. Pont, M.J. (2001) *Patterns for time-triggered embedded systems: Building reliable applications with the 8051 family of microcontroller*, Addison-Wesley / ACM Press.

- If you are using the code in a company, and (for example) ten people are using the code, the company should own ten copies of this book.
- If you are teaching in a university or college, you may freely distribute this code to your students without requiring a licence, as long as the code is used for teaching purposes and no commercial application is involved. Please note that teaching (by university or college staff, or anyone else) of 'short courses' for industry or for purposes of 'continuing professional development' does **not** fall into this category: if in doubt, please contact me for clarification.[2]
- You may not, **under any circumstances**, publish any of the source code included in the book or on the CD, in any form or by any means, without explicit written authorization from me. If you wish to publish limited code fragments then, in most circumstances, I will grant this permission, subject only to an appropriate acknowledgment accompanying the published material. If you wish to publish more substantial code listings, then payment of a fee may be required. Please contact me for further details.

IX How should this book be read?

This short book is intended to be read from cover to cover.

Access to a Windows PC while reading will be useful in later chapters, as this will allow you to try out the examples for yourself: however, this is not essential.

X What about bug reports and code updates?

There is fair amount of code involved in this project, both in the book itself and on the associated CD. I have personally tested all of the code that appears here. Nonetheless, errors can creep in.

If you think you have found a bug, please send me an e-mail (the address is at the end of this preface), and I will do my best to help.

XI What about other reader comments?

I began my first embedded project in 1986. When writing *Embedded C*, I wanted to, try and provide the kind of information that I needed (but could not find) at that time.

2. I can be contacted either by post (via the publishers, please), or much more efficiently by e-mail at the address given at the end of this preface.

I would appreciate your comments and feedback. For example, should the book be longer? Shorter? What other areas should I cover? What should I miss out? Would you like to see a future edition focusing on a different family of microcontrollers? If so, which one?

To ensure that any future editions continue to provide the information you need, I would be delighted to hear of your experiences (good or bad) using the book.

XII Credit where credit is due

The publication of this book would not have been possible without the help and support of a number of people.

In particular, I would like to thank:

- The 'Electronic and Software Engineering' students at the University of Leicester who have provided useful feedback on this material as they attended my introductory courses in embedded systems in recent years.
- Simon Plumtree at Pearson Education, who responded positively to my suggestion that this material was suitable for wider publication.
- Karen Sellwood at Pearson, who helped to keep the project on the rails.
- Chris Hills for reviewing the first draft of this book and – again – providing the core of the CD.
- Reinhard Keil for his review of the first draft of this book.
- Jim Cooling, for his review of the first draft of this book.
- Chris Stephens, for his review of the first draft of this book.
- Penelope Allport for managing the project.
- Sara Barnes for copy editing; Claire Brodmann for the design; Barbara Archer for proof reading and David Worthington for the index.
- Simon Key, Steve King, Fernando Schlindwein and Mike Shkolnitsky for spotting typos in the first print run.
- Barbara and Gordon Pont for proof reading.
- Sarah, for convincing me that 'No More Shall We Part' was worth listening to again.

Michael J. Pont

Great Dalby, February 2002

Michael.Pont@tesco.net

chapter 1

Programming embedded systems in C

1.1 Introduction

This is a short book for people who already know how to program desktop computers and now wish to develop software for embedded systems.

In this introductory chapter, we consider some important decisions that must be made at the start of any embedded project:

- The choice of processor.
- The choice of programming language.
- The choice of operating system.

We begin by considering the meaning of the phrase 'embedded system'.

1.2 What is an embedded system?

When we talk about 'embedded systems', what do we mean? Opinions vary. Throughout this book, we will use the following loose definition:

> An embedded system is an application that contains at least one programmable computer (typically in the form of a microcontroller, a microprocessor or digital signal processor chip) and which is used by individuals who are, in the main, unaware that the system is computer-based.

Typical examples of embedded applications that are constructed using the techniques discussed in this book include:

- **Mobile phone systems** (including both customer handsets and base stations).
- **Automotive applications** (including braking systems, traction control, airbag release systems, engine-management units, steer-by-wire systems and cruise-control applications).
- **Domestic appliances** (including dishwashers, televisions, washing machines, microwave ovens, video recorders, security systems, garage door controllers).
- **Aerospace applications** (including flight control systems, engine controllers, autopilots and passenger in-flight entertainment systems).
- **Medical equipment** (including anaesthesia monitoring systems, ECG monitors, drug delivery systems and MRI scanners).
- **Defence systems** (including radar systems, fighter aircraft flight control systems, radio systems and missile guidance systems).

Please note that our definition of embedded systems *excludes* applications such as 'personal digital assistants' (PDAs) running versions of Windows or similar operating systems: from a developer's perspective, these are best viewed as a cut-down version of a desktop computer system. This type of application makes up a very small percentage of the overall 'embedded' market and is not considered in this book.

1.3 Which processor should you use?

When desktop developers first think about working with embedded systems, there is a natural inclination to stick with what they know and look for a book which uses Pentium processors or other devices from this family (such as the 80486, or the Intel 188). However, if you open up the engine management unit or the airbag release system in your car, or take the back off your dishwasher, you will not find any of these processors sitting inside, nor will there be anywhere to plug in a keyboard, graphics display or mouse.

Typical desktop processors cost more than US $100.00 a piece (often much more). This cost puts them out of reach of all but the most expensive embedded application. (Who would pay more than US $100 for a TV remote-control unit?) In addition, a desktop processor requires numerous external support chips in order to function: this further increases the cost. The additional components also increase the physical size of the system, and the power consumption: both of these factors are major problems for battery-powered embedded devices. (Who would buy a portable music player that requires ten large batteries to run, and needs a trolley to transport it?)

Overall, the state-of-the art technology used in desktop processors matches the needs of the PC user very well: however, their key features – an ability to execute industry-standard code at a rate of more than 1000 million instructions per second – come with a heavy price tag and are simply not required in most embedded systems.

The 8051 device is very different. It is a well-tested design, introduced in its original form by Intel in 1980 (Figure 1.1). The development costs of this device have now been fully recovered, and prices of modern 8051 devices now start at less than US $1.00. At this price, you get a performance of around 1 million instructions per second, and 256 **bytes** (not megabytes!) of on-chip RAM. You also get 32 port pins and a serial interface. The 8051's profile (price, performance, available memory, serial interface) match the needs of many embedded systems very well. As a result, it is now produced in more than 400 different forms by a diverse range of companies including Philips, Infineon, Atmel and Dallas. Together, sales of this vast family are generally estimated to account for more than 50% of the 8-bit microcontroller market, and to have a large share (around 30%) of the microcontroller market as a whole. Versions of the 8051 are currently used in a long list of embedded products, from children's toys to automotive systems.

FIGURE 1.1 The external interface of a 'Standard' '8051' microcontroller (40-pin DIP package). Standard 8051s have four ports, and are pin compatible with the original 8051/8052 from Intel. Further information about the pin functions is given in Chapter 2

Building a desktop PC from an 8051 would not be a practical proposition, but it is an excellent device for building many embedded systems. One important factor is that the 8051 requires a minimum number of external components in order to operate. For example, Figure 1.2 shows the circuit diagram for a complete 8051-based application.

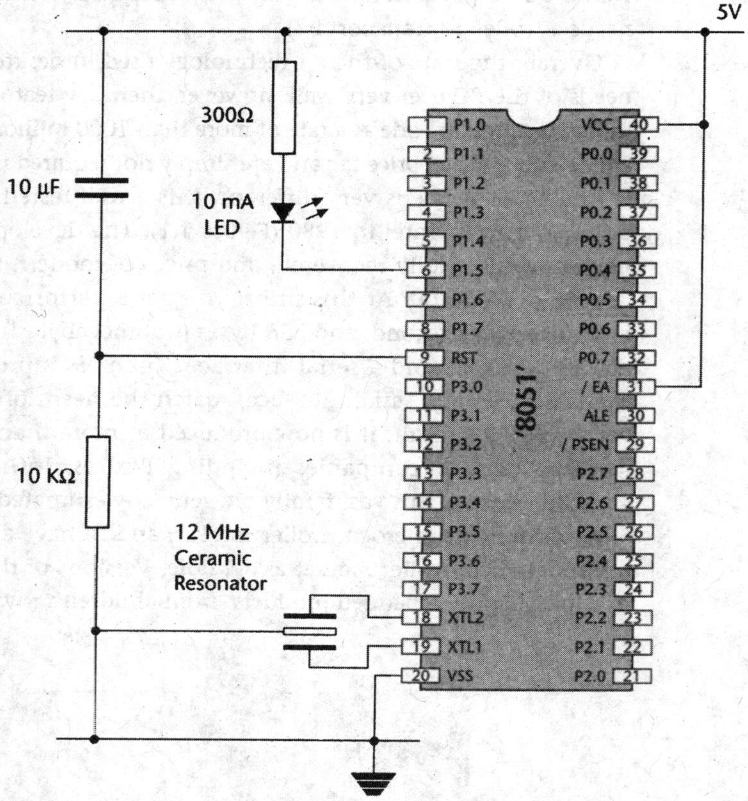

FIGURE 1.2 An example of an 8051 microcontroller in use. In this example, the microcontroller is intended to flash an LED connected to Pin 6. In addition to this LED, only a simple 'reset' circuit is required (the capacitor and resistor connected to Pin 9), plus an external oscillator (in this case, a 3-pin ceramic resonator). We will consider some software that could be used to control such an application in Chapter 3

The different nature of the embedded and desktop markets is emphasized by the fact that some of the more recent 8051 devices – far from being more powerful and having more features than the 1980 original – actually have *fewer* features. For example, as we will discuss in Chapter 2, the original 8051 (Figure 1.1) had 32 I/O pins and could – if necessary – be connected to up to 128 kbytes of external memory. By contrast, the more recent 'Small 8051' devices typically have only some 15 I/O pins, and do not support external memory. These devices are finding their way into applications that would have involved a small number of discrete components (transistors, diodes, resistors, capacitors) a few years ago, but which may now be implemented more cheaply using microcontrollers (Figure 1.3).

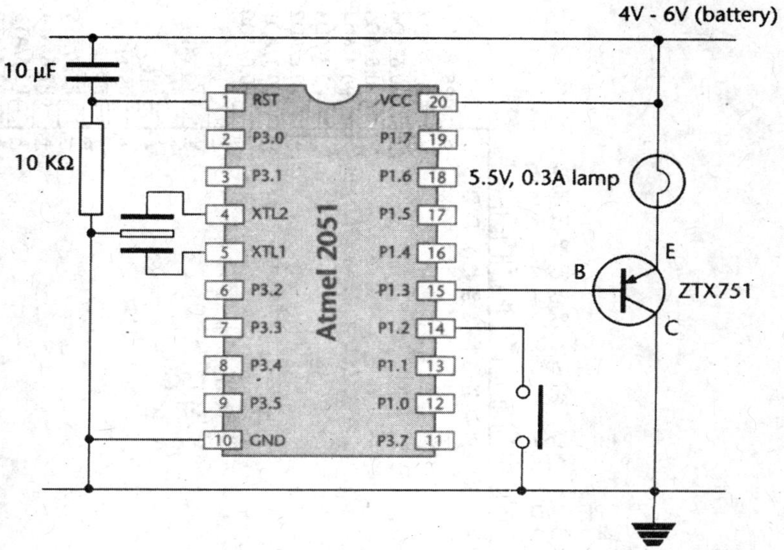

FIGURE 1.3 An example of a 'Small 8051' in use. Small 8051s are produced by Atmel and Philips. They have two ports (or less), and around 20 pins. In this case, an Atmel AT89C2051 is used, in a 'cupboard light' application. The circuit here is intended for use in a cupboard (closet), and will be battery powered. When the light is switched on (by pressing the switch), it will operate for 20 seconds. If, in this time, the user does not press the switch again (to turn off the light), the power will be removed automatically. This is a typical example of a very simple product that may now be economically produced using a microcontroller

Both the Standard and Small 8051s are aimed, largely, at low-performance application areas, where limited memory is required, and one of the most important considerations is product cost. This forms a large segment of the embedded market but – of course – not all projects take this form. To develop applications requiring additional hardware or larger amounts of memory, we can opt to switch to a 16-bit (or 32-bit) microcontroller environment – or even consider using a desktop microprocessor. However, such a move can require a major investment in staff, training and development tools. An alternative is to use one of the Extended 8051 devices introduced in recent years by a range of manufacturers (see Figure 1.4).

One important application area for Extended 8051s has been the automotive sector. Recent economic, legislative and technological developments in this sector mean that an increasing number of road vehicles contain embedded systems. Linking these systems together in many recent vehicles is a low-cost, two-wire Controller Area Network (CAN) computer bus. The CAN bus eliminates the expensive (and heavy) multi-wire looms, shaving around US $600 or more from production costs: a significant saving.

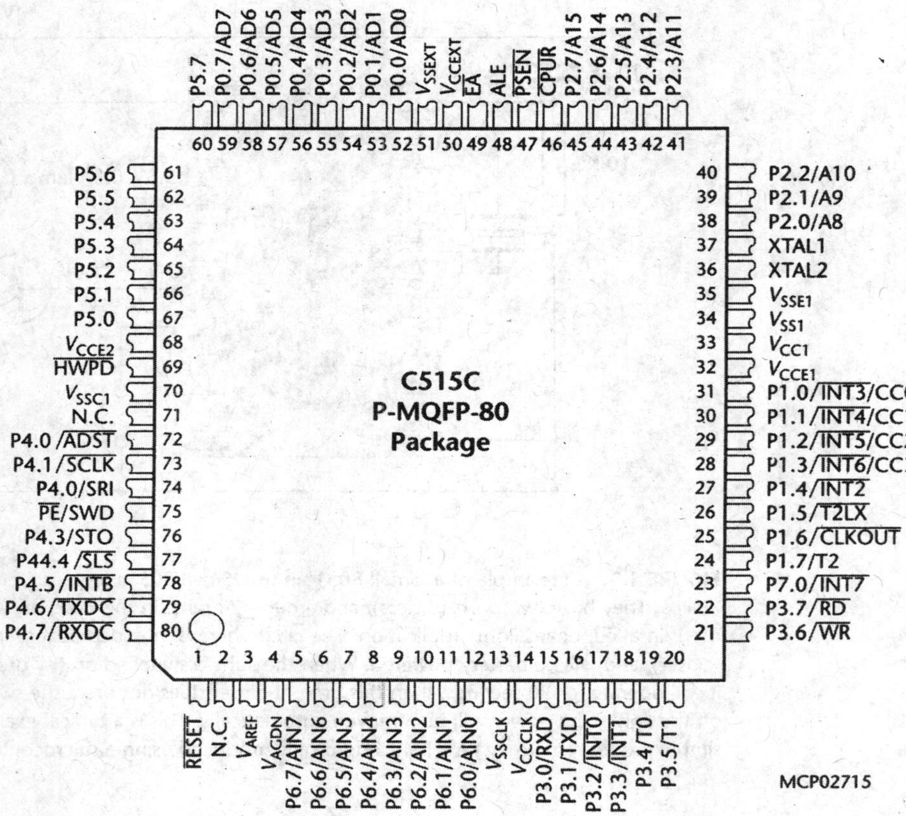

FIGURE 1.4 An example of an Extended 8051 device. Extended 8051s have additional on-chip facilities, and additional port pins. In the case of the Infineon C515C (shown here), the additional facilities include support for the 'Controller Area Network' (CAN) bus: this bus is widely used in the automotive sector and in industrial environments. Figure reproduced with permission from Infineon

This is not quite the end of the story. In order to connect to the CAN bus, the various devices – from door mirrors to braking systems – each require an embedded processor. As a consequence, a modern passenger car may typically have 50 processors on board. To use 50 desktop chips in these circumstances, we would need to spend around US $5000. This cost greatly outweighs any saving achieved through the use of the CAN bus in the first place: in addition, the desktop processor would not have on-chip support for CAN, so additional hardware would be needed in order to provide this, further increasing our costs and design complexity. As an alternative, various Extended 8051s have on-chip hardware support for

CAN (see Figure 1.4). The use of 50 such chips in a car design would not generally cost more than US $200. Using these processors, the switch to CAN may result in overall savings of around US $400 per vehicle.

The final thing to note about the 8051 architecture is that, if none of the 400 or so existing chips matches the needs of your application, you can now build your own device. For example, the Triscend[3] E5 series of devices have 8051 cores, plus an additional area of field-programmable gate arrays (FPGAs) with which you can create your own 'on chip' hardware. Alternatively, for even greater flexibility, Xilinx Foundation[4] provides a comprehensive set of tools for the programming of 'blank' FPGAs or Application-Specific ICs (ASICs). Compatible with these tools are a small range of 8051 'cores' which can be purchased – for example – from Dolphin Integration.[5] The use of such techniques allows you to create your own completely customized 8051 microcontroller, in order to match precisely your particular requirements.

Overall, the low cost, huge range, easy availability and widespread use of the 8051 architecture makes it an excellent platform for developing embedded systems: these same factors also make it an ideal platform for learning about embedded systems. Whether you will subsequently use 8-, 16- or 32-bit embedded processors, learning to work within the performance and memory limits of devices such as the 8051 is a crucial requirement in the cost-conscious embedded market. You simply cannot acquire these skills by developing code for a Pentium (or similar desktop) processor.

1.4 Which programming language should you use?

Having decided to use an 8051 processor as the basis of your embedded system, the next key decision that needs to be made is the choice of programming language. In order to identify a suitable language for embedded systems, we might begin by making the following observations:

- Computers (such as microcontroller, microprocessor or DSP chips) only accept instructions in 'machine code' ('object code'). Machine code is, by definition, in the language of the computer, rather than that of the programmer. Interpretation of the code by the programmer is difficult and error prone.
- All software, whether in assembly, C, C++, Java or Ada must ultimately be translated into machine code in order to be executed by the computer.

3. www.triscend.com 4. www.xilinx.com 5. www.dolphin.fr

- There is no point in creating 'perfect' source code, if we then make use of a poor translator program (such as an assembler or compiler) and thereby generate executable code that does not operate as we intended.
- Embedded processors – like the 8051 – have limited processor power and very limited memory available: the language used must be efficient.
- To program embedded systems, we need low-level access to the hardware: this means, at least, being able to read from and write to particular memory locations (using 'pointers' or an equivalent mechanism).

Of course, not all of the issues involved in language selection are purely technical:

- No software company remains in business for very long if it generates new code, from scratch, for every project. The language used must support the creation of flexible libraries, making it easy to re-use (well-tested) code components in a range of projects. It must also be possible to adapt complete code systems to work with a new or updated processor with minimal difficulty.
- Staff members change and existing personnel have limited memory spans. At the same time, systems evolve and processors are updated. As concern over the 'Year 2000' problem in recent years has illustrated, many embedded systems have a long lifespan. During this time, their code will often have to be maintained. Good code must therefore be easy to understand now, and in five years' time (and not just by those who first wrote it).
- The language chosen should be in common use. This will ensure that you can continue to recruit experienced developers who have knowledge of the language. It will also mean that your existing developers will have access to sources of information (such as books, training courses, WWW sites) which give examples of good design and programming practice.

Even this short list immediately raises the paradox of programming language selection. From one point of view, only machine code is safe, since every other language involves a translator, and any code you create is only as safe as the code written by the manufacturers of the translator. On the other hand, real code needs to be maintained and re-used in new projects, possibly on different hardware: few people would argue that machine code is easy to understand, debug or to port.

Inevitably, therefore, we need to make compromises; there is no perfect solution. All we can really say is that we require a language that is efficient, high-level, gives low-level access to hardware, and is well defined. In addition – of course – the language must be available for the platforms we wish to use. Against all of these points, C scores well.

We can summarize C's features as follows:

- It is 'mid-level', with 'high-level' features (such as support for functions and modules), and 'low-level' features (such as good access to hardware via pointers).
- It is very efficient.
- It is popular and well understood.
- Even desktop developers who have used only Java or C++ can soon understand C syntax.
- Good, well-proven compilers are available for every embedded processor (8-bit to 32-bit or more).
- Experienced staff are available.
- Books, training courses, code samples and WWW sites discussing the use of the language are all widely available.

Overall, C's strengths for embedded system development greatly outweigh its weaknesses. It may not be an ideal language for developing embedded systems, but it is unlikely that a 'perfect' language will ever be created.

1.5 Which operating system should you use?

Having opted to create our 8051-based applications using C, we can now begin to consider how this language can be used. In doing so, we will begin to probe some of the differences between software development for desktop and embedded systems.

In the desktop environment, the program the user requires (such as a word processor program) is usually loaded from disk on demand, along with any required data (such as a word processor file). Figure 1.5 shows a typical operating environment for such a word processor. Here the system is well insulated from the underlying hardware. For example, when the user wishes to save his or her latest novel on disk, the word processor delegates most of the necessary work to the operating system, which in turn may delegate many of the hardware-specific commands to the BIOS (basic input/output system).

The desktop PC does not *require* an operating system (or BIOS). However, for most users, the main advantage of a personal computer is its flexibility: that is, that the same piece of equipment has the potential to run many thousands of different programs. If the PC had no operating system, each of these programs would need to be able to carry out all the low-level functions for itself. This would be very inefficient and would tend to make systems more expensive. It would also be likely to lead to errors, as many simple functions would have to be duplicated in even the smallest of programs. One way of viewing this is that a desktop PC is used to run multiple programs, and the operating system provides the 'common code' (for printing, file storage, graphics, and so forth) that is required by this set of programs.

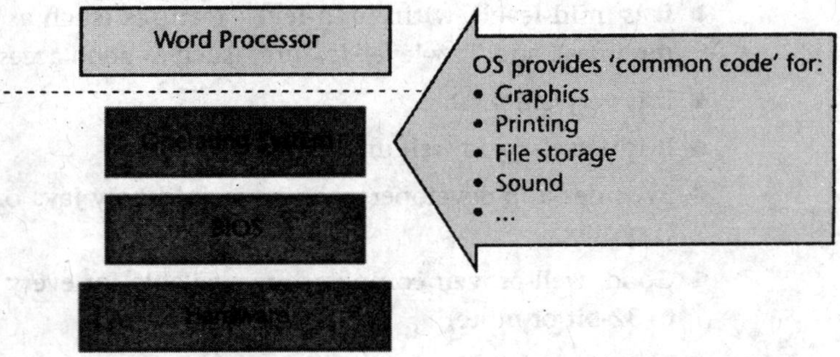

FIGURE 1.5 A schematic representation of the BIOS/OS sandwich from a desk-bound computer system running some word processor software

There are two fundamental differences between the embedded systems we are concerned with in this book and desktop computer systems:

1 The vast majority of embedded systems are required to run only one program: this program will start running when the microcontroller is powered up, and will stop running when the power is removed.

2 Many of the facilities provided by the modern desktop OS – such as the ability to display high-resolution graphics, printing facilities and efficient disk access – are of little value in embedded systems, where sophisticated graphics screens, printers and disks are generally unavailable.

As a consequence, the simplest architecture in an embedded system is typically a form of 'Super Loop' (see Listing 1.1).

Listing 1.1 Part of a simple Super Loop demonstration

```
void main(void)
   {
   // Prepare run function X
   X_Init();

   while(1) // 'for ever' (Super Loop)
      {
      X(); // Run function X()
      }
   }
```

It is important to appreciate that there is no operating system in use here. When power is applied to the system, the function `main()` will be called: having performed the initializations, the function `X()` will be called, repeatedly, until the system is disconnected from the power supply (or a serious error occurs).

For example, suppose we wish to develop a microcontroller-based control system to be used as part of the central-heating system in a building. The simplest version of this system might consist of a gas-fired boiler (which we wish to control), a sensor (measuring room temperature), a temperature dial (through which the desired temperature is specified) and the controller itself (Figure 1.6).

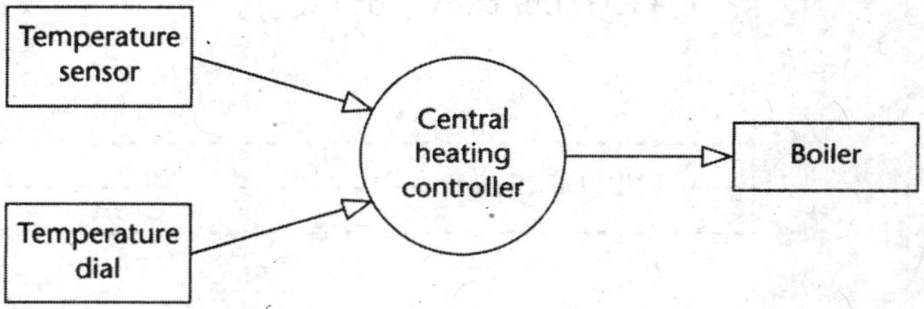

FIGURE 1.6 An overview of a central heating controller

We assume that the boiler, temperature sensor and temperature dial are connected to the system via appropriate ports.

Here, precise timing is not required, and a Super Loop framework similar to that shown in Listing 1.2 may be appropriate.

Listing 1.2 Part of the code for a simple central-heating system

```
/*------------------------------------------------------------------*-

   Main.C

   -------------------------------------------------------------------

   Framework for a central heating system using a Super Loop.
   [Compiles and runs but does nothing useful]
-*------------------------------------------------------------------*/
#include "Cen_Heat.h"
/*------------------------------------------------------------------*/
void main(void)
   {
   // Init the system
   C_HEAT_Init();
```

```
   while(1) // 'for ever' (Super Loop)
      {
      // Find out what temperature the user requires
      // (via the user interface)
      C_HEAT_Get_Required_Temperature();

      // Find out what the current room temperature is
      // (via temperature sensor)
      C_HEAT_Get_Actual_Temperature();

      // Adjust the gas burner, as required
      C_HEAT_Control_Boiler();
      }
   }
/*------------------------------------------------------------------*-
  ---- END OF FILE -------------------------------------------------
-*------------------------------------------------------------------*/
```

It should be noted that the Super Loop architecture employed in this central-heating system is not appropriate for all embedded applications. For more advanced applications, we will describe how to create your own embedded operating system in Chapter 7.

1.6 How do you develop embedded software?

The process of compiling, linking and executing the program shown (in part) in Listing 1.2 on a desktop PC is straightforward. In this environment, the executable code we create will, in almost all cases, be intended to run on a desktop computer similar to the one on which the code development is carried out. In the embedded environment this is rarely the case. For example, the 8051 devices we will use throughout this book do not have sufficient memory resources to allow them to be used for compiling programs, and they will not support a keyboard or graphics display. As a result, the code will be 'cross-compiled' on a desktop PC, generating machine code that is compatible with the 8051 family: this process will be examined in greater detail in Chapter 3.

Having created the required executable code, we need to test it and refine it. To do this, we need to do the following:

1 Build the hardware for the embedded system.

2 Transfer the executable code to the embedded hardware and test the system.

For programmers without experience of electronics, the process of building embedded hardware is a daunting one. A typical approach used to prototype small embedded applications is the 'breadboard'. This allows the microcontroller and associated components to be connected together, without soldering, in order to test and refine the hardware and software design.

For example, consider the breadboard shown in Figure 1.7. This code is for a simple alarm clock with an LED display and some switches to adjust the time and alarm settings. As the photograph makes clear, even in this simple application there are many opportunities for wiring errors. As a result – if the system does not operate correctly – it may not be clear whether this is as a result of software errors or hardware problems.

A means of transferring the program code to the microcontroller is also required. In examples such as the alarm clock shown in Figure 1.7, the microcontroller used will typically incorporate some form of 'flash' memory to store the program code.[6] To transfer the executable code to the microcontroller, we will use a 'flash' programmer. Flexible programmers (for use with the whole family of 8051 processors, and other devices) may cost several hundred dollars. Alternatively, 'hobby' developers often choose to save money by developing their own programmer at home: however, to do this, experience of electronics construction techniques is required.

Overall, the process of wiring up a breadboard to test your first simple embedded programs can be daunting, expensive and rather prone to error. Fortunately, there is now an alternative approach that can be used by those starting out in this area:

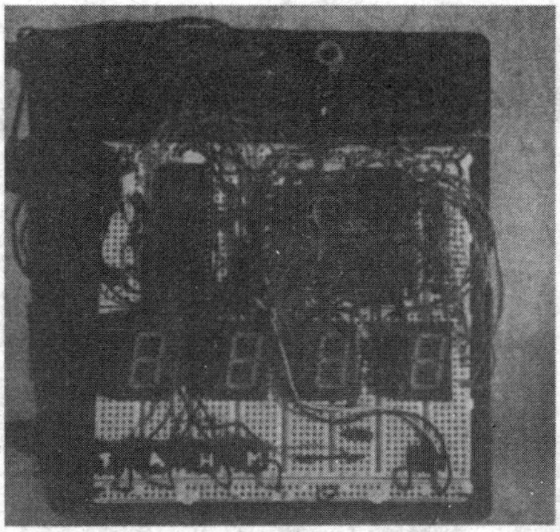

FIGURE 1.7 An example of a simple 8051-based alarm clock assembled on a breadboa
The board was assembled by Neeraj Kachhwaha, Bresley Lim, Melvin Lim and Henry T
Photograph by Michael Pont

6. We will consider the different types of available memory in greater detail in Chap

1 Create the executable code for the embedded system on a desktop PC using an appropriate cross-compiler and related tools (as above).

2 Use a **software simulator** (running on the desktop PC) to test the code.

3 Repeat Step 1 and Step 2, as necessary, until the software operates as required.

Throughout this book we will use such a simulator, produced by Keil Software. This provides you with a very flexible 'hardware' platform, on which you can gain experience of embedded software without simultaneously having to learn how to solder.

A copy of this simulator is included on the enclosed CD. Please note that this is an evaluation version of the simulator and has some restrictions compared with the full version: nonetheless, it can be used to run all of the examples in this book. We describe how to use this simulator in Chapter 3.

An example of the simulator in use is given in Figure 1.8. As we will see in subsequent chapters, this simulator accurately reproduces the activity of all key components in various members of the 8051 family.

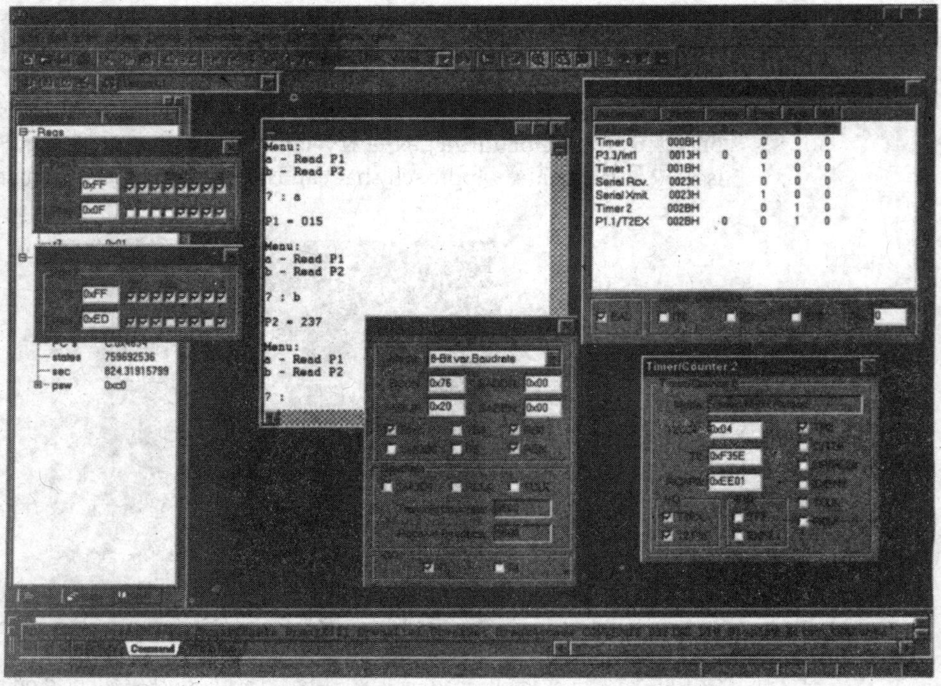

FIGURE 1.8 The Keil 8051 hardware simulator in use. We discuss the use of this simulator in detail in Chapter 3

Please note that these simulators are not simply 'toys' to be used only when learning how to develop embedded software. Even where hardware will be constructed, most developers will conduct early software tests on a simulator before using the hardware. This can greatly speed up the development process. For example, in applications using a serial interface (see Chapter 9), the simulator can determine the precise baud rate being generated by your software: this can avoid many subsequent problems. In addition, the simulator provides key facilities for debugging, such as support for 'profiling' the code, a process that will typically involve measuring the duration of particular functions. As we will see in subsequent chapters, timing plays a central role in most embedded applications, and the ability to measure function durations in a straightforward way makes the simulator a key debugging tool.

1.7 Conclusions

In this introductory chapter, we have considered:

- The type of embedded systems that will be discussed in this book.
- The choice of programming language for embedded systems.
- The choice of operating system for embedded systems.
- The process of creating executable code for an embedded processor on a desktop PC.
- The process of testing the embedded code.

In the next chapter, we will look more closely at the features of the 8051 microcontroller.

chapter 2

Introducing the 8051 microcontroller family

2.1 Introduction

In Chapter 1, we looked at some of the key features of 'embedded' software. In the remainder of the book, our focus will be on 8051-based embedded systems.

In this chapter, we consider some of the key features of the 8051 family.

2.2 What's in a name?

Before we look in more detail at the features of the various 8051 devices, we should note that the names given to the various family members is always a source of confusion to new developers. For example, the 8031, 8751, 8052, 8032, C505C, C515C, C509, C868, 80C517, 83C452, 80C390, ADµC812 and MAX7651 are all members of the 8051 family. The names of the devices provide little or no indication of the family connections.

Particular confusion arises over the labels '8051' and '8052'. The 8052 was launched (by Intel) shortly after the 8051 appeared. The architecture was the same, except that the 8052 had more on-chip RAM (256 bytes cf. 128 bytes), and also had an additional timer (Timer 2).

You should be aware that, despite the fact that they are described as '8051s', almost all current devices **are based on the slightly later 8052 architecture**. As the distinction between '8051' and '8052' is now purely of historical interest, we will follow this convention and use the label '8051' throughout this book.

If you want more information about the various 8051 devices that are available, you will find a large number of relevant data sheets on the CD. In addition, Keil

Software have a WWW site[7] with details of current 8051 variants (more than 400 devices are listed at the time of writing). This site is regularly updated. Another useful source of information about the different members of the 8051 family is the 'Micro Search' facility provided by Computer Solutions.[8]

2.3 The external interface of the Standard 8051

As we saw in Chapter 1, the 400 different devices in the 8051 family can be divided into three main groups: the Standard 8051s, the Small 8051s and the Extended 8051s (Figure 2.1).

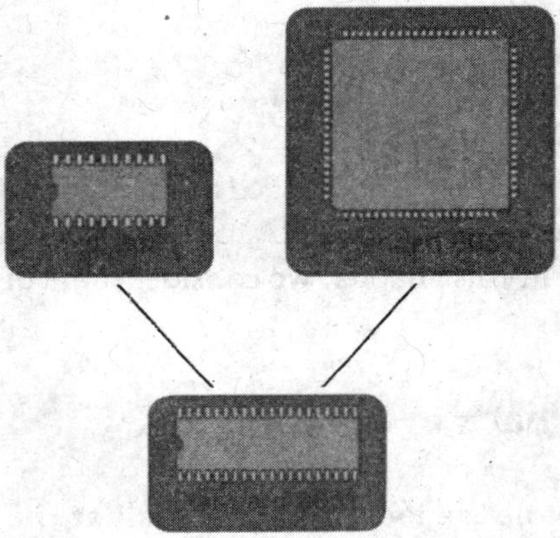

FIGURE 2.1 The relationship between the various 'clans' in the 8051 family. The Standard 8051s are modern implementations of the original 8051 / 8052 device. Both the Small 8051s and the Extended 8051s are derived from (and share key architectural features with) the Standard 8051s. From the developer's perspective, a key feature of this family is that a **single** compiler is required in order to generate code for all current devices

We will assume the use of Standard 8051 devices throughout this book. As the architecture of the Small and Extended 8051s is derived from that of the Standard 8051, the techniques we discuss may be applied with any 8051-based device, and the C compiler used throughout this book (and introduced in Chapter 3) can be used to develop code for all 8051 derivatives.

Figure 2.2 shows the external interface of the Standard 8051, and briefly summarizes the function of each of the port pins. Note that, in many cases, the port pins can serve more than one purpose.

7. www.keil.com 8. www.computer-solutions.co.uk

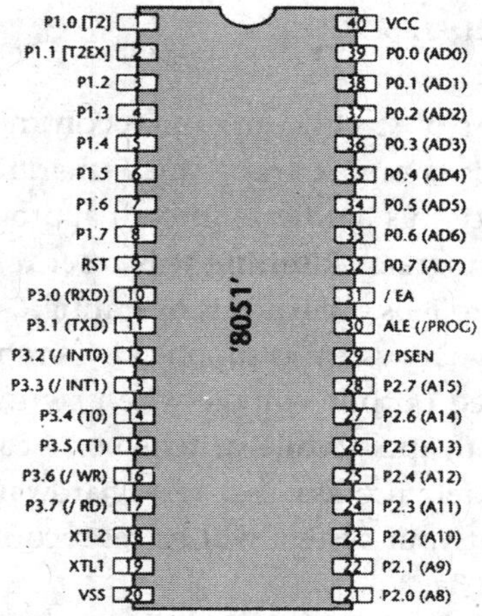

Pin(s)	Function
1–8	Port 1. The bi-directional pins on this port may be used for input and output: each pin may be individually controlled and – for example – some may be used for input while others on the same port are used for output. Use of these pins is discussed in detail in Chapter 3 and Chapter 4. In 8052-based designs, Pin 1 and Pin 2 have alternative functions associated with Timer 2 (see Section 2.8).
9	The 'Reset' pin. When this pin is held at Logic 0, the chip will run normally. If, while the oscillator is running, this pin is held at Logic 1 for two (or more) machine cycles, the microcontroller will be reset. An example of simple reset hardware is given in Section 2.4.
10–17	Port 3. Another bi-directional input port (same operation as Port 1). Each pin on this port also serves an additional function. Pin 10 and Pin 11 are used to receive and transmit (respectively) serial data using the 'RS-232' protocol. See Chapter 9 for details. Pin 12 and Pin 13 are used to process interrupt inputs. We say more about interrupts in Section 2.9. Pin 14 and Pin 15 have alternative functions associated with Timer 0 and Timer 1 (see Section 2.8). Pin 16 and Pin 17 are used when working with external memory (see Section 2.6).
18–19	These pins are used to connect an external crystal, ceramic resonator or oscillator module to the microcontroller. See Section 2.5 for further details.
20	Vss. This is the 'ground' pin.
21–28	Port 2. Another bi-directional input port (same operation as Port 1). These pins are also used when working with external memory (see Section 2.6).
29	Program Store Enable (PSEN) is used to control access to external CODE memory (if used). See Section 2.6.
30	Address Latch Enable (ALE) is used when working with external memory (see Section 2.6). Note that some devices allow ALE activity to be disabled (if external memory is not used): this can help reduce the level of electromagnetic interference (EMI) generated by your product. This pin is also used (<u>on some devices</u>) as the program pulse input (PROG) during Flash programming.
31	External Access (EA). To execute code from internal memory (e.g. on-chip Flash, where available) this pin must be connected to Vcc. To execute code from external memory, this pin must be connected to ground. Forgetting to connect this pin to Vcc is a common error when people first begin working with the 8051.
32–39	Port 0. Another bi-directional input port (same operation as Port 1). Note that – unlike Port 1, Port 2 and Port 3 – this port does NOT have internal pull-up resistors. See Chapter 4 for further details. These pins are also used when working with external memory (see Section 2.6).
40	Vcc. This is the '5V' pin (on 5V devices; 3V on 3V devices, etc).

FIGURE 2.2 The external interface to the standard '8051' microcontroller

2.4 Reset requirements

The process of starting any microcontroller is a non-trivial one. The underlying hardware is complex and a small, manufacturer-defined, 'reset routine' must be run to place this hardware into an appropriate state before it can begin executing the user program. Running this reset routine takes time, and requires that the microcontroller's oscillator is operating.

Where your system is supplied by a robust power supply, which rapidly reaches its specified output voltage when switched on, rapidly decreases to 0V when switched off, and – while switched on – cannot 'brown out' (drop in voltage), then you can safely use low-cost reset hardware based on a capacitor and a resistor to ensure that your system will be reset correctly: this form of reset circuit is shown in Figure 2.3a.

Where your power supply is less than perfect, and / or your application is safety related, the simple RC solution will not be suitable. Several manufacturers provide more sophisticated reset chips which may be used in these circumstances: Figure 2.3b illustrates one possibility.

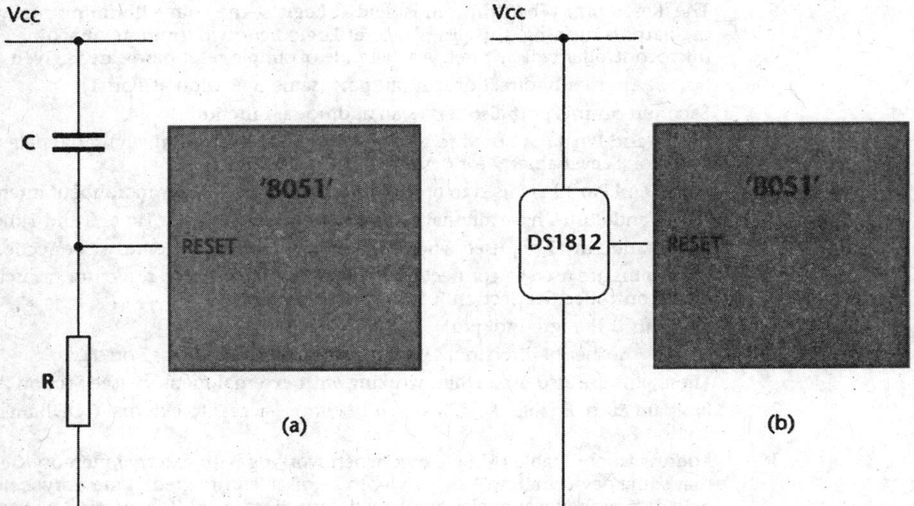

FIGURE 2.3a and b Two possible reset circuits for 8051-based designs. We will not consider hardware issues in detail in this book: please refer to Chapter 11 for sources of further information about this topic

2.5 Clock frequency and performance

All digital computer systems are driven by some form of oscillator circuit: the 8051 is certainly no exception (see Figure 2.4).

The oscillator circuit is the 'heartbeat' of the system and is crucial to correct operation. For example, if the oscillator fails, the system will not function at all; if the oscillator runs irregularly, any timing calculations performed by the system will be inaccurate.

We consider some important issues linked to oscillator frequency and performance in this section.

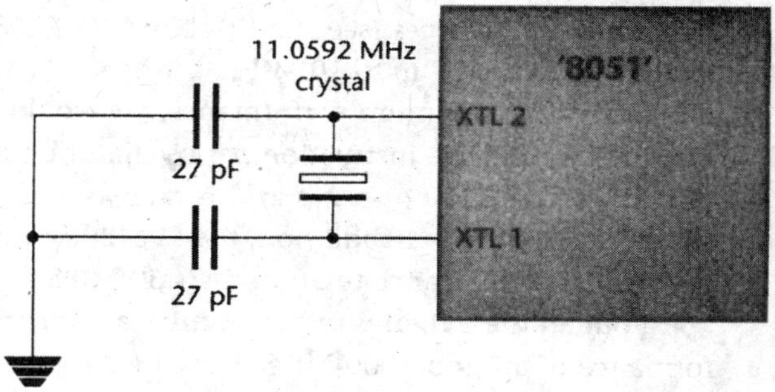

FIGURE 2.4 An example of a simple crystal oscillator circuit. We will not consider hardware issues in detail in this book: please refer to Chapter 11 for sources of further information about this topic

a) The link between oscillator frequency and machine-cycle period

One of the first questions to be asked when considering a microcontroller for a project is whether it has the required level of performance.

As a general rule, the speed at which your application runs is directly determined by the oscillator frequency: in most cases, if you double the oscillator frequency, the application will run twice as fast. When we want to compare different processors, we need a way of specifying performance in a quantitative manner. One popular measure is the number of machine instructions that may be executed in one second, usually expressed in 'MIPS' (Million Instructions Per Second). For example, in the original Intel 8051 microcontroller, a minimum of 12 oscillator cycles was required to execute a machine instruction. The original 8051 had a maximum oscillator frequency of 12 MHz and therefore a peak performance of 1 MIP.

A simple way of improving the 8051 performance is to increase the clock frequency. More modern (Standard) 8051 devices allow the use of clock speeds well beyond the 12 MHz limit of the original devices. For example, the Atmel AT89C55WD, allow clock speeds up to 33 MHz: this raises the peak performance to around 3 MIPS.

Another way of improving the performance is to make internal changes to the microcontroller so that fewer oscillator cycles are required to execute each machine instruction. The Dallas 'High Speed Microcontroller' devices (87C520, and similar) use this approach, so that only four oscillator cycles are required to execute a machine instruction. These Dallas devices also allow faster clock rates (typically up to 33 MHz). Combined, these changes give a total performance of around 8 MIPS. Similar changes are made in members of the Winbond family of Standard 8051 devices (see the Winbond W77E58, for example) resulting in performance figures of up to 10 MIPS.

Clearly, for maximum performance, we would like to execute instructions at a rate of one machine instruction per oscillator cycle. For example, the Dallas 'Ultra High Speed' 89C420 operates at this rate: as a result, it runs at 12 times the speed of the original 8051. In addition, the 89c420 can operate at up to 50 MHz, increasing overall performance to around 40–50 MIPS.

To put all these figures in perspective, a modern desktop PC has a potential performance of around 1000 MIPS. However, a good percentage of this performance (perhaps 50% or more) will be 'consumed' by the operating system. By contrast, the embedded operating system we will describe in Chapter 7 consumes less than 1% of the processor resources of the most basic 8051: this leaves sufficient CPU cycles to run a complex embedded application.

b) Why you should choose a low oscillator frequency

In our experience, many developers select an oscillator frequency that is at or near the maximum value supported by a particular device. For example, the Infineon C505/505C will operate with crystal frequency of 2–20 MHz, and many people automatically choose values at or near the top of this range, in order to gain maximum performance.

This can be a mistake, for the following reasons:

- Many applications do not require the levels of performance that a modern 8051 device can provide.
- In most modern (CMOS-based) 8051s, there is an almost linear relationship between the oscillator frequency and the power supply current. As a result, by using the lowest frequency necessary it is possible to reduce the power requirement: this can be useful, particularly in battery-powered applications.

- When accessing low-speed peripherals (such as slow memory, or liquid-crystal displays), programming and hardware design can be greatly simplified – and the cost of peripheral components, such as memory latches, can be reduced – if the chip is operating more slowly.
- The electromagnetic interference (EMI) generated by a circuit increases with clock frequency.

In general, you should operate at the *lowest* possible oscillator frequency compatible with the performance needs of your application. As we will see in later chapters, simulating the processor is a good way of determining the required operating frequency for a particular application.

2.6 Memory Issues

We consider some of the memory issues relating to the 8051 in this section.

a) Types of memory

On the desktop, most designers and programmers can safely ignore the type of memory they are using. This is seldom the case in embedded environments, and we therefore briefly review some of the different types of memory below.

First, a short history lesson, to explain the roots of an important acronym. On early mainframe and desktop computer systems, long-term data storage was carried out using computer tapes. Reading or writing to the tape took varying amounts of time, depending whether it involved, for example, rewinding the entire tape, or simply rewinding a couple of centimetres. In this context, new memory devices appeared that could be used to store data while the computer was running, but which lost these data when the power was removed. These read-write memory devices were referred to as 'random access memory' (RAM) devices, because – unlike tape-based systems – accessing any element of memory 'chosen at random' took the same amount of time.

Tapes have now largely disappeared, but the acronym RAM has not, and is still used to refer to memory devices that can be both read from and written to. However, since RAM was first introduced, new forms of memory devices have appeared, including various forms of ROM (read-only memory). Since these ROM devices are also 'random access' in nature, the acronym RAM is now best translated as 'Read-Write Memory'.

Dynamic RAM (DRAM)

Dynamic RAM is a read-write memory technology that uses a small capacitor to store information. As the capacitor will discharge quite rapidly, it must be frequently refreshed to maintain the required information: circuitry on the chip takes care of this refresh activity. Like most current forms of RAM, the information is lost when power is removed from the chip.

Static RAM (SRAM)

Static RAM is a read-write memory technology that uses a form of electronic flip-flop to store the information. No refreshing is required, but the circuitry is more complex and costs can be several times that of the corresponding size of DRAM. However, access times may be one-third those of DRAM.

Mask Read-Only Memory (ROM)

Mask ROM is – from the software developer's perspective – read only: however, the manufacturer is able to write to the memory, at the time the chip is created, according to a 'mask' provided by the company for which the chips are being produced. Such devices are therefore sometimes referred to as 'factory-programmed ROM'. Mask programming is not cheap, and is not a low-volume option: mistakes can be very expensive, and providing code for your first mask can be a character-building process. Access times are often slower than RAM: roughly 1.5 times that of DRAM.

Many members of the 8051 family are available with on-chip, mask-programmed, ROM.

Programmable Read-Only Memory (PROM)

PROM is a form of Write-Once, Read-Many (WORM) or 'One-Time Programmable' (OTP) memory. Basically, we use a PROM programmer to blow tiny 'fuses' in the device. Once blown, these fuses cannot be repaired; however, the devices themselves are cheap.

Many modern members of the 8051 family are available with OTP ROM.

UV Erasable Programmable Read-Only Memory (UV EPROM)

Like PROMs, UV EPROMs are programmed electrically. Unlike PROMs, they also have a quartz window which allows the memory to be erased by exposing the internals of the device to UV light. The erasure process can take several minutes and, after erasure, the quartz window will be covered with a UV-opaque label. This form of EPROM can withstand thousands of program / erase cycles.

More flexible than PROMs and once very common, UV EPROMs now seem rather primitive compared with EEPROMs (see below). They can be useful for prototyping but are prohibitively expensive for use in production.

Many older members of the 8051 family are available with on-board UV EPROM.

EEPROM and Flash ROM

Electrically-Erasable Programmable Read-Only Memory (EEPROMs) and 'Flash' ROMs are a more user-friendly form of ROM that can be both programmed and erased electrically.

EEPROM and Flash ROM are very similar. EEPROMs can usually be reprogrammed on a byte-by-byte basis, and are often used to store passwords or other 'persistent' user data. Flash ROMs generally require a block-sized 'erase' operation before they can be programmed: often the size of the block will be several kilobytes: such ROMs are often used for the storage of program code.

Many members of the 8051 family are available with on-board EEPROM or flash ROM, and some devices contain both types of memory.

b) Memory organization and 'hex'

As you will recall, all data items are represented in computer memory as binary codes, each containing a certain number of bits. To simplify the storage and retrieval of data items, these memory bits are organized into memory locations, each with a unique memory address. In a common byte-oriented memory (as used in desktop PCs and – with some exceptions – in the 8051), each memory location contains eight bits (one *byte*) of storage, and each byte has a unique address (Figure 2.5).

Address	Contents							
...	.	.	.	.	.	.	.	.
0x04	1	0	0	1	1	1	1	1
0x03	0	0	1	1	1	1	0	0
0x02	1	1	0	0	0	0	0	1
0x01	1	0	1	0	1	0	0	0
0x00	1	1	1	0	1	0	0	1

FIGURE 2.5 A segment of byte-oriented memory. Note that each **byte** (rather than each **bit**) has its own unique address, shown in hexadecimal notation here. See text for details

In Figure 2.5, the memory addresses are given in hexadecimal notation. This is a base-16 numbering scheme which provides a compact way of representing large binary numbers: it is widely used in embedded systems. Note that the prefix '0x' is used in C (and elsewhere) to indicate that a number is in 'hex' notation.

Table 2.1 shows a list of numbers with their hex, binary and 'ordinary' decimal representations.

TABLE 2.1 Different number representations. See text for details

Hexadecimal (base 16)	Binary (base 2)	Decimal (base 10)
0x00	00000000	0
0xFF	11111111	255
0x0F	00001111	15
0xF0	11110000	240
0xAA	10101010	170
0xFFFF	1111111111111111	65535
0xFFAA	1111111110101010	65450

c) The 8051 memory architecture

Having considered some of the basic memory types available and some general features of computer memory organization, we are now in a position to consider the memory architecture of the 8051.

There are two distinct memory regions in an 8051 device: the DATA area and the CODE area. We will consider each region in turn here.

DATA memory

DATA memory is used to store variables and the program stack while the program is running. The DATA area will be implemented using some form of RAM.

Most of the DATA area has a byte-oriented memory organization. However, within the DATA area is a 16-byte BDATA area which can also be accessed using bit addresses. This area can be used to store bit-sized variables (see Figure 2.6). The 8051 has machine instructions which allow bit variables to be manipulated very efficiently. These instructions can be easily utilized from C, as we will demonstrate in Chapter 3.

Byte address	Bit address							
0x2F	0x7F	0x7E	0x7D	0x7C	0x7B	0x7A	0x79	0x78
0x2E	0x77	0x76	0x75	0x74	0x73	0x72	0x71	0x70
0x2D	0x6F	0x6E	0x6D	0x6C	0x6B	0x6A	0x69	0x68
0x2C	0x67	0x66	0x65	0x64	0x63	0x62	0x61	0x60
0x2B	0x5F	0x5E	0x5D	0x5C	0x5B	0x5A	0x59	0x58
0x2A	0x57	0x56	0x55	0x54	0x53	0x52	0x51	0x50
0x29	0x4F	0x4E	0x4D	0x4C	0x4B	0x4A	0x49	0x48
0x28	0x47	0x46	0x45	0x44	0x43	0x42	0x41	0x40
0x27	0x3F	0x3E	0x3D	0x3C	0x3B	0x3A	0x39	0x38
0x26	0x37	0x36	0x35	0x34	0x33	0x32	0x31	0x30
0x25	0x2F	0x2E	0x2D	0x2C	0x2B	0x2A	0x29	0x28
0x24	0x27	0x26	0x25	0x24	0x23	0x22	0x21	0x20
0x23	0x1F	0x1E	0x1D	0x1C	0x1B	0x1A	0x19	0x18
0x22	0x17	0x16	0x15	0x14	0x13	0x12	0x11	0x10
0x21	0x0F	0x0E	0x0D	0x0C	0x0B	0x0A	0x09	0x08
0x20	0x07	0x06	0x05	0x04	0x03	0x02	0x01	0x00

FIGURE 2.6 On-chip RAM memory in the 8051: The BDATA area. See text for details

Note that the various locations can be accessed either via their byte addresses (0x20 to 0x2F) or via their bit addresses (0x00 to 0x7F).

Note also that there is an area where the bit addresses and the byte addresses are the same. For example, within byte address 0x24, there is a bit location with address 0x27: there is also a byte with address 0x27 in the BDATA area. It may appear that this will cause problems for the compiler. However, no conflicts will arise because the compiler can always determine from the context (that is, the type of data being manipulated) whether the bit address or byte address should be used.

CODE memory

Not surprisingly, the CODE area is used to store the program code, usually in some form of ROM ('read-only memory').

Please note:

- The CODE area may also contain read-only variables ('constants'), such as filter co-efficients or data for speech playback.
- On a desktop PC, code is copied from disk to RAM when you run the program. It is then executed from RAM. In most embedded systems, like the 8051, code is 'executed in place', from ROM.

- One consequence of the 'execute in place' operation is that, in most applications, while you may require up to 10 kbytes of CODE memory, you will rarely need much DATA memory. This is reflected in the fact that many 8051 devices have 20 kbytes or more of on-chip ROM, but will often have no more than 256 bytes of RAM. This is an appropriate mix for most general applications.

d) 8-bit family, 16-bit address space

The Standard 8051 can be described as an 8-bit microcontroller with a 16-bit address space.

Here the fact that it is an '8-bit microcontroller' refers to the size of the registers and data bus. This means that the family will handle 8-bit data very quickly and process 16-bit or 32-bit data rather less efficiently.

The 16-bit address space means that the device can directly address 2^{16} bytes of memory: that is, 64 kbytes. Note that the (Harvard-like) architecture of the 8051 means that it can access both 64 kbytes of CODE memory and 64 kbytes of DATA memory. These figures refer to the total amount of memory you can access: to reach these limits, you will need to connect memory devices to the external interface (Figure 2.7).

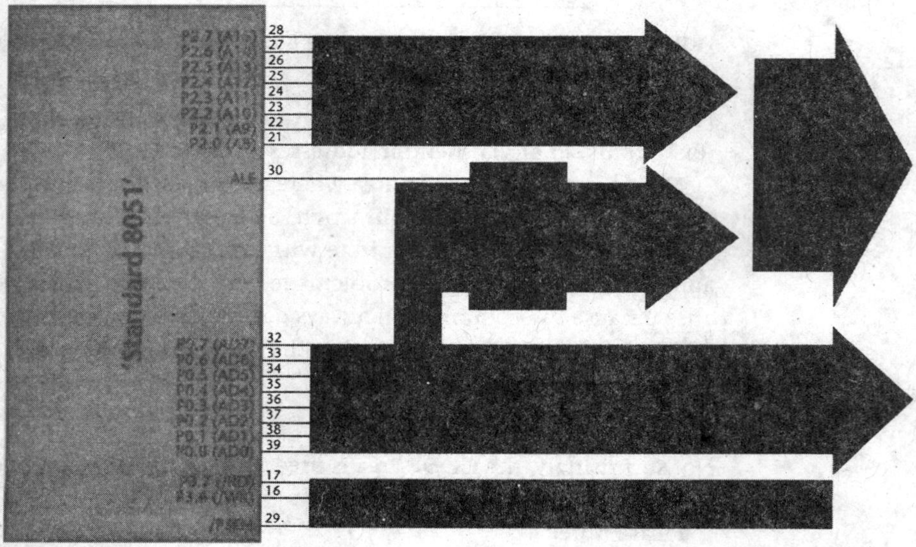

FIGURE 2.7 The 8051 external memory interface. Use of this external memory interface involves the use of the whole of Port 0 and Port 2, plus some of Port 3. We will not consider hardware issues in detail in this book: please refer to Chapter 11 for sources of further information about this topic

Where possible, it is better to use a device with all the required memory on the chip: this can improve reliability, reduce costs, reduce the application size, and reduce power consumption.

Finally, please note that – while all 8051s are 8-bit microcontrollers – some more recent devices (like the Dallas 80c390) support an address space greater than 16 bits. This allows access to much larger amounts of memory. Please refer to the 80c390 data sheet (on the CD) for details.

2.7 I/O pins

Much of the activity in embedded systems involves reading pins (which may, for example, be connected to switches or keypads) and altering the value of other pins (which may, in turn, control anything, from an LED to a 5-tonne industrial robot). The 8051 architecture has a number of features which make it very well suited to such applications.

Most 8051s have four 8-bit ports, giving a total of 32 pins you can individually read from or control. All of the ports are bidirectional: that is, they may be used for both input and output. To limit the size of the device, some of the port pins have alternate functions. For example, as we saw in the previous section, Ports 0, 2 (and part of Port 3) together provide the address and data bus used to support access to external memory. Similarly, two further pins on Port 3 (Pin 16 and Pin 17) also provide access to the on-chip UART (see Section 2.10). When in their 'alternative roles', these pins cannot be used for ordinary input or output. For example, if using a Standard 8051 device with external memory, Port 1 is the only (complete) port available for general-purpose I/O operations.

The comments above all refer to the Standard 8051: the number of available ports on 8051 microcontrollers varies enormously: the Small 8051s have the equivalent of approximately two ports, and the Extended 8051s have up to ten ports. Despite these differences, the control of ports on all members of the 8051 family is carried out in the same way.

We will consider how to use the port pins for input and output in Chapter 3 and Chapter 4.

2.8 Timers

All members of the 8051 family have at least two timer/counters, known as Timer 0 and Timer 1: most also have an additional timer (Timer 2). These are 16-bit timers, which means they can hold values from 0 to 65535 (decimal).

Timers like these are crucial to the development of embedded systems. To see why, you need to appreciate that, when configured appropriately, the timers are incremented periodically: specifically, in most 8051 devices, the timers are incremented every 12 oscillator cycles. Thus, assuming we have a 12 MHz oscillator, the timer will be incremented 1 million times per second.

There are many things we can do with such a timer:

- We can use it to measure intervals of time. For example, we can measure the duration of a function by noting the value of a timer at the beginning and end of the function call, and comparing the two results.
- We can use it to generate precise hardware delays, as we discuss in Chapter 6.
- We can use it to generate 'time out' facilities: this is a key requirement in systems with real-time constraints (see Chapter 6).
- Most important of all, we can use it to generate regular 'ticks', and drive an operating system: we say a little more about this in the next section.

2.9 Interrupts

If you were to ask developers who are experienced in embedded systems to sum up in one word the difference between desktop software and embedded software, many would probably choose the word 'interrupt'.

From a low-level perspective, an interrupt is a hardware mechanism used to notify a processor that an 'event' has taken place: such events may be 'internal' events (such as the overflow of a timer) or 'external' events (such as the arrival of a character through a serial interface).

Viewed from a high-level perspective, interrupts provide a mechanism for creating multitasking applications: that is applications which, apparently, perform more than one task at a time using a single processor. To illustrate this, a schematic representation of interrupt handling in an embedded system is shown in Figure 2.8.

In Figure 2.8 the system executes two (background) functions, Function 1 and Function 2. During the execution of Function 1, an interrupt is raised, and an 'interrupt service routine' (ISR1) deals with this event. After the execution of ISR1 is complete, Function 1 resumes its operation. During the execution of Function 2, another interrupt is raised, this time dealt with by ISR2.

The original '8051' ('8052') architecture supported seven interrupt sources:[9]

- Two or three timer/counter interrupts (related to Timer 0, Timer 1 and – in the 8052 – Timer 2).

9. More recent devices support larger numbers of interrupts without altering the core architecture.

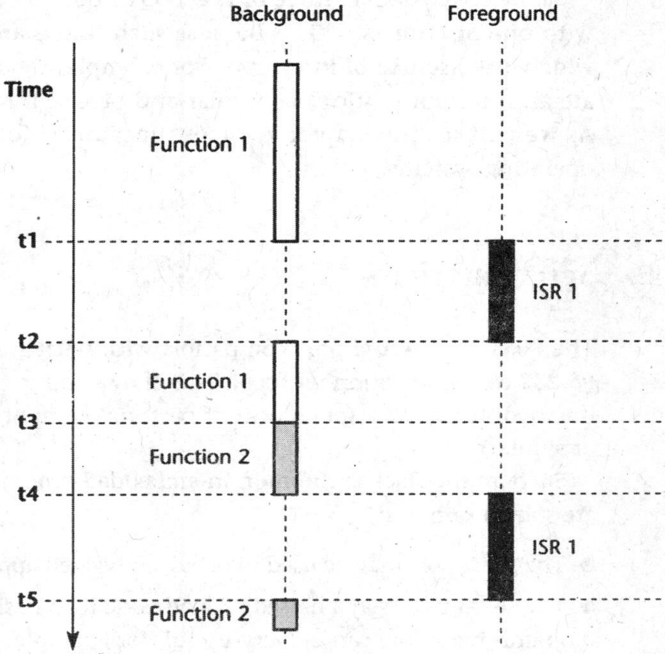

FIGURE 2.8 A schematic representation of interrupt handling in an embedded system

- Two UART-related interrupts (note: these share the same interrupt vector, and can be viewed as a single interrupt source).
- Two external interrupts.

In addition, there is one further interrupt source over which the programmer has minimal control:

- The 'power-on reset' (POR) interrupt.

When an interrupt is generated, the processor 'jumps' to an address at the bottom of the CODE memory area. These locations must contain suitable code with which the microcontroller can respond to the interrupt. In most cases, the locations will include another 'jump' instruction, giving the address of suitable 'interrupt service routine' located elsewhere in (CODE) memory.

This process may sound complicated but, from the perspective of the C programmer, an interrupt service routine is simply a function that is 'called by the microcontroller', as a result of a particular hardware event. As we will see in later chapters, use of interrupts in a high-level language is a straightforward process.

As we noted above, three of the '8051 / 8052' interrupt sources are associated with on-chip timers. This is because such timers are a particularly effective and widely-used source of interrupts. For example, we can use such timers to generate an interrupt (a 'tick') at regular and precise intervals of (say) 1 millisecond. As we will see in Chapter 7, such 'timer ticks' form the basis of all real-time operating systems.

2.10 Serial interface

The 8051 has a serial port compatible with what is commonly referred to as the RS-232 communication protocol. This allows you to transfer data between an 8051 microcontroller and some form of personal computer (desktop PC, notebook PC or similar).

Such an interface is common in embedded processors, and is widely used. Here are some examples:

- The serial port may be used to debug embedded applications, using a desktop PC.
- The serial port may be used to load code into flash memory for 'in circuit programming'. This can be very useful, for example, when code must be updated 'in situ' (for example, when the product is already installed in a vehicle, or on a production line).
- The serial port may be used to transfer data from embedded data acquisition systems to a PC, or to other embedded processors.

We will consider the use of the serial interface in detail in Chapter 9.

2.11 Power consumption

The final issue we need to address is power consumption.

On a desktop PC, processor power consumption is not generally a major concern. In such an environment, the typical CRT-based screen, DVD/CD drive and hard disk will consume much more power than the processor itself: efforts at saving power therefore tend to focus on 'shutting down' peripheral components rather than optimizing the processor itself.

The embedded environment is very different, particularly where battery-powered applications are being developed. In such applications, the microcontroller is often the main drain on our battery power. To achieve longer battery life, all modern implementations of 8051 processors have at least three operating modes:

- Normal mode.
- Idle Mode.
- Power-Down Mode.

The 'Idle' and 'Power Down' modes are intended to be used to save power at times when no processing is required. Typical current requirements for the various modes are shown in Table 2.2. Note that the original 'Intel 8051' figure (for the 1980 processor) is shown for comparative purposes: this did not have power-saving modes.

TABLE 2.2 Typical current consumption figures for a selection of Standard 8051 devices. Note that figures vary (approximately linearly) with oscillator frequency: in this case, the clock frequency is assumed at 12 MHz for each device

Device	Normal	Idle	Power Down
Intel 8051	160 mA	-	-
Atmel 89S53	11 mA	2 mA	60 uA
Dallas 87C520	15 mA	8 mA	50 μA
Intel 80C51	16 mA	4 mA	50 μA

To put these figures in context, bear in mind that – for reasonable battery life – we generally aim for an average power consumption of less than 10 mA. As the table makes clear, this means that operating in 'Normal' mode for extended periods is not a practical option.

The Infineon C501 is an example of a Standard 8051 device, which offers power-down modes identical to those available in the 8052 and many other modern devices. The following description of the C501 idle modes, adapted from the user manual, describes these modes in detail. Please note that this description applies equally well to most Standard 8051s.

a) Idle mode

In the idle mode the oscillator of the C501 continues to run, but the CPU is gated off from the clock signal. However, the interrupt system, the serial port and all timers are connected to the clock. The CPU status is preserved in its entirety.

The reduction of power consumption which can be achieved by this feature depends on the number of peripherals running. If all timers are stopped and the serial interface is not running, the maximum power reduction can be achieved: the developer has to determine which peripheral must continue to run and which may be stopped.

The idle mode is entered by setting the flag bit IDLE (PCON.0). The easiest way to set the IDLE bit is with the following 'C' statement:

```
PCON |= 0x01; // Enter idle mode
```

There are two ways to terminate idle mode:

- Activate any enabled interrupt. This interrupt will be serviced and the program will continue by executing the instruction following the instruction that sets the IDLE bit.
- Perform a hardware reset.

b) Power-down mode

In the power-down mode, the on-chip oscillator is stopped. Therefore all functions are stopped; only the contents of the on-chip RAM are maintained.

The power-down mode is entered by setting the flag bit PDE (PCON.1). This is most easily done in 'C' as follows:

```
PCON |= 0x02; // Enter power-down mode
```

The only exit from power-down mode is a hardware reset.

2.12 Conclusions

All members of the 8051 family provide the hardware components – multiple port pins, timers, interrupt handling, serial interface and memory – required in embedded applications. We will describe how to make full use of these components in the remainder of this book.

In Chapter 3, we describe how the operation of the 8051 can be simulated on a desktop PC.

chapter 3

Hello, Embedded World

3.1 Introduction

FIGURE 3.1 A desk-bound computer (left) sporting general-purpose input and output facilities (keyboard and high-resolution graphics screen), compared with an embedded, single-board computer system which lacks any high-level I/O facilities

When you first started programming a desktop computer, you probably wrote a program similar to the example shown in Listing 3.1 for every language you learned.

Listing 3.1 A simple desktop C program

```
#include <stdio.h>

int main(void)
  {
  printf("Hello world\n");

  return 0;
  }
```

In this chapter, we will dissect a 'Hello World' program written for the 8051 microcontroller. Like the desktop program, this will be designed to introduce key features of the development tools and the environment. Unlike the desktop version, we have no screen on which to display text (Figure 3.1): instead, the code will be designed to flash an LED on for one second, off for one second, *ad infinitum*.

The program we will use to do this is shown (in part) in Listing 3.2.

Listing 3.2 Part of the 'Hello, Embedded World' example code

```
void main(void)
   {
   LED_FLASH_Init();

   while(1)
      {
      // Change the LED state (OFF to ON, or vice versa)
      LED_FLASH_Change_State();

      // Delay for *approx* 1000 ms
      DELAY_LOOP_Wait(1000);
      }
   }
```

We begin by considering the Keil tools that will be used to develop this software. We will then consider the various components of the program in detail.

3.2 Installing the Keil software and loading the project

To make full use of the material in this chapter, you need to install the Keil C51 development tools: these are included on the CD. Please refer to p.304 (the last page of this book) for details.

Note: the example projects for this book are NOT loaded automatically when you install the Keil compiler. Instead, these files are stored on the CD in a directory '/Pont'. The files are arranged by chapter: the project discussed here is in the directory '/Pont/ Ch03_00 – Hello'.

Rather than using the projects on the CD (where changes cannot be saved), please copy the files from the CD onto an appropriate directory on your hard disk. Note: you will need to change the file properties after copying: files transferred from the CD will be 'read only'.

When you have copied the files onto your hard disk, please run the Keil µVision application, and use the 'Open Project' option (from the 'Project' menu) to load the 'Hello' example. You will then be able to work with this project by following the example described in the remainder of this chapter.

3.3 Configuring the simulator

Having loaded the 'Hello' project in the Keil µVision environment, we will begin by exploring the project settings.

First, using the Project menu, we will look at the 8051 device which we are intending to use for this application (Figure 3.2).

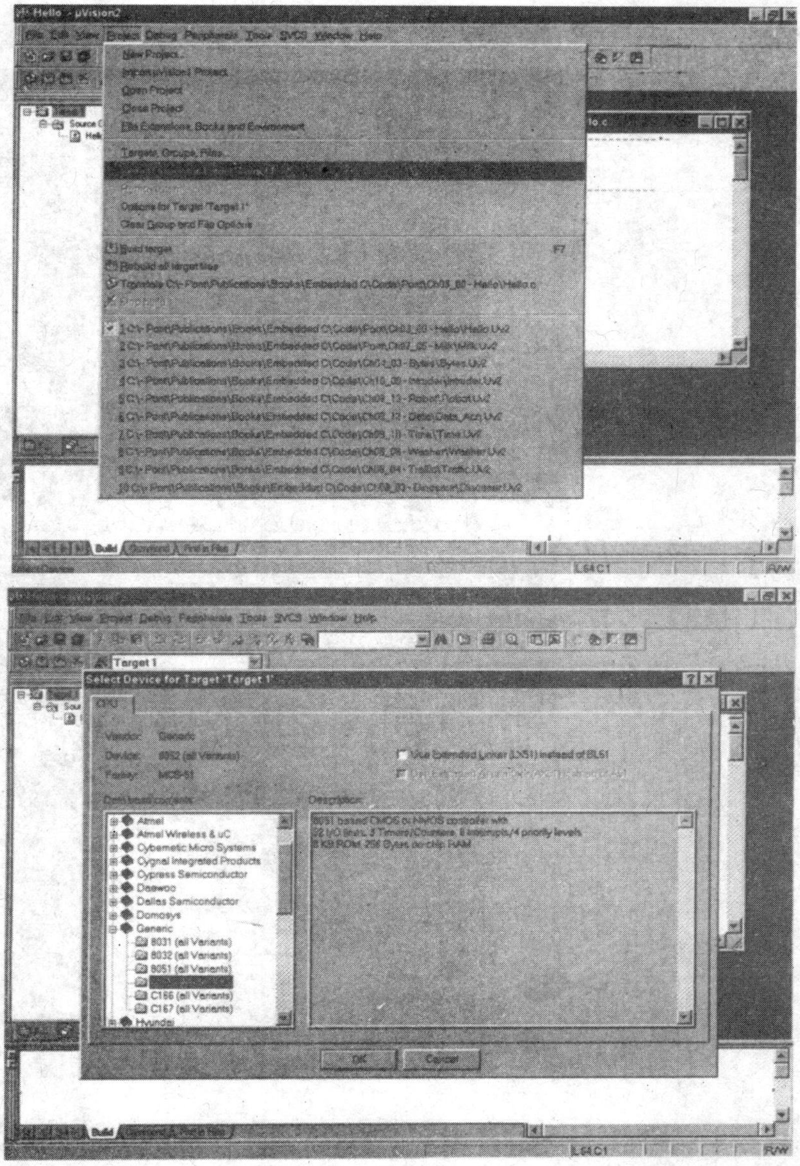

FIGURE 3.2 This is how we choose which particular 8051 chip the hardware will simulate. In this project, we are using a 'generic' 8052 driver. This driver will work with all of the examples in this book

In this case, we will use a generic '8052' driver: as we discussed in Chapter 2, the 8052 architecture forms the basis of the great majority of current '8051' devices. This driver can be used with all of the examples in this book.

The next thing we need to check is the oscillator frequency. As we also discussed in Chapter 2, the choice of oscillator frequency has a large impact on 8051-based applications. In most examples in this book, we will assume that the oscillator frequency is 12 MHz. Figure 3.3 shows how to inspect and – if required – alter this frequency.

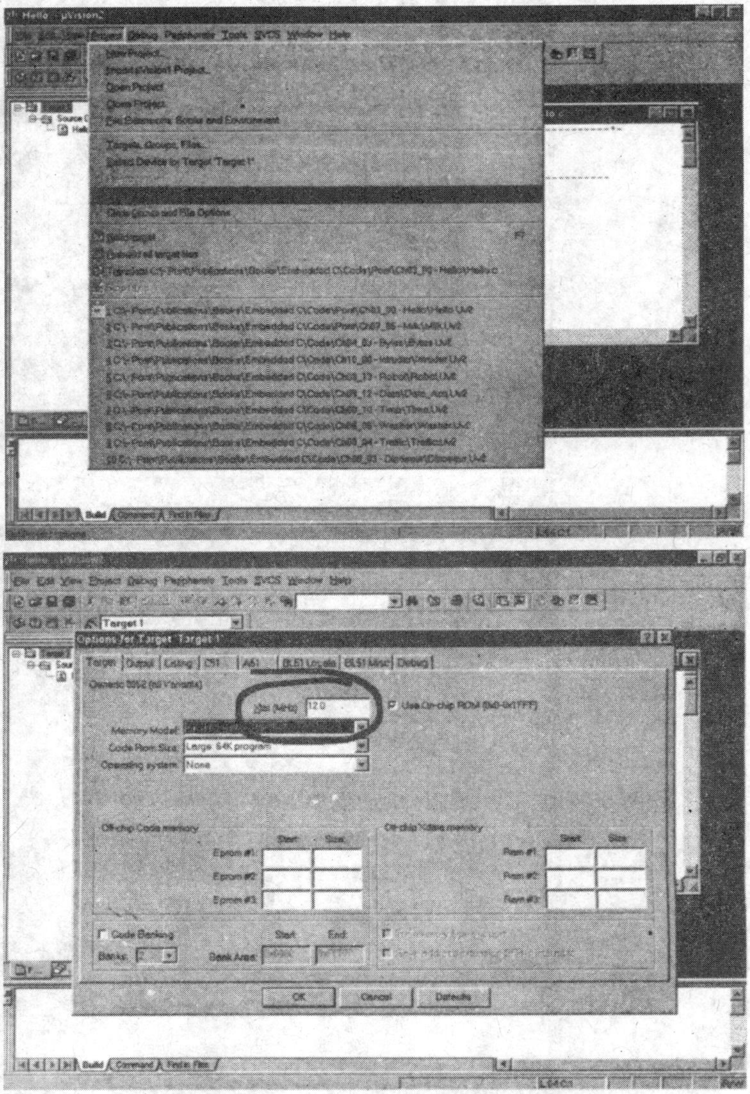

FIGURE 3.3 Viewing and – if necessary – changing the oscillator frequency

Note: one of the key reasons for setting the oscillator frequency in the simulator is that any attempting at 'profiling' the application (for example, measuring function durations) will only be successful if the oscillator frequency in the simulator matches the frequency that will be used in the real system hardware (see Section 3.6e).

3.4 Building the target

We next need to build the 'target', as illustrated in Figure 3.4.

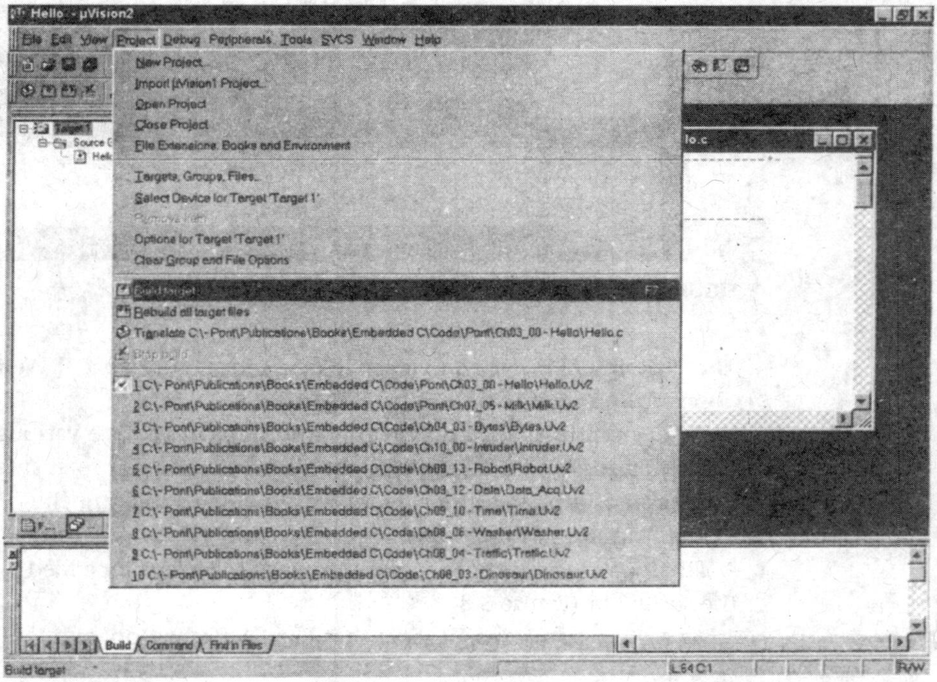

FIGURE 3.4 Building the target (compiling and linking your source files) in the Keil environment

3.5 Running the simulation

Having successfully built the target, we are now ready to start the debug session and run the simulator.

First, start a debug session (Figure 3.5).

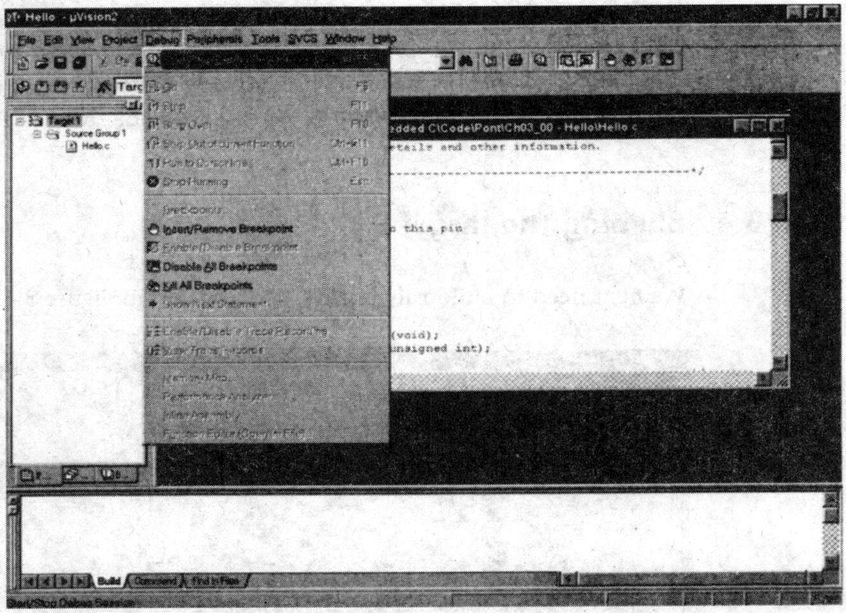

FIGURE 3.5 Starting the simulator (debugger)

The 'flashing LED' we will view will be connected to Port 1. We therefore want to observe the activity on this port (Figure 3.6).

By default, to speed up the simulation, updates to the various components are carried out only on demand. For our purposes, we want to ensure that the simulator regularly updates the screen: we do this by ticking the 'Periodic Window Update' option in the 'View' menu (Figure 3.7).

Finally, we are ready to start running our 'Hello, Embedded World' program in the simulator (Figure 3.8).

As the program runs, observe that Pin 1.5 flashes 'on' and 'off', as required.

Please note:

The simulator does <u>**NOT**</u> operate in real time. What this means is that – except by chance – the port pin will not flash on for one second, off for one second, when you execute this program.

To determine the speed at which the code will execute on the real system, you need to use the 'Performance Analyzer' functions provided in the simulator: we discuss these functions in Section 3.6e.

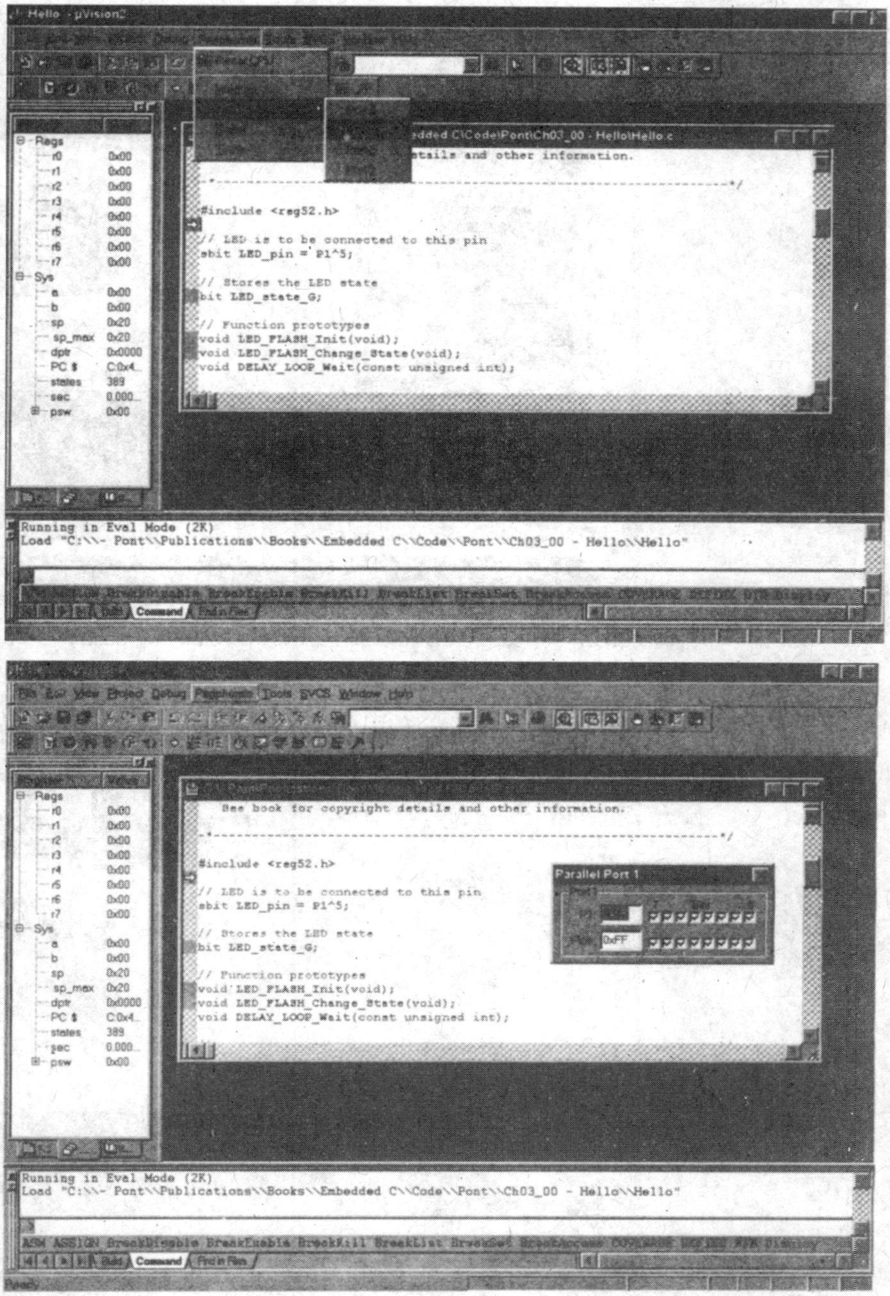

FIGURE 3.6 The flashing LED will be connected to Port 1. We therefore need to have the simulator display the activity on this port

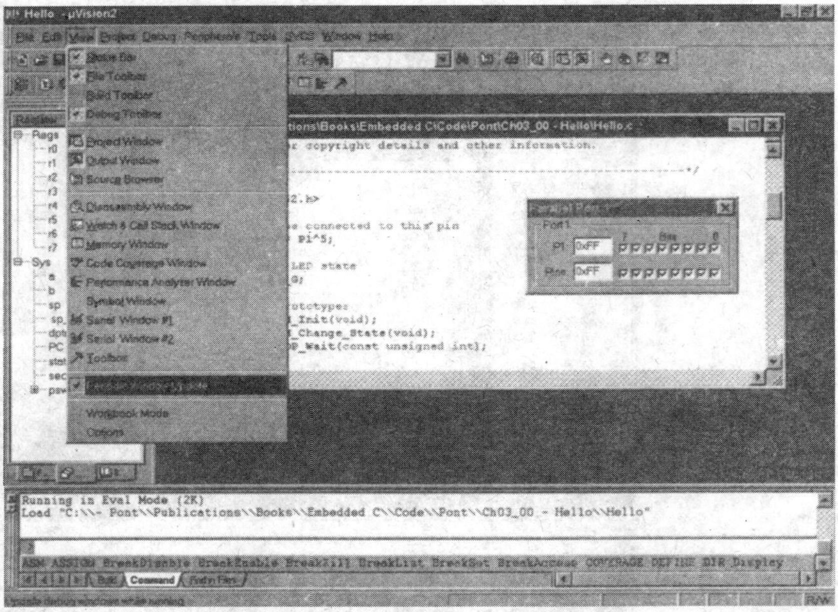

FIGURE 3.7 To ensure that the port activity is visible, we need to set the 'Periodic Window Update' flag

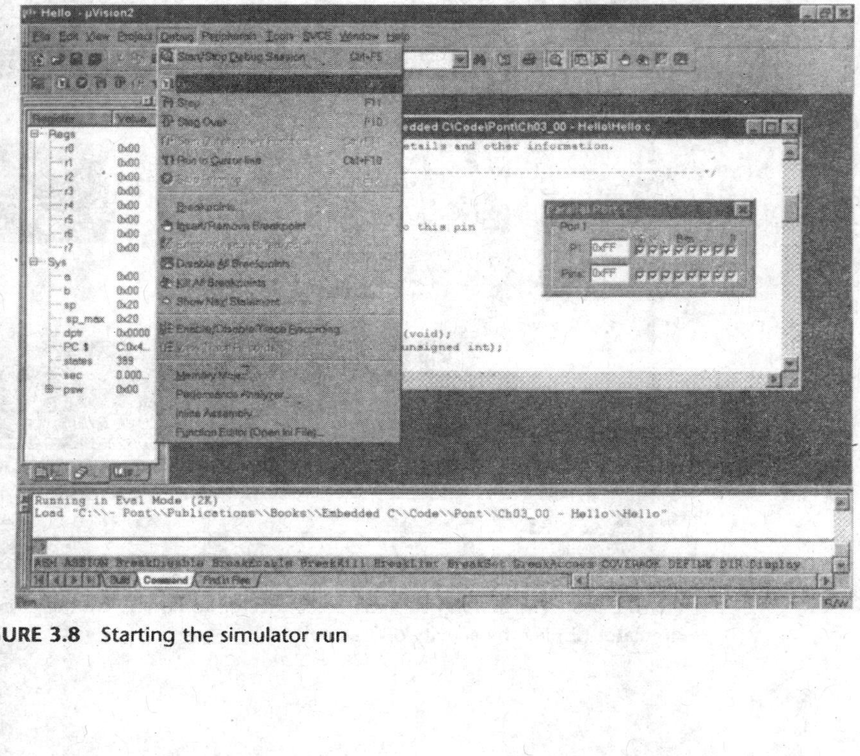

FIGURE 3.8 Starting the simulator run

3.6 Dissecting the program

So far in this chapter we have simply demonstrated the operation of the Keil 8051 simulator.

We now begin to consider how the code in Listing 3.2 actually works.

a) The complete program

The complete 'Hello, Embedded World' program is shown in Listing 3.3.

Listing 3.3 The complete 'Hello, Embedded World' program

```
/*------------------------------------------------------------------*-

   Hello.C (v1.00)

   ------------------------------------------------------------------

   A "Hello Embedded World" test program for 8051.

-*------------------------------------------------------------------*/

#include <reg52.h>

// LED is to be connected to this pin
sbit LED_pin = P1^5;

// Stores the LED state
bit LED_state_G;

// Function prototypes
void LED_FLASH_Init(void);
void LED_FLASH_Change_State(void);
void DELAY_LOOP_Wait(const unsigned int);

/*..................................................................*/

void main(void)
   {
   LED_FLASH_Init();

   while(1)
      {
      // Change the LED state (OFF to ON, or vice versa)
      LED_FLASH_Change_State();
```

```
      // Delay for *approx* 1000 ms
      DELAY_LOOP_Wait(1000);
      }
   }

/*------------------------------------------------------------------*-

   LED_FLASH_Init()
   Prepare for LED_Change_State() function - see below.

-*------------------------------------------------------------------*/
void LED_FLASH_Init(void)
   {
   LED_state_G = 0;
   }

/*------------------------------------------------------------------*-

   LED_FLASH_Change_State()

   Changes the state of an LED (or pulses a buzzer, etc) on a
   specified port pin.

   Must call at twice the required flash rate: thus, for 1 Hz
   flash (on for 0.5 seconds, off for 0.5 seconds),
   this function must be called twice a second.

-*------------------------------------------------------------------*/
void LED_FLASH_Change_State(void)
   {
   // Change the LED from OFF to ON (or vice versa)
   if (LED_state_G == 1)
      {
      LED_state_G = 0;
      LED_pin = 0;
      }
   else
      {
      LED_state_G = 1;
      LED_pin = 1;
      }
   }

/*------------------------------------------------------------------*-
```

```
   DELAY_LOOP_Wait()

   Delay duration varies with parameter.

   Parameter is, *ROUGHLY*, the delay, in milliseconds,
   on 12MHz 8051 (12 osc cycles).

   You need to adjust the timing for your application!

-*------------------------------------------------------------*/
void DELAY_LOOP_Wait(const unsigned int DELAY)
   {
   unsigned int x, y;

   for (x = 0; x <= DELAY; x++)
      {
      for (y = 0; y <= 120; y++);
      }
   }

/*------------------------------------------------------------*-
  ---- END OF FILE -------------------------------------------
-*------------------------------------------------------------*/
```

We will consider the various parts of this program in detail in the sections below.

b) The Super Loop architecture

The main function (shown in Listing 3.4) is a classic example of a Super Loop architecture introduced in Chapter 1.

Listing 3.4 Part of the 'Hello, Embedded World' example code

```
void main(void)
   {
   LED_FLASH_Init();

   while(1)
      {
      // Change the LED state (OFF to ON, or vice versa)
      LED_FLASH_Change_State();

      // Delay for *approx* 1000 ms
      DELAY_LOOP_Wait(1000);
      }
   }
```

In this function, we perform some initialization operations (considered below), then we enter the endless loop. In this loop, we alternately call a function to 'flash' the LED, and a one-second-delay function.

The functions `LED_FLASH_Init()`, `LED_FLASH_Change_State()`, and `DELAY_ LOOP_Wait()` are discussed below.

c) Controlling the port pins

We next consider the functions used to control the LED.

Listing 3.5 highlights several key features from this part of the program.

Listing 3.5 Part of the 'Hello, Embedded World' example code

```
. . .

#include <reg52.h>

. . .

// ------ Port pins ----------------------------------------
sbit LED_pin = P1^5;

// ------ Private variable definitions ----------------------
bit LED_state_G;

. . .

/*------------------------------------------------------------*-

  LED_FLASH_Init()

  Prepare for LED_Change_State() function - see below.

-*------------------------------------------------------------*/
void LED_FLASH_Init(void)
   {
   LED_state_G = 0;
   }

/*------------------------------------------------------------*-

  LED_FLASH_Change_State()

  Changes the state of an LED (or pulses a buzzer, etc) on a
  specified port pin.
```

```
  Must call at twice the required flash rate: thus, for 1 Hz
  flash (on for 0.5 seconds, off for 0.5 seconds) must call
  every 0.5 seconds.

-*------------------------------------------------------------------*/
void LED_FLASH_Change_State(void)
   {
   // Change the LED from OFF to ON (or vice versa)
   if (LED_state_G == 1)
      {
      LED_state_G = 0;
      LED_pin = 0;
      }
   else
      {
      LED_state_G = 1;
      LED_pin = 1;
      }
   }
```

To understand Listing 3.5, recall that – as we discussed in Chapter 2 – Standard 8051s have four 8-bit ports. The ports are referred to as Port 0, Port 1, Port 2 and Port 3. All ports are bidirectional: that is, they may be used for both input and output.

Control of the ports is carried out using what are known as 'special function registers' (SFRs). The SFRs are 8-bit latches: in practical terms, this means that the values written to the port are held there until a new value is written or the device is reset. Each of the four ports is represented by an SFR: these are named, appropriately, P0, P1, P2 and P3. Physically, each SFR is an area of memory in the upper areas of internal RAM: P0 is at address 0x80, P1 at address 0x90, P2 at address 0xA0 and P3 at address 0xB0.

Table 3.1 shows the representation of the ports in the SFR area of memory.

TABLE 3.1 On-chip RAM memory in the 8051: The SFR area. See text for details

Byte address	Bit address								
0xB0	Pin 3.7 0xB7	Pin 3.6 0xB6	Pin 3.5 0xB5	Pin 3.4 0xB4	Pin 3.3 0xB3	Pin 3.2 0xB2	Pin 3.1 0xB1	Pin 3.0 0xB0	Port 3
...									
0xA0	Pin 2.7 0xA7	Pin 2.6 0xA6	Pin 2.5 0xA5	Pin 2.4 0xA4	Pin 2.3 0xA3	Pin 2.2 0xA2	Pin 2.1 0xA1	Pin 2.0 0xA0	Port 2
...									
0x90	Pin 1.7 0x97	Pin 1.6 0x96	Pin 1.5 0x95	Pin 1.4 0x94	Pin 1.3 0x93	Pin 1.2 0x92	Pin 1.1 0x91	Pin 1.0 0x90	Port 1
...									
0x80	Pin 0.7 0x87	Pin 0.6 0x86	Pin 0.5 0x85	Pin 0.4 0x84	Pin 0.3 0x83	Pin 0.2 0x82	Pin 0.1 0x81	Pin 0.0 0x80	Port 0

If we want to write to the ports, we need to write to these addresses. Assuming that we are using a C compiler, the process of writing to an address is usually carried out by means of a SFR variable declaration,[10] hidden in a header file.

In Listing 3.5, the first `#include` directive ensures that a copy of the Keil 'reg52' file is inserted into the source file before compilation. Note that this file matches the '8052' register set, and is compatible with the selection of 8052 as the target hardware (see Section 3.3).

The key part of this file as far as this program is concerned is as follows:

```
. . .

/* BYTE Registers */
sfr P0 = 0x80;
sfr P1 = 0x90;
sfr P2 = 0xA0;
sfr P3 = 0xB0;

. . .
```

Having declared the SFR variables, we can write to the ports in a straightforward manner. For example, we can send some data to Port 1 as follows:

10. Reminder. A variable definition consumes memory. A variables declaration does not consume memory, it simply associates a name with an area of memory defined elsewhere in the program. Variable definitions are also variable declarations, but the reverse is not true.

```
unsigned char Port_data;

// REMEMBER:
// 0x identifies the number as hexadecimal (base 16)
// 0x0F (hexadecimal) = 00001111 (binary)
Port_data = 0x0F;

P1 = Port_data; // Write 00001111 to Port 1
```

Please note that, for experienced C programmers, this code may appear to be incorrect: P1 represents an *address*, and the correct C syntax would appear to be:

```
*P1 = Port_data; // Surely this is correct?
```

However, because the compiler knows how to deal with SFRs, the use of the indirection operator is not necessary (and code using it will not work as intended).

The example above assumed that we wished to control the whole of Port 1. In the 'Hello, Embedded World' program, we simply wish to control an individual port pin. Control of the Pin 1.5 is achieved through the following variable declaration in Listing 3.3:

```
// ------ Port pins ----------------------------------------
sbit LED_pin = P1^5;
```

The variable type here is `sbit`: this is not ISO / ANSI C, but is a Keil extension. Use of this keyword allows you to declare bit variables which are part of already-defined (byte-sized) variables. Note also the use of the '^' symbol to access a particular pin: this is again a Keil-specific operation.

Following this declaration, we can control the status of this individual pin by writing, for example:

```
LED_pin = 1;
```

This is exactly what we do later in the program:

```
// Change the LED from OFF to ON (or vice versa)
if (LED_state_G == 1)
   {
   LED_state_G = 0;
   LED_pin = 0;
   }
else
   {
```

```
LED_state_G = 1;
LED_pin = 1;
}
```

d) Creating and using a bit variable

Listing 3.3 also includes the definition of the bit variable LED_state_G:

```
// ------ Private variable definitions --------------------
bit LED_state_G;
```

As we discussed in Chapter 2, the 8051 device has a BDATA area (16-bytes in size) in which user-defined bit-sized variables may be stored. (You may like to refer back to Figure 2.6 for details for this).

In this case, we are using the Keil keyword bit to define LED_state_G, a bit-sized variable that will be stored in the BDATA area. LED_state_G can (of course) take on the values of only 1 or 0. It is used in the program to store the current state of the LED (ON or OFF):

```
if (LED_state_G == 1)
   {
   LED_state_G = 0;
   LED_pin = 0;
   }
```

e) The delay function

The next key component of the 'Hello, Embedded World' program is a delay function.

The creation of accurate delays is a key requirement in many embedded applications. One way of creating such delays is by using a loop delay, implemented as follows:

```
void Loop_Delay(void)
   {
   unsigned int x;

   for (x=0; x <= 65535; x++);
   }
```

If we find that these delays are not long enough, we can easily extend them by adding additional layers, as shown in Longer_Loop_Delay():

```
void Longer_Loop_Delay(void)
   {
   unsigned int x;
   unsigned int y;

   for (x=0; x <= 65535; x++)
      {
      for (y=0; y <= 65535; y++);
      }
   }
```

Listing 3.6 shows how the 1-second delay required in this application is achieved using this approach.

Listing 3.6 Part of the 'Hello, Embedded World' example code

```
/*------------------------------------------------------------------*-

  DELAY_LOOP_Wait()

  Delay duration varies with parameter.

  Parameter is, *ROUGHLY*, the delay, in milliseconds,
  on 12MHz 8051 (12 osc cycles).

  You need to adjust the timing for your application!

-*------------------------------------------------------------------*/
void DELAY_LOOP_Wait(const unsigned int DELAY)
   {
   unsigned int x, y;

   for (x = 0; x <= DELAY; x++)
      {
      for (y = 0; y <= 120; y++);
      }
   }
```

Note: there is nothing miraculous about the values used in this listing: they were determined by trial and error. If you use this (or similar) code in a real application, the delays will vary with compiler optimization settings and other factors. **They must always be checked carefully as part of the final pre-release tests.**[11]

11. Please note that some more robust techniques for generating delays are considered in Chapter 6.

To check the delay durations, run the Keil simulator as shown earlier. While the simulation is running, view the Performance Analyzer (Figure 3.9).

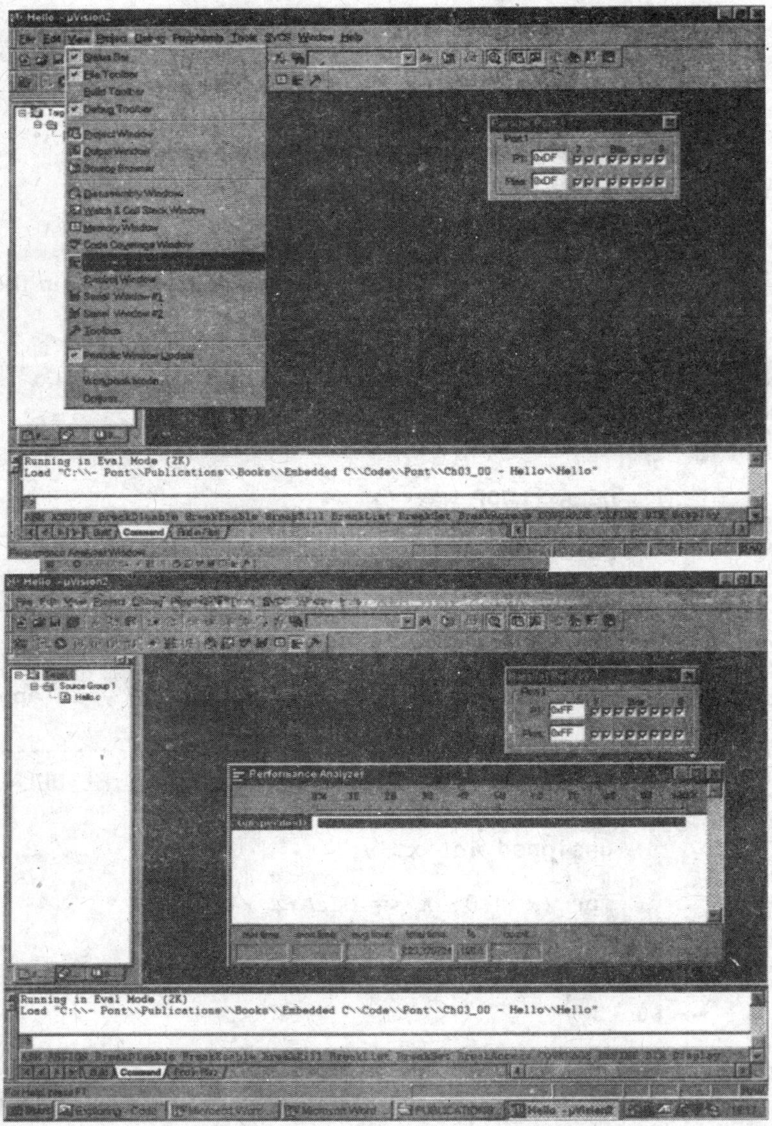

FIGURE 3.9 Running the Performance Analyzer in order to measure the duration of the loop delay function

At this stage, 100% of the processor time is devoted to 'Unspecified' activities. We now need to indicate that we wish to measure the duration of the loop delay functions (Figure 3.10).

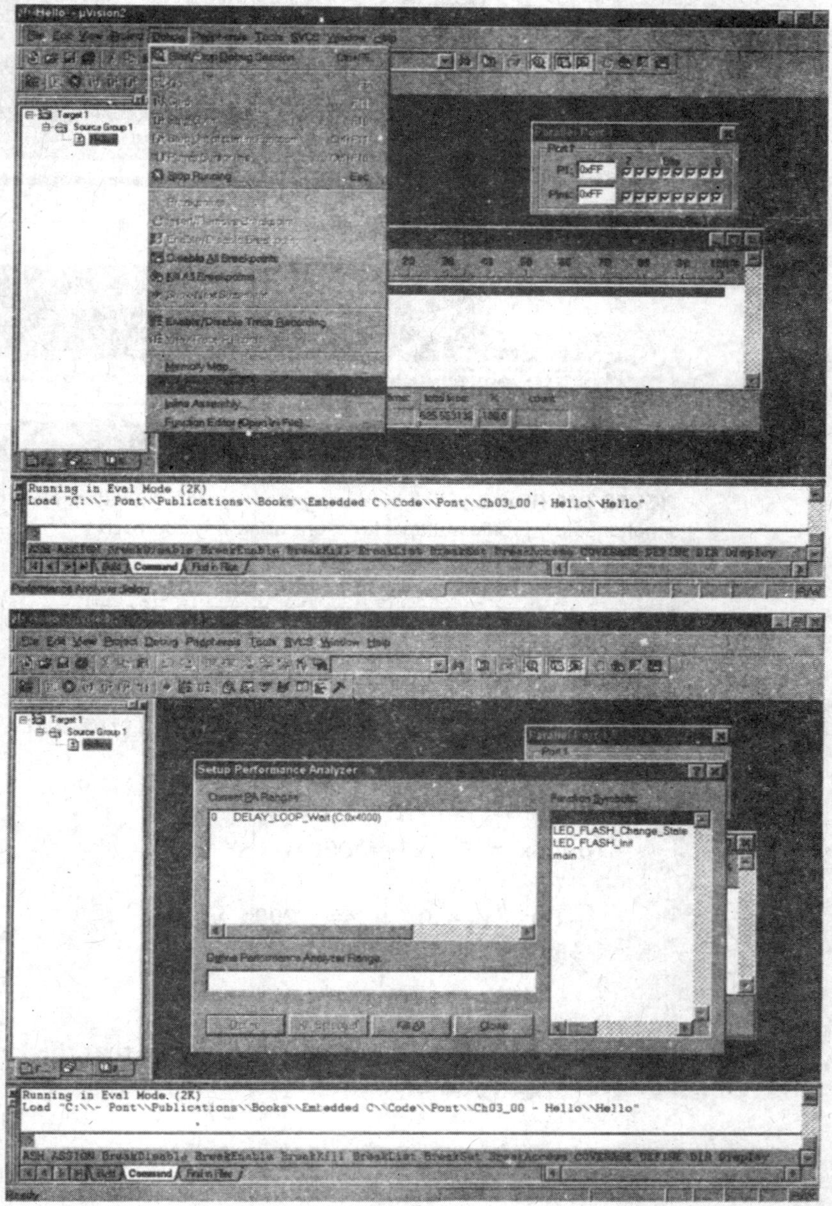

FIGURE 3.10 (Part 1 of 2) Measuring the duration of the loop delay. Note that we can profile multiple functions simultaneously using this approach

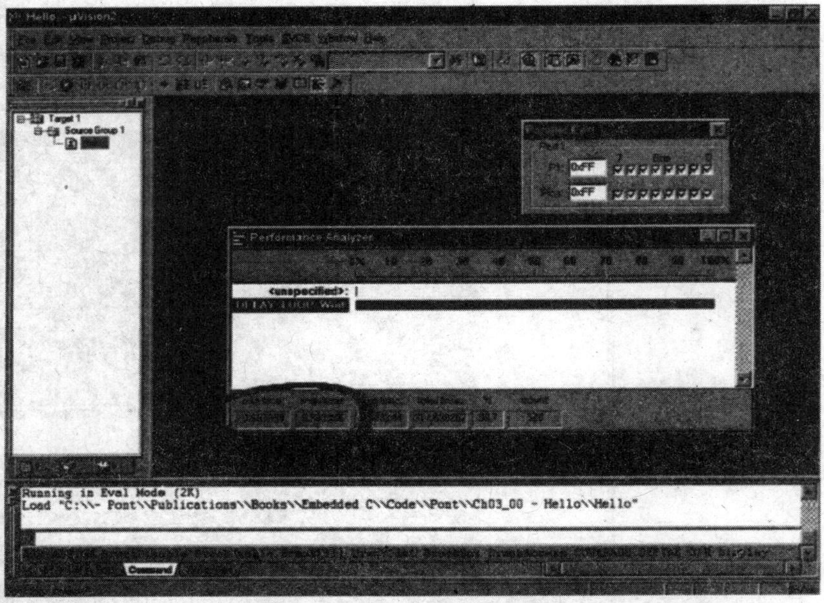

FIGURE 3.10 (Part 2 of 2) Measuring the loop delay duration. Note that we can simultaneously profile multiple functions using this approach

Figure 3.10 (Part 2) reveals that the duration of the loop delay is very close to the required value.

We can go back and alter the delay code:

```
void DELAY_LOOP_Wait(const unsigned int DELAY)
   {
   unsigned int x, y;

   for (x = 0; x <= DELAY; x++)
      {
      for (y = 0; y <= 1200; y++);
      }
   }
```

If we then repeat the simulation,[12] we can see that the loop delay duration has increased precisely as expected (Figure 3.11).

12. To make this change, you need to: [1] stop the simulation; [2] end the debug session; [3] edit the file and re-build the target; [4] re-start the debug session.

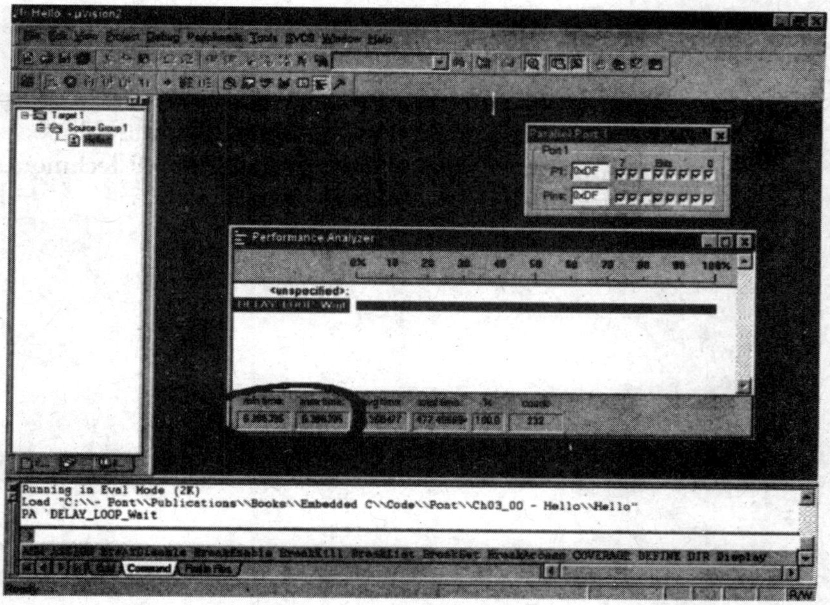

FIGURE 3.11 The result of altering the loop delay code

3.7 Aside: Building the hardware

This book is largely 'hardware free'. However, for the benefit of those readers who – having got this far – would like to run their program on 'real' hardware, we provide some suggestions here.

To make your life easier, you should base your design around an 8051 device with flash memory: for example, the Atmel AT89C52 is widely available, at low cost.

The required hardware schematic is given in Figure 1.2. This may be assembled on a breadboard of the type illustrated in Figure 1.7.

You will also require a suitable programmer with which to program your chosen microcontroller. Various companies produce suitable devices. Alternatively, if you have some experience in electronic construction (or simply enjoy a challenge), you will find an Application Note from Atmel on the CD ROM which describes how to construct a suitable programmer. Software to drive the programmer is also included on the CD.

3.8 Conclusions

The purpose of this chapter was to show how simple C programs can be developed and tested using the software tools included with this book.

In the next chapter, we will go on to look at techniques for reading port pins and working with mechanical switches.

chapter 4

Reading switches

4.1 Introduction

In earlier chapters, we have considered some of the fundamental differences between software development for desktop systems and embedded systems. We've noted that embedded systems usually execute one program, which begins running when the device is powered up. We've begun to look at a simple software architecture – the Super Loop – that is used at the heart of many embedded systems.

Another key challenge for desktop programmers moving into the embedded market is the implementation of the user interface. On the desktop, design of the user interface means working with a high-resolution graphics screen, some form of mouse (or equivalent 'pointing' device), and a large keyboard. Design freedom is restricted by the fact that the user of your application wants to have a similar 'look and feel' to other applications that he or she uses. To match these design constraints – and speed up the development process – developers will typically use some form of standard code library when building applications, rather than attempting to create all the code from scratch (Figure 4.1).

In the embedded world, it may appear – at first sight at least – that there are fewer constraints. Instead, it can seem that there is a 'free for all' where every developer will implement a different interface to their system. However, there is at least one common denominator: embedded systems usually use switches as part of their user interface (see Figure 4.2). This general rule applies from the most basic remote-control system for opening a garage door, right up to the most sophisticated aircraft autopilot system. Whatever the system you create, you need to be able to create a reliable switch interface.

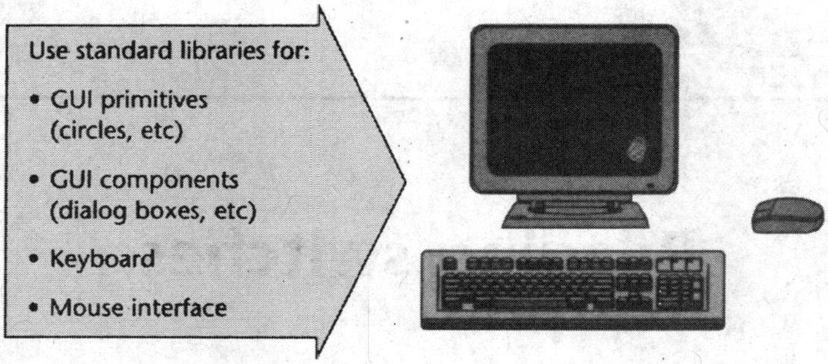

FIGURE 4.1 Developing the user interface for a modern desktop application will almost invariably mean working with a high-resolution graphics screen, a keyboard and a mouse, using code libraries written in, say, Java or C++

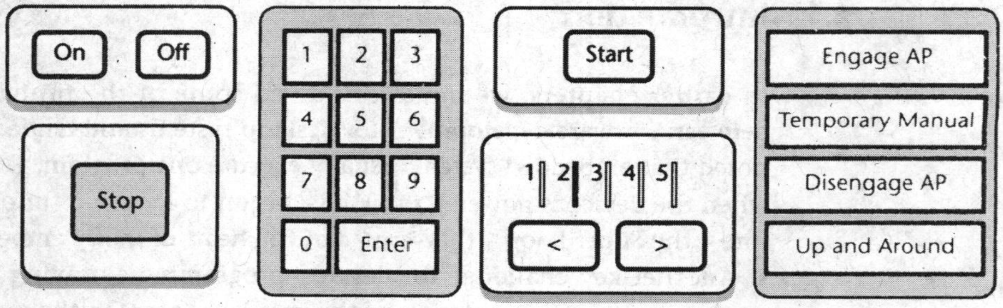

FIGURE 4.2 A collection of user-interface components taken from a range of different embedded systems. Most such interfaces contain at least one switch

In this chapter, we consider how you can read inputs from mechanical switches in your embedded application. Before considering some important characteristics of the switches themselves, we will consider the process of reading the state of port pins to which the switches will be connected.

4.2 Basic techniques for reading from port pins

As we saw in Chapter 3, control of the 8051 ports is carried out using 8-bit latches (SFRs). We can send some data to Port 1 as follows:[13]

```
sfr P1 = 0x90; // Usually in header file
P1 = 0x0F;     // Write 00001111 to Port 1
```

13. Remember: numbers beginning 'Ox...' are in hexadecimal. 'Hex' was reviewed in Chapter 2.

In exactly the same way, we can read from Port 1 as follows:

```
unsigned char Port_data;

P1 = 0xFF; // Set the port to 'read mode'
Port_data = P1; // Read from the port
```

Note: because of the underlying hardware, we can only read from a pin **if the corresponding latch contains a '1'**. In practice, this means that – in order to read from a pin – we need to ensure that the last thing written to the pin was a '1'.

After the 8051 microcontroller is reset, the port latches all have the value 0xFF (11111111 in binary): that is, all the port-pin latches are set to values of '1'. It is tempting to assume that writing data to the port is therefore unnecessary, and that we can get away with the following version:

```
unsigned char Port_data;

// Assume nothing written to port since reset
// - DANGEROUS!!!
Port_data = P1;
```

The problem with this code is that, in simple test programs it works: this can lull the developer into a false sense of security. If, at a later date, someone modifies the program to include a routine for writing to all or part of the same port, this code will not generally work as required:

```
unsigned char Port_data;

P1 = 0x00;

. . .

// Assumes nothing written to port since reset
// - WON'T WORK
Port_data = P1;
```

In most cases, initialization functions are used to set the port pins to a known state at the start of the program. Where this is not possible, it is safer to always write '1' to any port pin before reading from it.

4.3 Example: Reading and writing bytes

Listing 4.1 is a simple example which illustrates how we can read from one port on an 8051 microcontroller and 'echo' the result on another port.

As with the examples in Chapter 3, the Keil hardware simulator (included on the CD) will allow you to simulate suitable hardware for use with this program. Figure 4.3 shows the output from one such simulation.

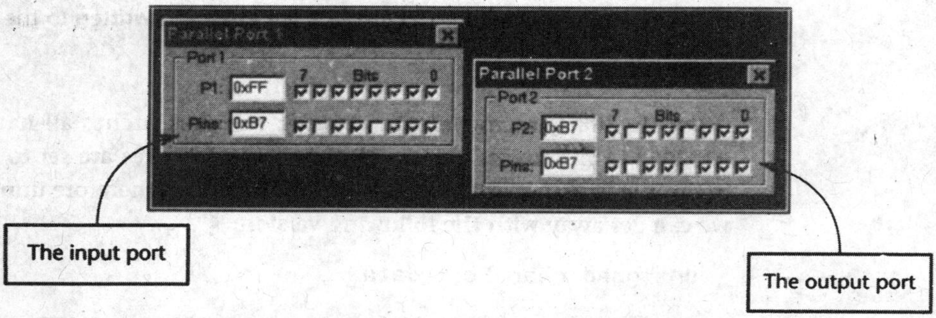

FIGURE 4.3 The output from the program in Listing 4.1 produced using the Keil hardware simulator included on the CD. Note the difference between the Port 1 latch value (0xFF) and the pin value (0xB7)

Listing 4.1 A simple 'Super Loop' application which copies the values from P1 to P2.

```
/*-------------------------------------------------------------------*-

   Bytes.C (v1.00)

   ------------------------------------------------------------------

   Reads from P1 and copies the value to P2.

-*-------------------------------------------------------------------*/

#include <Reg52.H>

/* ............................................................... */

void main (void)
   {
   unsigned char Port1_value;

   // Must set up P1 for reading
   P1 = 0xFF;
```

```
while(1)
  {
  // Read the value of P1
  Port1_value = P1;

  // Copy the value to P2
  P2 = Port1_value;
  }
}

/*------------------------------------------------------------------*-
  ---- END OF FILE -------------------------------------------------
-*------------------------------------------------------------------*/
```

4.4 Example: Reading and writing bits (simple version)

Listing 4.1 demonstrated how to read from or write to an entire port. However, suppose we have a switch connected to Pin 1.0 and an LED connected to Pin 1.1. We might also have input and output devices connected to the other pins on Port 1. These pins may be used by totally different parts of the same system, and the code to access them may be produced by other team members, or other companies. It is therefore essential that we are able to read-from or write-to individual port pins without altering the values of other pins on the same port.

We provided a simple example in which we controlled an individual pin in Chapter 3. Listing 4.2 goes one step further and illustrates how we can read from Pin 1.0, and write to Pin 1.1, without disrupting any other pins on this (or any other) port.

Listing 4.2 Reading and writing bits (simple version)

```
/*------------------------------------------------------------------*-

   Bits1.C (v1.00)

  ------------------------------------------------------------------

   Reading and writing individual port pins.

   NOTE: Both pins on the same port

-*------------------------------------------------------------------*/
```

```
#include <Reg52.H>

sbit Switch_pin = P1^0;
sbit LED_pin = P1^1;

/* ............................................................ */

void main (void)
   {
   bit x;

   // Set switch pin for reading
   Switch_pin = 1;

   while(1)
      {
      x = Switch_pin; // Read Pin 1.0
      LED_pin = x;    // Write to Pin 1.1
      }
   }

/*------------------------------------------------------------*-
  ---- END OF FILE -------------------------------------------
-*------------------------------------------------------------*/
```

Experienced 'C' programmers please note these lines:

```
sbit Switch_pin = P1^0;
sbit LED_pin = P1^1;
```

Here we gain access to two port pins through the use of an `sbit` variable declaration. The symbol '^' is used, but the XOR bitwise operator is NOT involved.

For programmers with less experience, we say more about the bitwise operators in the next section.

4.5 Example: Reading and writing bits (generic version)

We can make Listing 4.2 more flexible by making use of the bitwise AND, OR and 'complement' operators.

Even if you have programmed in C before on a desktop computer, you may not have come across the bitwise operators (&, |, ^, <<, >>, ~). These are not widely used by desktop programmers, but they allow a number of data manipulations that are very useful in embedded applications, including the introductory examples presented in this chapter. We will therefore briefly review the use of these operators here.

The six bitwise operators are listed in Table 4.1.

TABLE 4.1 The C bitwise operators

Operator	Description
&	Bitwise AND
|	Bitwise OR (inclusive OR)
^	Bitwise XOR (exclusive OR)
<<	Left shift
>>	Right shift
~	One's complement

To remind you, a summary of the AND, OR and XOR operations is given in Table 4.2.

TABLE 4.2 The AND, OR and XOR operations

A	B	A AND B	A OR B	A XOR B
0	0	0	0	0
0	1	0	1	1
1	0	0	1	1
1	1	1	1	0

Some examples of the use of all six of the bitwise operators are given in Listing 4.3. Note that this program is written in 'Desktop C': it cannot be compiled using the Keil tools.

Listing 4.3 Demonstrating the C bitwise operators.

```
/*------------------------------------------------------------------*-

   Main.C

  ------------------------------------------------------------------

   Illustrating the use of bitwise operators

-*------------------------------------------------------------------*/
```

```
#include <stdio.h>

void Display_Byte(const unsigned char);

/* ............................................................ */

int main()
  {
  unsigned char x = 0xFE;
  unsigned int y = 0x0A0B;

  printf("%-35s","x");
  Display_Byte(x);

  printf("%-35s","1s complement [~x]");
  Display_Byte(~x);

  printf("%-35s","Bitwise AND [x & 0x0f]");
  Display_Byte(x & 0x0f);

  printf("%-35s","Bitwise OR [x | 0x0f]");
  Display_Byte(x | 0x0f);

  printf("%-35s","Bitwise XOR [x ^ 0x0f]");
  Display_Byte(x ^ 0x0f);

  printf("%-35s","Left shift, 1 place [x <<= 1] ");
  Display_Byte(x <<= 1);

  x = 0xfe; /* Return x to original value */
  printf("%-35s","Right shift, 4 places [x >>= 4]");
  Display_Byte(x >>= 4);

  printf("\n\n");

  printf("%-35s","Display MS byte of unsigned int y");
  Display_Byte((unsigned char) (y >> 8));

  printf("%-35s","Display LS byte of unsigned int y");
  Display_Byte((unsigned char) (y & 0xFF));

  return 0;
  }

/* ------------------------------------------------------------ */
```

```
void Display_Byte(const unsigned char CH)
   {
   unsigned char i, c = CH;
   unsigned char Mask = 1 << 7;

   for (i = 1; i <= 8; i++)
      {
      putchar(c & Mask ? '1' : '0');
      c <<= 1;
      }

   putchar('\n');
   }

/*------------------------------------------------------------------*-
  ---- END OF FILE -------------------------------------------------
-*------------------------------------------------------------------*/
```

The output from the program in Listing 4.3 is as follows:

x	11111110
1s complement [~x]	00000001
Bitwise AND [x & 0x0f]	00001110
Bitwise OR [x | 0x0f]	11111111
Bitwise XOR [x ^ 0x0f]	11110001
Left shift, 1 place [x <<= 1]	11111100
Right shift, 4 places [x >>= 4]	00001111
Display MS byte of unsigned int y	00001010
Display LS byte of unsigned int y	00001011

The use of some of these operators in an embedded application is illustrated in Listing 4.4 which echoes the input on Pin X to Pin Y on Port 1.

Note that:

- The function `Read_Bit_P1()` allows the programmer to specify the particular pin (on Port 1) that is to be read.
- The function `Write_Bit_P1()` allows the programmer to specify both the pin to be written to, and the value to be written (1 or 0).

Listing 4.4 Reading and writing bits (generic version). See text for details

```
/*------------------------------------------------------------------*-

   Bits2.C (v1.00)

   ------------------------------------------------------------------

   Reading and writing individual port pins.

   NOTE: Both pins on the same port

   --- Generic version ---

-*------------------------------------------------------------------*/

#include <reg52.H>

// Function prototypes
void Write_Bit_P1(const unsigned char, const bit);
bit Read_Bit_P1(const unsigned char);

/* ................................................................ */

void main (void)
   {
   bit x;

   while(1)
     {
     x = Read_Bit_P1(0); // Read Port 1, Pin 0
     Write_Bit_P1(1,x);  // Write to Port 1, Pin 1
     }
   }

/* ---------------------------------------------------------------- */

void Write_Bit_P1(const unsigned char PIN, const bit VALUE)
   {
   unsigned char p = 0x01; // 00000001

   // Left shift appropriate number of places
   p <<= PIN;

   // If we want 1 output at this pin
   if (VALUE == 1)
```

```
   {
   P1 |= p; // Bitwise OR
   return;
   }

  // If we want 0 output at this pin
  p = ~p; // Complement
  P1 &= p; // Bitwise AND
  }

/* ------------------------------------------------------------- */

bit Read_Bit_P1(const unsigned char PIN)
  {
  unsigned char p = 0x01; // 00000001

  // Left shift appropriate number of places
  p <<= PIN;

  // Write a 1 to the pin (to set up for reading)
  Write_Bit_P1(PIN, 1);

  // Read the pin (bitwise AND) and return
  return (P1 & p);
  }

/*------------------------------------------------------------------*-
  ---- END OF FILE --------------------------------------------------
-*------------------------------------------------------------------*/
```

4.6 The need for pull-up resistors

In our discussions in this chapter, we have assumed that we were reading from port pins in the simulator: we have not yet considered how a switch will actually be connected to the 8051 port pin in a real application. Figure 4.4 illustrates one possibility.

This hardware operates as follows:

- When the switch is open, it has no impact on the port pin. An internal resistor on the port 'pulls up' the pin to the supply voltage of the microcontroller (typically 5V). If we read the pin, we will see the value '1'. (We say more about pull-up resistors below).

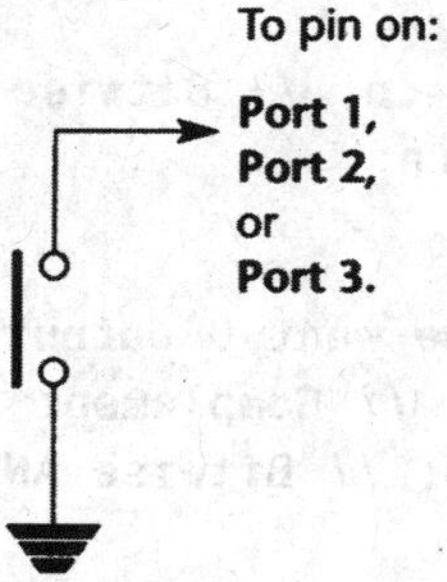

FIGURE 4.4 Connecting a switch to an 8051 port pin. See text for details

- When the switch is closed (pressed), the pin voltage will be 0V. If we read the the pin, we will see the value '0'.

The internal 'pull up' resistors referred to above can be thought of as small springs, connecting the port pin to a '1' value. To change the port setting, we need to 'push' the pin down to 0, against the force of the spring (Figure 4.5).

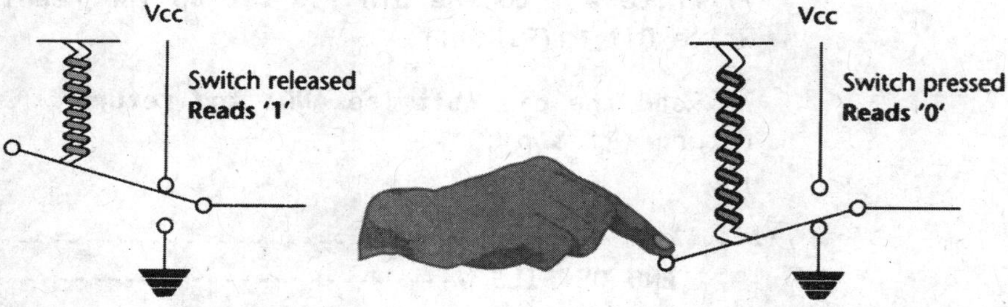

FIGURE 4.5 A schematic representation of a switch connected to a port (with internal pull-up resistors). See text for details

Where there is no pull-up resistor, changing the state of the input pin is not possible: not matter how hard we push, the pin will always read '0' (Figure 4.6).

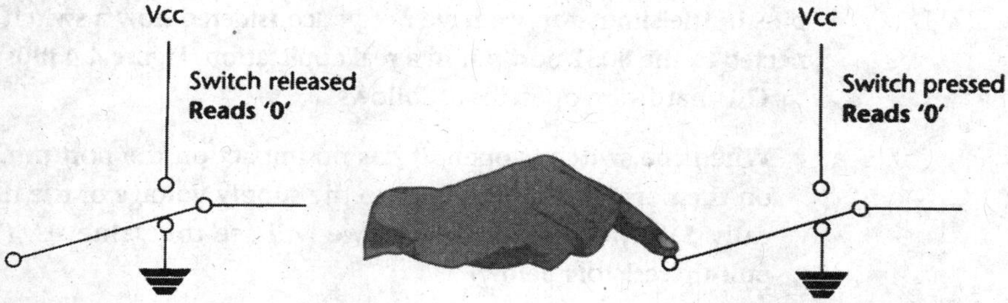

FIGURE 4.6 A schematic representation of a switch connected to a port (**without** internal pull-up resistors). See text for details

Returning to Figure 4.4, please note that the simple switch arrangement shown only applies to Port 1, Port 2 and Port 3, since these ports all have internal pull-up resistors. This arrangement does not apply to Port 0, which has no internal pull-ups. If you need to connect a switch (or similar device) to Port 0, you can do so, but you need to add an *external* pull-up resistor: a resistance of 10 KΩ is appropriate here (see Figure 4.7).

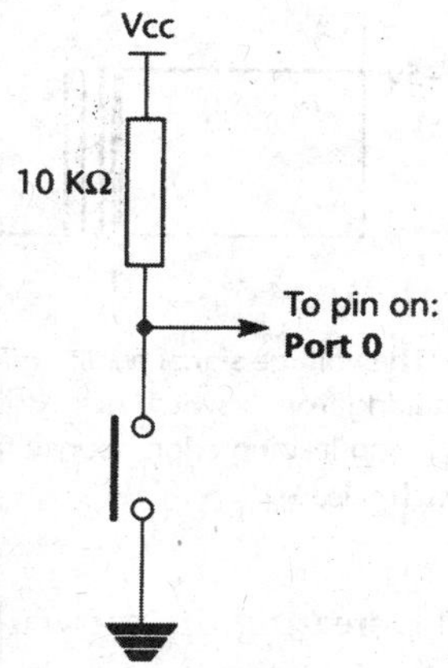

FIGURE 4.7 An example of a push-button ('normally open') switch input. Where there is no internal pull-up, this arrangement must be used

4.7 Dealing with switch bounce

In an ideal world, this change in voltage obtained by connecting a switch to the port pin of an 8051 microcontroller would take the form illustrated in Figure 4.8 (top). In practice, all mechanical switch contacts *bounce* (that is, turn on and off, repeatedly, for a short period of time) after the switch is closed or opened. As a result, the actual input waveform looks more like that shown in Figure 4.8 (bottom). Usually, switches bounce for less than 20 ms: however large mechanical switches exhibit bounce behaviour for 50 ms or more.

When you turn on the lights in your home or office with a mechanical switch, the switches will bounce. As far as humans are concerned, this bounce is imperceptible. However, as far as the microcontroller is concerned, each 'bounce' is equivalent to one press and release of an 'ideal' switch. Without appropriate software design, this can give rise to a number of problems, not least:

- Rather than reading 'A' from a keypad, we may read 'AAAAA'.
- Counting the number of times that a switch is pressed becomes extremely difficult.
- If a switch is depressed once, and then released some time later, the 'bounce' may make it appear as if the switch has been pressed again (at the time of release).

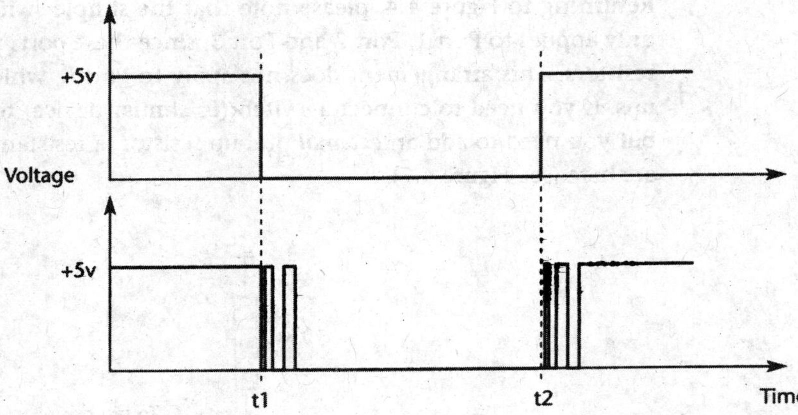

FIGURE 4.8 The voltage signal resulting from the switch shown in Figure 4.7. [Top] Idealized waveform resulting from a switch depressed at time t1 and released at time t2. [Bottom] Actual waveform showing leading edge bounce following switch depression and trailing edge bounce following switch release

Fortunately, creating the software needed to check for a valid switch input is straightforward:

1 We read the relevant port pin.

2 If we think we have detected a switch depression, we wait for 20 ms and then read the pin again.

3 If the second reading confirms the first reading, we assume the switch really has been depressed.

Note that the figure of '20 ms' will, of course, depend on the switch used: the data sheet of the switch will provide this information. If you have no data sheet, you can either experiment with different figures, or measure directly using an oscilloscope.

4.8 Example: Reading switch inputs (basic code)

In this example, we present a simple code library for reading the input from a mechanical switch. The code implements – directly – the algorithm described in Section 4.7: that is, it tests the switch state and – if the switch is pressed – executes a 'debounce delay' before testing the switch again.

This switch-reading code is adequate if we want to perform operations such as:

- Drive a motor while a switch is pressed.
- Switch on a light while a switch is pressed.
- Activate a pump while a switch is pressed.

These operations could be implemented using an electrical switch, without using a microcontroller; however, use of a microcontroller may well be appropriate if we require more complex behaviour. For example:

- Drive a motor while a switch is pressed
  Condition: If the safety guard is not in place, don't turn the motor. Instead sound a buzzer for 2 seconds.
- Switch on a light while a switch is pressed
  Condition: To save power, ignore requests to turn on the light during daylight hours.
- Activate a pump while a switch is pressed
  Condition: If the main water reservoir is below 300 litres, do not start the main pump: instead, start the reserve pump and draw the water from the emergency tank.

The key to this library is the function `SWITCH_Get_Input()`, which is shown in context in Listing 4.5.

Listing 4.5 Reading switch inputs (basic code)

```
/*------------------------------------------------------------------*-

   Switch_read.C (v1.00)

  ------------------------------------------------------------------

   A simple 'switch input' program for the 8051.
   - Reads (and debounces) switch input on Pin1^0
   - If switch is pressed, changes Port 3 output

-*------------------------------------------------------------------*/

#include <Reg52.h>

// Connect switch to this pin
sbit Switch_pin = P1^0;

// Display switch status on this port
#define Output_port P3
```

```
// Return values from Switch_Get_Input()
#define SWITCH_NOT_PRESSED (bit) 0
#define SWITCH_PRESSED (bit) 1

// Function prototypes
void SWITCH_Init(void);
bit SWITCH_Get_Input(const unsigned char DEBOUNCE_PERIOD);
void DISPLAY_SWITCH_STATUS_Init(void);
void DISPLAY_SWITCH_STATUS_Update(const bit);
void DELAY_LOOP_Wait(const unsigned int DELAY_MS);

/* ------------------------------------------------------------------ */
void main(void)
   {
   bit Sw_state;

   // Init functions
   SWITCH_Init();
   DISPLAY_SWITCH_STATUS_Init();

   while(1)
      {
      Sw_state = SWITCH_Get_Input(30);

      DISPLAY_SWITCH_STATUS_Update(Sw_state);
      }
   }

/*------------------------------------------------------------------*-

   SWITCH_Init()

   Initialisation function for the switch library.

-*------------------------------------------------------------------*/
void SWITCH_Init(void)
   {
   Switch_pin = 1; // Use this pin for input
   }

/*------------------------------------------------------------------*-

  SWITCH_Get_Input()

  Reads and debounces a mechanical switch as follows:
```

```
   1. If switch is not pressed, return SWITCH_NOT_PRESSED.

   2. If switch is pressed, wait for DEBOUNCE_PERIOD (in ms),
      then:
      a. If switch is still pressed, return SWITCH_PRESSED.
      b. If switch is not pressed, return SWITCH_NOT_PRESSED

   See Switch_Wait.H for details of return values.

-*------------------------------------------------------------------*/
bit SWITCH_Get_Input(const unsigned char DEBOUNCE_PERIOD)
   {
   bit Return_value = SWITCH_NOT_PRESSED;

   if (Switch_pin == 0)
      {
      // Switch is pressed

      // Debounce - just wait...
      DELAY_LOOP_Wait(DEBOUNCE_PERIOD);

      // Check switch again
      if (Switch_pin == 0)
         {
         Return_value = SWITCH_PRESSED;
         }
      }

   // Now return switch value
   return Return_value;
   }
/*------------------------------------------------------------------*-

  DISPLAY_SWITCH_STATUS_Init()

  Initialization function for the DISPLAY_SWITCH_STATUS library.

-*------------------------------------------------------------------*/
void DISPLAY_SWITCH_STATUS_Init(void)
   {
   Output_port = 0xF0;
   }
```

```
/*------------------------------------------------------------------*-

  DISPLAY_SWITCH_STATUS_Update()

  Simple function to display data (SWITCH_STATUS)
  on LEDs connected to port (Output_Port)

-*------------------------------------------------------------------*/
void DISPLAY_SWITCH_STATUS_Update(const bit SWITCH_STATUS)
   {
   if (SWITCH_STATUS == SWITCH_PRESSED)
      {
      Output_port = 0x0F;
      }
   else
      {
      Output_port = 0xF0;
      }
   }
/*------------------------------------------------------------------*-

  DELAY_LOOP_Wait()

  Delay duration varies with parameter.

  Parameter is, *ROUGHLY*, the delay, in milliseconds,
  on 12MHz 8051 (12 osc cycles).

  You need to adjust the timing for your application!

-*------------------------------------------------------------------*/
void DELAY_LOOP_Wait(const unsigned int DELAY_MS)
   {
   unsigned int x, y;

   for (x = 0; x <= DELAY_MS; x++)
      {
      for (y = 0; y <= 120; y++);
      }
   }

/*------------------------------------------------------------------*-
  ---- END OF FILE -------------------------------------------------
-*------------------------------------------------------------------*/
```

Figure 4.9 shows this program running in the simulator.

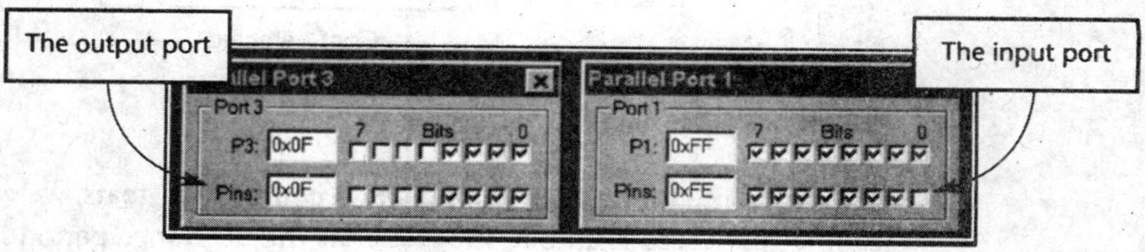

FIGURE 4.9 Running the code from Listing 4.5 in the simulator. Changing the status of the switch pin (Pin 1.0) alters the output on Port 3

4.9 Example: Counting goats

Variations of the simple switch-reading code presented in Listing 4.5 are currently in use in many embedded systems. However, this code is not suitable for all purposes.

With this simple code, problems can arise whenever a switch is pressed for a period longer than the debounce interval. This is a concern, because in many cases, users will press switches for at least 500 ms (or until they receive feedback that the system has detected the switch press). As a result, a user typing 'Hello' on a keypad may see 'HHHHHHHHHeeeeeeeeellllllllllllllllooooooooooo' appear on the screen.

One consequence is that this code is not suitable for applications where we need to count the number of times that a switch is pressed and then released. For example, suppose we wish to use this code to count the number of goats passing into a milking parlour (Figure 4.10). We assume that the optical sensor arrangement gives a 'Logic 0' output while a goat is passing and a 'Logic 1' output at other times (Figure 4.11).

FIGURE 4.10 A system for counting the number of goats passing into a milking parlour

FIGURE 4.11 The output of the 'goat sensor'

If we try to use the code in Listing 4.5 to count these goats, we will get a very misleading result. For example, suppose that the debounce period is 20 ms. If a goat takes – say – around five seconds to pass the sensor, then the `SWITCH_Get_Input()` function will count a total of around 250 goats every time one goat passes (250 = 5000 ms / 20 ms): **in other words, the goat sensor will not allow us to count the number of goats but will instead provide an indication of the time taken for the goats to pass the sensor**.

A simple way to solve such problems is to wait until a switch is released before returning from a switch-test function. This approach is illustrated in the function `SWITCH_Get_Input()` in Listing 4.6. The code in this listing is used to do two things:

- Debounce the switch input.
- Count the number of times that a switch is pressed and then released.

This code could be applied – for example – to count the number of (human) visitors entering a museum. It could also be used to measure the speed of rotating machinery, or the flow of liquid through pipes, assuming that an appropriate sensor was employed.[14]

Listing 4.6 A simple program for counting the number of times that a switch is pressed and released

```
/*------------------------------------------------------------------*-

   Switch_count.C (v1.00)

   ------------------------------------------------------------------

   A 'goat counting' program for the 8051...

-*------------------------------------------------------------------*/

#include <Reg52.h>
```

14. See the 'milk pasteurization' example in Chapter 7 (p. 174) for further details.

```
// Connect switch to this pin
sbit Switch_pin = P1^0;

// Display count (binary) on this port
#define Count_port P3

// Return values from Switch_Get_Input()
#define SWITCH_NOT_PRESSED (bit) 0
#define SWITCH_PRESSED (bit) 1

// Function prototypes
void SWITCH_Init(void);
bit  SWITCH_Get_Input(const unsigned char);
void DISPLAY_COUNT_Init(void);
void DISPLAY_COUNT_Update(const unsigned char);
void DELAY_LOOP_Wait(const unsigned int);

/* ------------------------------------------------------------ */
void main(void)
  {
  unsigned char Switch_presses = 0;

  // Init functions
  SWITCH_Init();
  DISPLAY_COUNT_Init();

  while(1)
     {
     if (SWITCH_Get_Input(30) == SWITCH_PRESSED)
        {
        Switch_presses++;
        }

     DISPLAY_COUNT_Update(Switch_presses);
     }
  }

/*------------------------------------------------------------

  SWITCH_Init()

  Initialisation function for the switch library.

-*------------------------------------------------------------*/
void SWITCH_Init(void)
```

```
   {
   Switch_pin = 1; // Use this pin for input
   }

/*------------------------------------------------------------------*-

  SWITCH_Get_Input()

  Reads and debounces a mechanical switch as follows:

  1. If switch is not pressed, return SWITCH_NOT_PRESSED.

  2. If switch is pressed, wait for DEBOUNCE_PERIOD (in ms).
     a. If switch is not pressed, return SWITCH_NOT_PRESSED.
     b. If switch is pressed, wait (indefinitely) for
        switch to be released, then return SWITCH_PRESSED

  See Switch_Wait.H for details of return values.

-*------------------------------------------------------------------*/
bit SWITCH_Get_Input(const unsigned char DEBOUNCE_PERIOD)
   {
   bit Return_value = SWITCH_NOT_PRESSED;

   if (Switch_pin == 0)
      {
      // Switch is pressed

      // Debounce - just wait...
      DELAY_LOOP_Wait(DEBOUNCE_PERIOD);

      // Check switch again
      if (Switch_pin == 0)
         {
         // Wait until the switch is released.
         while (Switch_pin == 0);
         Return_value = SWITCH_PRESSED;
         }
      }

   // Now (finally) return switch value
   return Return_value;
   }
/*------------------------------------------------------------------*-

  DISPLAY_COUNT_Init()
```

```
   Initialisation function for the DISPLAY COUNT library.

-*------------------------------------------------------------*/
void DISPLAY_COUNT_Init(void)
   {
   Count_port = 0x00;
   }

/*------------------------------------------------------------*-

   DISPLAY_COUNT_Update()

   Simple function to display tByte data (COUNT)
   on LEDs connected to port (Count_Port)

-*------------------------------------------------------------*/
void DISPLAY_COUNT_Update(const unsigned char COUNT)
   {
   Count_port = COUNT;
   }

/*------------------------------------------------------------*-

   DELAY_LOOP_Wait()

   Delay duration varies with parameter.

   Parameter is, *ROUGHLY*, the delay, in milliseconds,
   on 12MHz 8051 (12 osc cycles).

   You need to adjust the timing for your application!

-*------------------------------------------------------------*/
void DELAY_LOOP_Wait(const unsigned int DELAY_MS)
   {
   unsigned int x, y;

   for (x = 0; x <= DELAY_MS; x++)
      {
      for (y = 0; y <= 120; y++);
      }
   }

/*------------------------------------------------------------*-
  ---- END OF FILE --------------------------------------------
-*------------------------------------------------------------*/
```

Figure 4.12 shows the program in Listing 4.6 running in the simulator.

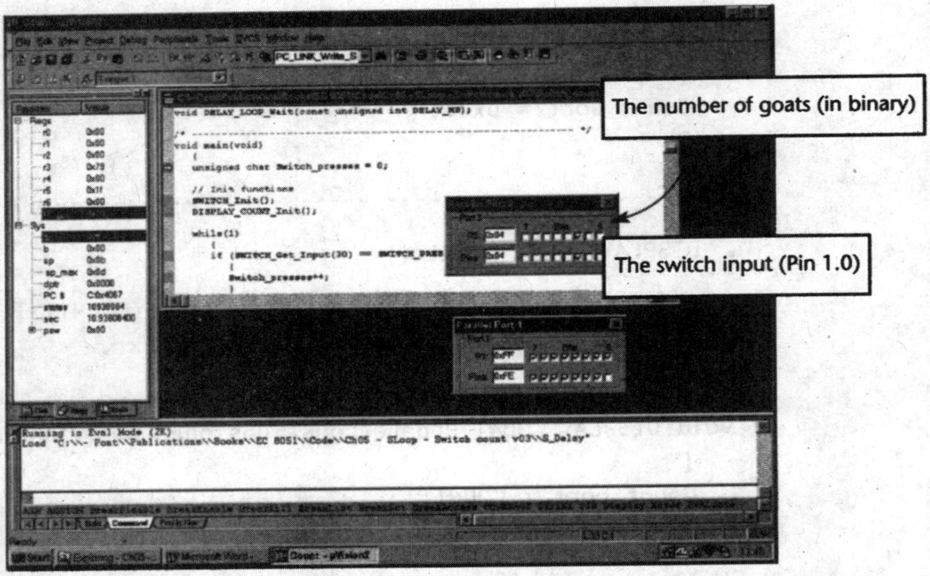

FIGURE 4.12 Counting the number of goats using the hardware simulator. The switch input is on Pin 1.0: the count is shown (in binary) on Port 3

4.10 Conclusions

The switch interface code presented and discussed in this chapter has allowed us to do two things:

- To perform an activity while a switch is depressed.
- To respond to the fact that a user has pressed – and then released – a switch.

In both cases, we have illustrated how the switch may be 'debounced' in software.

In Chapter 5, we turn our attention to techniques that can help you re-use the code you develop in subsequent projects.

chapter 5

Adding structure to your code

5.1 Introduction

In addition to the key technical issues we have examined in previous chapters (such as the use of a Super Loop, or the design and implementation of an appropriate switch interface), there are other factors which need to be considered by desktop developers migrating to the desktop area. For example, we made the following observations in Chapter 1:

- No software company remains in business for very long if it generates new code, from scratch, for every project. The language used must support the creation of flexible libraries, making it easy to re-use (well-tested) code components in a range of projects. It must also be possible to adapt complete code systems to work with a new or updated processor with minimal difficulty.
- Staff members change and existing personnel have limited memory spans. At the same time, systems evolve and processors are updated. As concern over the 'Year 2000' problem in recent years has illustrated, many embedded systems have a long lifespan. During this time, their code will often have to be maintained. Good code must therefore be easy to understand now, and in five years' time (and not just by those who first wrote it).

To support these activities, we will do three things in this chapter:

1 We will describe how to use an object-oriented style of programming with C programs, allowing the creation of libraries of code that can be easily adapted for use in different embedded projects.

2 We will describe how to create and use a 'Project Header' file. This file encapsulates key aspects of the hardware environment, such as the type of processor to be used, the oscillator frequency and the number of oscillator cycles required to execute each instruction. This helps to document the system, and makes it easier to port the code to a different processor.

3 We will describe how to create and use a 'Port Header' file. This brings together all details of the port access from the whole system. Like the Project Header, this helps during porting and also serves as a means of documenting important system features.

We will use all three of these techniques in the code examples presented in subsequent chapters.

We begin by discussing how to use object-oriented styles of programming with the C language.

5.2 Object-oriented programming with C

One way in which the different programming languages may be classified is as a series of generations (see Table 5.1).

TABLE 5.1 The classification of programming languages into different generations. Please note that some people consider O-O languages to be 5GLs: however, this distinction will not have an impact on our discussions here

Language generation	Example languages
–	Machine Code
First-Generation Language (1GL)	Assembly Language.
Second-Generation Languages (2GLs)	COBOL, FORTRAN
Third-Generation Languages (3GLs)	C, Pascal, Ada 83
Fourth-Generation Languages (4GLs)	C++, Java, Ada 95

It is often argued that object-oriented (O-O) design – and O-O programming languages – have advantages when compared with those from earlier generations. For example, as Graham notes:[15]

> *[The phrase] 'object-oriented' has become almost synonymous with modernity, goodness and worth in information technology circles.*

15. Graham, I. (1994) *Object-Oriented Methods*, (2nd edn) Addison-Wesley, Harlow, England, p. 1.

A frequent argument is that the O-O approach is more effective than those previously used because it represents 'a more natural way' of thinking about problems. As Jalote notes:[16]

One main claimed advantage of using object orientation is that an OO model closely represents the problem domain, which makes it easier to produce and understand designs.

You might reasonably ask why this book uses C, rather than a language from a later generation (such as C++ or Java). The reason is that O-O languages are not readily available for small embedded systems, primarily because of the overheads inherent in the O-O approach.

It is easy to see the source of these overheads. Suppose, for example, we have a C program with a variable Xyz that we wish to set to some value and then display. We might do so using the following code:

```
...
int Xyz;

Xyz = 3;

...

printf("%d", Xyz);
```

Now, consider the following O-O version, using C++:

```
class cClass
  {
  public:
     int  Get_Xyz(void) const;
     void Set_Xyz(const int);
  private:
     int _Xyz; // Encapsulated data
  };

...

cClass abc;

abc.Set_Xyz(3);

...

cout << abc.Get_Xyz();
```

16. Jalote, P. (1997) *An Integrated Approach to Software Engineering,* (2nd edn) Springer-Verlag, New York.

The C++ version has both strengths and weaknesses:

☺ **In the C++ code, the data (_Xyz) are encapsulated in the class: access to these data is controlled because it is possible only via the two member functions. By contrast, the data (Xyz) in the C version are 'global' variables and can be altered anywhere in the program. From a design perspective, the C++ code is more elegant. It may also prove easier to maintain.**

☹ There is a CPU time overhead associated with the C++ code: this is, at least, the cost of two (member) function calls. In real applications, such overheads can be substantial: even Stroustrup, creator of the C++ programming language, has acknowledged that a C++ implementation is likely to run 25% more slowly than an equivalent application in FORTRAN.[17] This can have implications for embedded projects where speed of processing is a primary concern. For example, Sommerville cites the case of an aircraft system in which an O-O solution was abandoned due to the impact of these overheads.[18]

One solution to such performance problems is to 'in line' the member functions: this can greatly reduce the CPU overhead, but a penalty will then be paid in terms of memory usage.[19]

Neither the CPU performance load nor the alternative memory load present a significant problem on multi-megabyte desktop PCs, but – on the type of embedded projects considered in this book (where teams may struggle with code to save one or two bytes of memory) a 'pure' O-O approach is rarely practical.

Does this mean that O-O design principles need (or should) be avoided by C programmers? Fortunately it does not. For many years before O-O techniques entered the mainstream, C programmers used a 'modular' style of programming which is well supported by the language. Using this approach, it is possible to create 'file-based-classes' in C without imposing a significant memory or CPU load:

```
// BEGIN: File XYZ.C

static int Xyz;

Xyz = 3;

...

printf("%d", Xyz);

// END: File XYZ.C
```

17. Stroustrup, B. (1994) *The Design of C++*, University Video Communications, Stanford CA, USA. Recorded 2 March, 1994.
18. Sommerville, I. (1996) *Software Engineering*, (5th edn) Addison-Wesley, London, p. 301.
19. Pont, M.J. (1996) *Software Engineering with C++ and CASE Tools*, (1st edn) Addison-Wesley, London, pp. 191–93.

The change here is minor: we have simply used the (ISO/ANSI) C keyword `static` to ensure that only functions within the file `XYZ.c` are able to access the data `Xyz`. As a consequence, the source file becomes our 'class' and the 'static' data in that file become private data members of that class. The functions defined within the file become the member functions in our class, and our whole program may be split into a number of clearly-defined (file-based) classes (Figure 5.1).

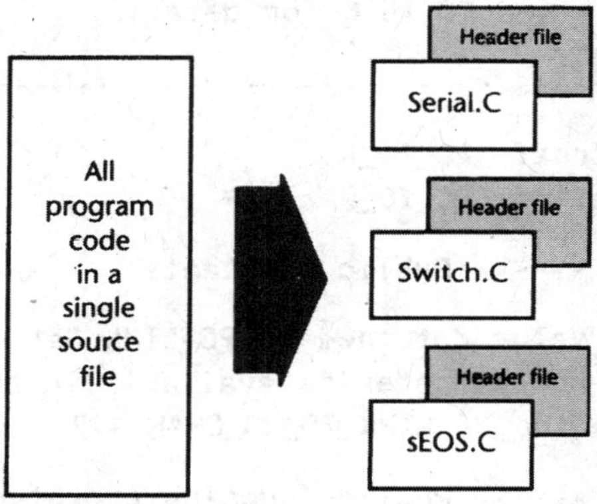

FIGURE 5.1 Turning a monolithic program into object-oriented C. See text for details

Note that we can also create 'private' member functions (which are accessible only by functions defined within a particular file) simply by including the prototypes for the function in the .C file (rather than the .H file) for the particular class.

This process is illustrated in Listing 5.1 and Listing 5.2. These files are part of a library of code designed to allow an 8051 microcontroller to use a serial interface. Please note that we will not be concerned with the operation of this code here (that will be considered in Chapter 9): at this time, we are simply concerned with the library structure.

As you look at this code, please note the presence of:

- Public 'member' functions, such as `PC_LINK_IO_Write_String_To_Buffer()`. Such functions have their prototypes in the H file.
- A private 'member' function, `PC_LINK_IO_Send_Char()`. Such `static` functions have their prototypes in the C file.
- A public constant (`PC_LINK_IO_NO_CHAR`), with a value which must be accessed by the rest of the program (see the H file).
- A limited number of public variables (e.g. `In_read_index_G`), defined in the C file (without the use of the `static` keyword).
- Numerous private constants and private variables (e.g. `RECV_BUFFER_LENGTH`), which are 'invisible' outside the C file.

Listing 5.1 An example of a file-based C class (H file). See text for details

```
/*------------------------------------------------------------------*-

  PC_IO.H (v1.00)

  ------------------------------------------------------------------

  - see PC_IO.C for details.

-*------------------------------------------------------------------*/

#ifndef _PC_IO_H
#define _PC_IO_H

// ------ Public constants -----------------------------------------

// Value returned by PC_LINK_Get_Char_From_Buffer if
// no character is available in buffer
#define PC_LINK_IO_NO_CHAR 127

// ------ Public function prototypes -------------------------------

void PC_LINK_IO_Write_String_To_Buffer(const char* const);
void PC_LINK_IO_Write_Char_To_Buffer(const char);

char PC_LINK_IO_Get_Char_From_Buffer(void);

// Must call this function frequently...
void PC_LINK_IO_Update(void);

#endif

/*------------------------------------------------------------------*-
  ---- END OF FILE -------------------------------------------------
-*------------------------------------------------------------------*/
```

Listing 5.2 An example of a file-based C class (C file). See text for details

```
/*------------------------------------------------------------------*-

  PC_IO.C (v1.00)

  ------------------------------------------------------------------

  Core files for simple PC link library for 8051 family
```

```
   Uses the UART, and Pins 3.1 (Tx) and 3.0 (Rx)

   [INCOMPLETE - STRUCTURE ONLY - see Chap 9 for complete library]

-*------------------------------------------------------------------*/

#include "Main.H"
#include "PC_IO.H"

// ------ Public variable definitions --------------------------

tByte In_read_index_G; // Data in buffer that has been read
tByte In_waiting_index_G; // Data in buffer not yet read

tByte Out_written_index_G; // Data in buffer that has been written
tByte Out_waiting_index_G; // Data in buffer not yet written

// ------ Private function prototypes --------------------------

static void PC_LINK_IO_Send_Char(const char);

// ------ Private constants ------------------------------------

// The receive buffer length
#define RECV_BUFFER_LENGTH 8

// The transmit buffer length
#define TRAN_BUFFER_LENGTH 50

#define XON 0x11
#define XOFF 0x13

// ------ Private variables ------------------------------------

static tByte Recv_buffer[RECV_BUFFER_LENGTH];
static tByte Tran_buffer[TRAN_BUFFER_LENGTH];

/*------------------------------------------------------------------*/
void PC_LINK_IO_Update(...)
   {
   ...
   }

/*------------------------------------------------------------------*/
void PC_LINK_IO_Write_Char_To_Buffer(...)
   {
   ...
   }
```

```
/*------------------------------------------------------------------*/
void PC_LINK_IO_Write_String_To_Buffer(...)
   {
   ...
   }

/*------------------------------------------------------------------*/
char PC_LINK_IO_Get_Char_From_Buffer(...)
   {
   ...
   }

/*------------------------------------------------------------------*/
void PC_LINK_IO_Send_Char(...)
   {
   ...
   }

/*------------------------------------------------------------------*-
  ---- END OF FILE -------------------------------------------------
-*------------------------------------------------------------------*/
```

Overall, this approach is very common in C programs. If used with care (and, where necessary, enforced by company coding guidelines) it can provide many of the benefits of an O-O language without the corresponding performance or memory costs.

5.3 The Project Header (Main.H)

The 'Project Header' is simply a header file, included in all projects, that groups the key information about the 8051 device you have used, along with other key parameters – such as the oscillator frequency – in one file (Figure 5.2). As such, it is a practical implementation of a standard software design guideline: 'Do not duplicate information in numerous files; place the information in one place, and refer to it where necessary.'[20]

In the case of the great majority of the examples in this book, we use a Project Header file. This is always called `Main.H`. An example of a typical project header file is included in Listing 5.3.

20. In a database system (for example) this rule will be expressed more formally by the requirement that your data should be in 'First Normal Form'. See Date, C.J. (1999) *An Introduction to Database Systems*, (7th edn) Addison-Wesley, London.

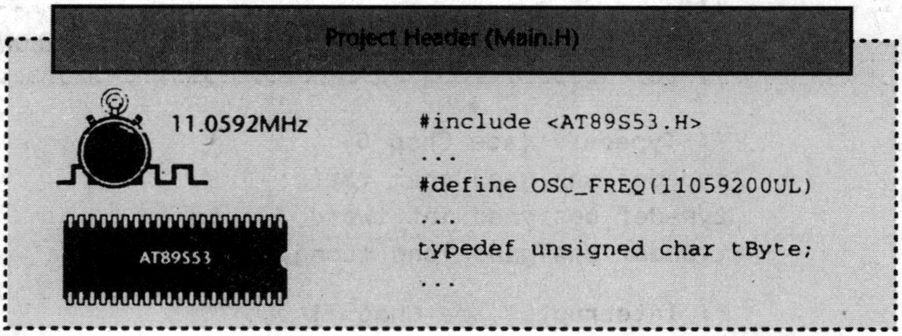

FIGURE 5.2 A schematic representation of the project header file

Listing 5.3 An example of a typical project header file (`Main.H`)

```
/*------------------------------------------------------------------*-

   Main.H (v1.00)

   ------------------------------------------------------------------

   'Project Header' for project HELLO2 (see Chap 5)

-*------------------------------------------------------------------*/

#ifndef _MAIN_H
#define _MAIN_H

//------------------------------------------------------------------
// WILL NEED TO EDIT THIS SECTION FOR EVERY PROJECT
//------------------------------------------------------------------

// Must include the appropriate microcontroller header file here
#include <reg52.h>

// Oscillator / resonator frequency (in Hz) e.g. (11059200UL)
#define OSC_FREQ (12000000UL)

// Number of oscillations per instruction (12, etc)
// 12 - Original 8051 / 8052 and numerous modern versions
//  6 - Various Infineon and Philips devices, etc.
//  4 - Dallas 320, 520 etc.
//  1 - Dallas 420, etc.

#define OSC_PER_INST (12)
```

```
//-----------------------------------------------------------
// SHOULD NOT NEED TO EDIT THE SECTIONS BELOW
//-----------------------------------------------------------

// Typedefs (see Chap 5)
typedef unsigned char tByte;
typedef unsigned int tWord;
typedef unsigned long tLong;

// Interrupts (see Chap 7)
#define INTERRUPT_Timer_0_Overflow 1
#define INTERRUPT_Timer_1_Overflow 3
#define INTERRUPT_Timer_2_Overflow 5

#endif

/*----------------------------------------------------------*-
  ---- END OF FILE -------------------------------------------
-*----------------------------------------------------------*/
```

We consider the various components of this file in the sub-sections below.

a) The device header

The first entry in the project header is the link to the appropriate 'device header' file.

We discussed one such file ('reg52.h') in Chapter 3. These files will, in most cases, have been produced by your compiler manufacturer, and will include the addresses of the special function registers (SFRs) used for port access, plus similar details for other on-chip components such as analog-to-digital converters.

For example, Listing 5.4 shows part of the device header for an Extended 8051, the Infineon C515C. This device has eight ports, a watchdog unit, analog-to-digital converter and other components, all made accessible through the device header.

Listing 5.4 Part of a device header file (Infineon C515C). Copyright Keil Elektronik GmbH

```
/*-----------------------------------------------------------
  REG515C.H

  Header file for the Infineon C515C

  Copyright (c) 1995-1999 Keil Elektronik GmbH All rights
  reserved.
-----------------------------------------------------------*/
```

```
. . .
/* A/D Converter */
sfr ADCON0 = 0xD8;
. . .
/* Interrupt System */
sfr  IEN0    = 0xA8;
. . .
/* Ports */
sfr  P0       = 0x80;
sfr  P1       = 0x90;
sfr  P2       = 0xA0;
sfr  P3       = 0xB0;
sfr  P4       = 0xE8;
sfr  P5       = 0xF8;
sfr  P6       = 0xDB;
sfr  P7       = 0xFA;
. . .
/*  Serial Channel    */
sfr   SCON   = 0x98;
. . .
/*  Timer0 / Timer1 */
sfr   TCON   = 0x88;
. . .
/*  CAP/COM Unit / Timer2 */
sfr   CCEN   = 0xC1;
. . .
/*  Watchdog */
sfr   WDTREL = 0x86;

/*  Power Save Modes */
sfr   PCON   = 0x87;
sfr   PCON1  = 0x88;
```

b) Oscillator frequency and oscillations per instruction

If you create an application using a particular 8051 device operating at a particular oscillator frequency, with a particular number of oscillations per instruction, this information will be required when compiling many of the different source files in your project. For example – in many cases – we can create code for generating delays (and similar purposes) if we store information about the oscillator frequency and number of oscillations-per-instruction in an appropriate form. This is done in the `Main.H` file as follows:

```
// Oscillator / resonator frequency (in Hz) e.g. (11059200UL)
#define OSC_FREQ (12000000UL)

// Number of oscillations per instruction (12, etc)
// 12 - Original 8051 / 8052 and numerous modern versions
//  6 - Various Infineon and Philips devices, etc.
//  4 - Dallas 320, 520 etc.
//  1 - Dallas 420, etc.

#define OSC_PER_INST (12)
```

We will demonstrate how to use this information in Chapter 6 (for creating delays), Chapter 7 (for controlling timing in an operating system) and Chapter 9 (for controlling the baud rate in a serial interface).

c) Common data types

The next part of the Project Header file in Listing 5.3 includes three `typedef` statements:

```
typedef unsigned char tByte;
typedef unsigned int tWord;
typedef unsigned long tLong;
```

In C, the typedef keyword allows us to provide aliases for data types: we can then use these aliases in place of the original types. Thus, in the projects you will see code like this:

```
tWord Temperature;
```

Rather than:

```
unsigned int Temperature;
```

The main reason for using these `typedef` statements is to simplify – and promote – the use of unsigned data types. This is a good idea for two main reasons:

- The 8051 does not support signed arithmetic and extra code is required to manipulate signed data: this reduces your program speed and increases the program size. Wherever possible, it makes sense to use unsigned data, and these `typedef` statements make this easier.
- Use of bitwise operators (see Chapter 4) generally makes sense only with unsigned data types: use of '`typedef`' variables reduces the likelihood that programmers will inadvertently apply these operators to signed data.

Finally, as in desktop programming, use of the `typedef` keyword in this way can make it easier to adapt your code for use on a different processor (for example, when you move your 8051 code to a 32-bit environment). In many circumstances, you will simply be able to change the `typedef` statements in `Main.H`, rather than editing every source file in your project.

d) Interrupts

As we noted in Chapter 2, interrupts are a key component of most embedded systems.

The following lines in the Project Header are intended to make it easier for you to use (timer-based) interrupts in your projects:

```
#define INTERRUPT_Timer_0_Overflow 1
#define INTERRUPT_Timer_1_Overflow 3
#define INTERRUPT_Timer_2_Overflow 5
```

We discuss how to make use of this facility in Chapter 7.

e) Summary: Use of a Project Header?

Use of Project Header can help to make your code more readable, not least because anyone using your projects knows where to find key information, such as the model of microcontroller and the oscillator frequency required to execute the software.

The use of a Project Header can help to make your code more easily portable, by placing some of the key microcontroller-dependent data in one place: if you change the processor or the oscillator used then – in many cases – you will need to make changes only to the Project Header.

Almost every example project on the CD includes a Project Header file. Search for the file `Main.H` on the CD to see further examples.

5.4 The Port Header (Port.H)

In a typical embedded project, you may have a user interface created using an LCD, a keypad, and one or more single LEDs. There may be a serial (RS-485) link to another microcontroller board. There may be one or more high-power devices (say 3-phase industrial motors) to be controlled.

Each of these (software) components in your application will require exclusive access to one or more port pins. Following the structure discussed in Section 5.2, the project may include 10–20 different source files, created – perhaps – by five different people. How do you ensure that changes to port access in one component does not impact on another? How do you ensure that it is easy to adapt the application to an environment where different port pins must be used?

These issues are addressed through the use of a simple Port Header file (Figure 5.3). Using a Port Header, you pull together the different port access features for the whole project into a single (header) file. Use of this technique can ease project development, maintenance and porting.

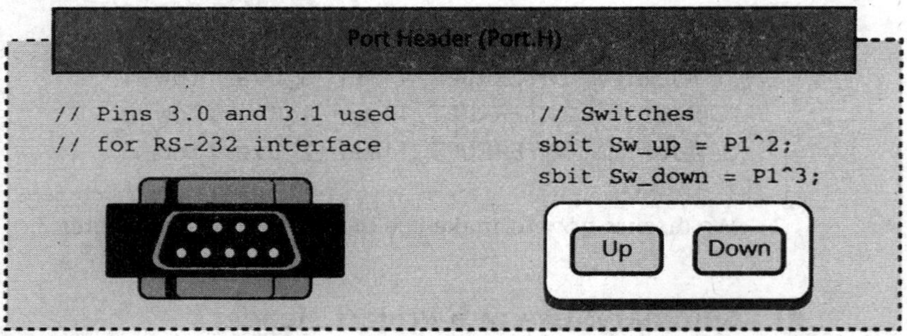

FIGURE 5.3 A schematic representation of the port header file

The Port Header file is simple to understand and easy to apply. Consider, for example, that we have three C files in a project (A, B, C), each of which require access to one or more port pins, or to a complete port.

File A may include the following:

```
// File A
sbit Pin_A = P3^2;
```

File B may include the following:

```
// File B

#define Port_B P0

. . .
```

File C may include the following:

```
// File C

sbit Pin_C = P2^7;

. . .
```

In this version of the code, all of the port access requirements are spread over multiple files. Instead of this, there are many advantages obtained by integrating all port access in a single `Port.H` header file:

```
// ----- Port.H -----

// Port access for File B
#define Port_B P0

// Port access for File A
sbit Pin_A = P3^2;

// Port access for File C
sbit Pin_C = P2^7;

...
```

Each of the remaining project files will then '`#include`' the file '`Port.H`'.

Listing 5.5 shows a complete example of a `Port.H` file from a real application.

Listing 5.5 An example of a real Port Header file (Port.H) from a project using an interface consisting of a keypad and liquid crystal display

```
/*------------------------------------------------------------------*-

  Port.H (v1.00)

  ------------------------------------------------------------------
```

```
   'Port Header' (see Chap 5) for project DATA_ACQ (see Chap 9)

-*------------------------------------------------------------*/

#ifndef _PORT_H
#define _PORT_H

#include 'Main.H'

// ------ Menu_A.C ------------------------------------------
// Uses whole of Port 1 and Port 2 for data acquisition
#define Data_Port1 P1
#define Data_Port2 P2

// ------ PC_IO.C -------------------------------------------

// Pins 3.0 and 3.1 used for RS-232 interface

#endif

/*------------------------------------------------------------*-
  ---- END OF FILE -----------------------------------------
-*------------------------------------------------------------*/
```

Despite its simplicity, use of a Port Header file can improve reliability and safety, because it avoids potential conflicts between port pins, particularly during the maintenance phase of the project when developers (who may not have been involved in the original design) are required to make code changes.

A Port Header is itself portable: it can be used with any microcontroller, and is not linked to the 8051 family. Use of a Port Header also improves portability, by making accessible, in one location, all of the port access requirements of the application.

5.5 Example: Restructuring the Hello, Embedded World example

We present here the complete source code listing for the 'Hello, Embedded World' example introduced in Chapter 3. This time, the code is restructured to match the layout suggestions given in this chapter.

The complete code for this project is also included on the CD.

Listing 5.6 Part of the 'Hello, Embedded World' example (restructured version)

```
/*------------------------------------------------------------------*-

   Main.H (v1.00)

   -----------------------------------------------------------------

   'Project Header'

-*------------------------------------------------------------------*/

#ifndef _MAIN_H
#define _MAIN_H

//------------------------------------------------------------------
// WILL NEED TO EDIT THIS SECTION FOR EVERY PROJECT
//------------------------------------------------------------------

// Must include the appropriate microcontroller header file here
#include <reg52.h>

// Oscillator / resonator frequency (in Hz) e.g. (11059200UL)
#define OSC_FREQ (12000000UL)

// Number of oscillations per instruction (12, etc)
// 12 - Original 8051 / 8052 and numerous modern versions
//  6 - Various Infineon and Philips devices, etc.
//  4 - Dallas 320, 520 etc.
//  1 - Dallas 420, etc.
#define OSC_PER_INST (12)

//------------------------------------------------------------------
// SHOULD NOT NEED TO EDIT THE SECTIONS BELOW
//------------------------------------------------------------------

// Typedefs (see Chap 5)
typedef unsigned char tByte;
typedef unsigned int tWord;
typedef unsigned long tLong;

// Interrupts (see Chap 7)
#define INTERRUPT_Timer_0_Overflow 1
```

```
#define INTERRUPT_Timer_1_Overflow 3
#define INTERRUPT_Timer_2_Overflow 5

#endif

/*------------------------------------------------------------------*-
  ---- END OF FILE -------------------------------------------------
-*------------------------------------------------------------------*/
```

Listing 5.7 Part of the 'Hello, Embedded World' example (restructured version)

```
/*------------------------------------------------------------------*-

   Port.H (v1.00)

  ------------------------------------------------------------------

   'Port Header' for project HELLO2 (see Chap 5)

-*------------------------------------------------------------------*/

#ifndef _PORT_H
#define _PORT_H

// ------ LED_Flash.C -----------------------------------------------

// Connect LED to this pin, via appropriate resistor
sbit LED_pin = P1^5;

#endif

/*------------------------------------------------------------------*-
  ---- END OF FILE -------------------------------------------------
-*------------------------------------------------------------------*/
```

Listing 5.8 Part of the 'Hello, Embedded World' example (restructured version)

```
/*------------------------------------------------------------------*-

   Main.C (v1.00)

  ------------------------------------------------------------------

   A "Hello Embedded World" test program for 8051.

   (Re-structured version - multiple source files)

-*------------------------------------------------------------------*/
```

```
#include "Main.H"
#include "Port.H"

#include "Delay_Loop.h"
#include "LED_Flash.h"

void main(void)
   {
   LED_FLASH_Init();

   while(1)
      {
      // Change the LED state (OFF to ON, or vice versa)
      LED_FLASH_Change_State();

      // Delay for *approx* 1000 ms
      DELAY_LOOP_Wait(1000);
      }
   }

/*------------------------------------------------------------------*-
  ---- END OF FILE -------------------------------------------------
-*------------------------------------------------------------------*/
```

Listing 5.9 Part of the 'Hello, Embedded World' example (restructured version)

```
/*------------------------------------------------------------------*-

   LED_flash.H (v1.00)

  ------------------------------------------------------------------

   - See LED_flash.C for details.

-*------------------------------------------------------------------*/

#ifndef _LED_FLASH_H
#define _LED_FLASH_H

// ------ Public function prototypes -------------------------

void LED_FLASH_Init(void);
void LED_FLASH_Change_State(void);

#endif

/*------------------------------------------------------------------*-
  ---- END OF FILE -------------------------------------------------
-*------------------------------------------------------------------*/
```

Listing 5.10 Part of the 'Hello, Embedded World' example (restructured version)

```
/*------------------------------------------------------------------*-

  LED_flash.C (v1.00)

  ------------------------------------------------------------------

  Simple 'Flash LED' test function.

-*------------------------------------------------------------------*/

#include "Main.H"
#include "Port.H"

#include "LED_flash.H"

// ------ Private variable definitions ------------------------------

static bit LED_state_G;

/*------------------------------------------------------------------*-

  LED_FLASH_Init()

  Prepare for LED_Change_State() function - see below.

-*------------------------------------------------------------------*/
void LED_FLASH_Init(void)
   {
   LED_state_G = 0;
   }

/*------------------------------------------------------------------*-

  LED_FLASH_Change_State()

  Changes the state of an LED (or pulses a buzzer, etc) on a
  specified port pin.

  Must call at twice the required flash rate: thus, for 1 Hz
  flash (on for 0.5 seconds, off for 0.5 seconds) must call
  every 0.5 seconds.

-*------------------------------------------------------------------*/
void LED_FLASH_Change_State(void)
```

```
    {
    // Change the LED from OFF to ON (or vice versa)
    if (LED_state_G == 1)
        {
        LED_state_G = 0;
        LED_pin = 0;
        }
    else
        {
        LED_state_G = 1;
        LED_pin = 1;
        }
    }

/*------------------------------------------------------------------*-
  ---- END OF FILE -------------------------------------------------
-*------------------------------------------------------------------*/
```

Listing 5.11 Part of the 'Hello, Embedded World' example (restructured version)

```
/*------------------------------------------------------------------*-

   Delay_Loop.H (v1.00)

  ------------------------------------------------------------------

   - See Delay_Loop.C for details.

-*------------------------------------------------------------------*/

#ifndef _DELAY_LOOP_H
#define _DELAY_LOOP_H

// ------ Public function prototype -------------------------------
void DELAY_LOOP_Wait(const tWord);

#endif

/*------------------------------------------------------------------*-
  ---- END OF FILE -------------------------------------------------
-*------------------------------------------------------------------*/
```

Listing 5.12 Part of the 'Hello, Embedded World' example (restructured version)

```
/*------------------------------------------------------------------*-

   Delay_Loop.C (v1.00)

  ------------------------------------------------------------------

   Create a simple software delay using a loop.

-*------------------------------------------------------------------*/

#include "Main.H"
#include "Port.H"

#include "Delay_loop.h"

/*------------------------------------------------------------------*-

  DELAY_LOOP_Wait()

  Delay duration varies with parameter.

  Parameter is, *ROUGHLY*, the delay, in milliseconds,
  on 12MHz 8051 (12 osc cycles).

  You need to adjust the timing for your application!

-*------------------------------------------------------------------*/
void DELAY_LOOP_Wait(const tWord DELAY_MS)
   {
   tWord x, y;

   for (x = 0; x <= DELAY_MS; x++)
      {
      for (y = 0; y <= 120; y++);
      }
   }

/*------------------------------------------------------------------*-
  ---- END OF FILE -------------------------------------------------
-*------------------------------------------------------------------*/
```

5.6 Example: Restructuring the goat-counting example

In Chapter 4 (Section 4.9), we presented an example in which the number of goats passing a sensor was measured and displayed on a port. Here we present another version of this example, restructured according to the guidelines presented in this chapter.

Listing 5.13 Part of the 'Goat' example (restructured version)

```
/*------------------------------------------------------------------*-

   Main.H (v1.00)

  ------------------------------------------------------------------

   'Project Header' (see Chapter 5).

-*------------------------------------------------------------------*/

#ifndef _MAIN_H
#define _MAIN_H

//------------------------------------------------------------------
// WILL NEED TO EDIT THIS SECTION FOR EVERY PROJECT
//------------------------------------------------------------------

// Must include the appropriate microcontroller header file here
#include <reg52.h>

// Oscillator / resonator frequency (in Hz) e.g. (11059200UL)
#define OSC_FREQ (12000000UL)

// Number of oscillations per instruction (12, etc)
// 12 - Original 8051 / 8052 and numerous modern versions
//  6 - Various Infineon and Philips devices, etc.
//  4 - Dallas 320, 520 etc.
//  1 - Dallas 420, etc.

#define OSC_PER_INST (12)

//------------------------------------------------------------------
// SHOULD NOT NEED TO EDIT THE SECTIONS BELOW
//------------------------------------------------------------------

// Typedefs (see Chap 5)
typedef unsigned char tByte;
```

```
typedef unsigned int tWord;
typedef unsigned long tLong;

// Interrupts (see Chap 7)
#define INTERRUPT_Timer_0_Overflow 1
#define INTERRUPT_Timer_1_Overflow 3
#define INTERRUPT_Timer_2_Overflow 5

#endif

/*------------------------------------------------------------------*-
  ---- END OF FILE -------------------------------------------------
-*------------------------------------------------------------------*/
```

Listing 5.14 Part of the 'Goat' example (restructured version)

```
/*------------------------------------------------------------------*-

   Port.H (v1.00)

   -----------------------------------------------------------------

   'Port Header' for project GOATS2 (see Chap 5)

-*------------------------------------------------------------------*/

#ifndef _PORT_H
#define _PORT_H

// ------ Switch_Wait.C -----------------------------------------------
// Connect switch to this pin
sbit Switch_pin = P1^0;

// ------ Display_count.C --------------------------------------------
// Display count (binary) on this port
#define Count_port P3

#endif

/*------------------------------------------------------------------*-
  ---- END OF FILE -------------------------------------------------
-*------------------------------------------------------------------*/
```

Listing 5.15 Part of the 'goat' example (restructured version)

```
/*------------------------------------------------------------------*-

   Main.C (v1.00)

  ------------------------------------------------------------------

   A 'switch count' program for the 8051.

-*------------------------------------------------------------------*/

#include "Main.H"
#include "Port.H"

#include "Switch_wait.H"
#include "Display_count.H"

/* --------------------------------------------------------------- */
void main(void)
   {
   tByte Switch_presses = 0;

   // Init functions
   SWITCH_Init();
   DISPLAY_COUNT_Init();

   while(1)
      {
      if (SWITCH_Get_Input(30) == SWITCH_PRESSED)
         {
         Switch_presses++;
         }

      DISPLAY_COUNT_Update(Switch_presses);
      }
   }

/*------------------------------------------------------------------*-
  ---- END OF FILE -------------------------------------------------
-*------------------------------------------------------------------*/
```

Listing 5.16 Part of the 'goat' example (restructured version)

```
/*------------------------------------------------------------------*-

   Switch_wait.H (v1.00)

  ------------------------------------------------------------------

   - See Switch_wait.C for details.

-*------------------------------------------------------------------*/

#ifndef _SWITCH_WAIT_H
#define _SWITCH_WAIT_H

// ------ Public constants ------------------------------------------
// Return values from Switch_Get_Input()
#define SWITCH_NOT_PRESSED (bit) 0
#define SWITCH_PRESSED (bit) 1

// ------ Public function prototype ---------------------------------
void SWITCH_Init(void);
bit SWITCH_Get_Input(const tByte);

#endif

/*------------------------------------------------------------------*-
  ---- END OF FILE -------------------------------------------------
-*------------------------------------------------------------------*/
```

Listing 5.17 Part of the 'goat' example (restructured version)

```
/*------------------------------------------------------------------*-

   Switch_Wait.C (v1.00)

  ------------------------------------------------------------------

   Simple library for debouncing a switch input.

   NOTE: Duration of function is highly variable!

-*------------------------------------------------------------------*/

#include "Main.H"
#include "Port.H"
```

```
#include "Switch_wait.h"
#include "Delay_loop.h"

/*------------------------------------------------------------------*-

  SWITCH_Init()

  Initialisation function for the switch library.

-*------------------------------------------------------------------*/
void SWITCH_Init(void)
   {
   Switch_pin = 1; // Use this pin for input
   }

/*------------------------------------------------------------------*-

  SWITCH_Get_Input()

  Reads and debounces a mechanical switch as follows:

  1. If switch is not pressed, return SWITCH_NOT_PRESSED.

  2. If switch is pressed, wait for DEBOUNCE_PERIOD (in ms).
     a. If switch is not pressed, return SWITCH_NOT_PRESSED.
     b. If switch is pressed, wait (indefinitely) for
        switch to be released, then return SWITCH_PRESSED

  See Switch_Wait.H for details of return values.

-*------------------------------------------------------------------*/
bit SWITCH_Get_Input(const tByte DEBOUNCE_PERIOD)
   {
   bit Return_value = SWITCH_NOT_PRESSED;

   if (Switch_pin == 0)
      {
      // Switch is pressed

      // Debounce - just wait...
      DELAY_LOOP_Wait(DEBOUNCE_PERIOD);

      // Check switch again
      if (Switch_pin == 0)
         {
         // Wait until the switch is released.
```

```
            while (Switch_pin == 0);
            Return_value = SWITCH_PRESSED;
            }
         }

      // Now (finally) return switch value
      return Return_value;
      }

/*------------------------------------------------------------------*-
  ---- END OF FILE -------------------------------------------------
-*------------------------------------------------------------------*/
```

Listing 5.18 Part of the 'goat' example (restructured version)

```
/*------------------------------------------------------------------*-

   Display_count.H (v1.00)

  ------------------------------------------------------------------

   - See Display_count.C for details.

-*------------------------------------------------------------------*/

#ifndef _DISPLAY_COUNT_H
#define _DISPLAY_COUNT_H

// ------ Public function prototypes -------------------------------
void DISPLAY_COUNT_Init(void);
void DISPLAY_COUNT_Update(const tByte);

#endif

/*------------------------------------------------------------------*-
  ---- END OF FILE -------------------------------------------------
-*------------------------------------------------------------------*/
```

Listing 5.19 Part of the 'goat' example (restructured version)

```
/*------------------------------------------------------------------*-

   Display_count.C (v1.00)

  ------------------------------------------------------------------
```

```
   Display an unsigned char on a port.

-*--------------------------------------------------------------*/

#include "Main.H"
#include "Port.H"

#include "Display_Count.H"

/*--------------------------------------------------------------*-

  DISPLAY_COUNT_Init()

  Initialisation function for the DISPLAY COUNT library.

-*--------------------------------------------------------------*/
void DISPLAY_COUNT_Init(void)
   {
   Count_port = 0x00;
   }

/*--------------------------------------------------------------*-

  DISPLAY_COUNT_Update()

  Simple function to display tByte data (COUNT)
  on LEDs connected to port (Count_Port)

-*--------------------------------------------------------------*/
void DISPLAY_COUNT_Update(const tByte COUNT)
   {
   Count_port = COUNT;
   }

/*--------------------------------------------------------------
  ---- END OF FILE ---------------------------------------------
-*--------------------------------------------------------------
```

Listing 5.20 Part of the 'goat' example (restructured version)

```
/*--------------------------------------------------------------

   Delay_Loop.H (v1.00)

  ------------------------------------------------------------

   - See Delay_Loop.C for details.

-*--------------------------------------------------------------
```

```
#ifndef _DELAY_LOOP_H
#define _DELAY_LOOP_H

// ------ Public function prototype -----------------------
void DELAY_LOOP_Wait(const tWord);

#endif

/*------------------------------------------------------------*-
  ---- END OF FILE ---------------------------------------------
-*------------------------------------------------------------*/
```

Listing 5.21 Part of the 'goat' example (restructured version)

```
/*------------------------------------------------------------*-

   Delay_Loop.C (v1.00)

   ------------------------------------------------------------

   Create a simple software delay using a loop.

-*------------------------------------------------------------*/

#include "Main.H"
#include "Port.H"

#include "Delay_loop.h"

/*------------------------------------------------------------*-

  DELAY_LOOP_Wait()

  Delay duration varies with parameter.

  Parameter is, *ROUGHLY*, the delay, in milliseconds,
  on 12MHz 8051 (12 osc cycles).

  You need to adjust the timing for your application!

-*------------------------------------------------------------*/
void DELAY_LOOP_Wait(const tWord DELAY_MS)
  {
  tWord x, y;

  for (x = 0; x <= DELAY_MS; x++)
     {
```

```
        for (y = 0; y <= 120; y++);
        }
    }

/*------------------------------------------------------------------*-
  ---- END OF FILE -------------------------------------------------
-*------------------------------------------------------------------*/
```

5.7 Further examples

For further examples of structured code, `Port.H` files and `Main.H` files throughout the remaining chapters in this book – please refer to the CD for details.

5.8 Conclusions

Over the course of the first five chapters of this book, we have reached the stage where we can create a simple – but functional – code framework for an embedded application.

In the remainder of this book, much of what we do will involve examining and refining different parts of this framework until – by the time we reach the case study in Chapter 11 – we will be in a position to assemble a range of complete embedded projects.

chapter 6

Meeting real-time constraints

6.1 Introduction

In this chapter, we begin to consider the issues involved in the accurate measurement of time. These issues are important because many embedded systems must satisfy real-time constraints.

For example, consider the aircraft autopilot application illustrated in Figure 6.1. Here we assume that the pilot has entered the required course heading, and that the system must make regular and frequent changes to the rudder, elevator, aileron and engine settings (for example) in order to keep the aircraft following this path.

An important characteristic of this embedded system is the need to process inputs and generate outputs very rapidly, on a time-scale measured in milliseconds. In this case, even a slight delay in making changes to the rudder setting (for example) may cause the plane to oscillate very unpleasantly or, in extreme circumstances, even to crash. However, in order to be able to have such an autopilot system certified for use, ensuring that the processing was 'as fast as we could make it' would not be enough to satisfy the relevant authorities: in this situation, as in many other real-time applications, the key characteristic is *deterministic* processing. What this means is that in many real-time embedded systems we need to be able to *guarantee* that a particular activity will always be completed within (say) 2 ms: if the processing does not match this specification, then the application is not simply slower than we would like, it is useless.

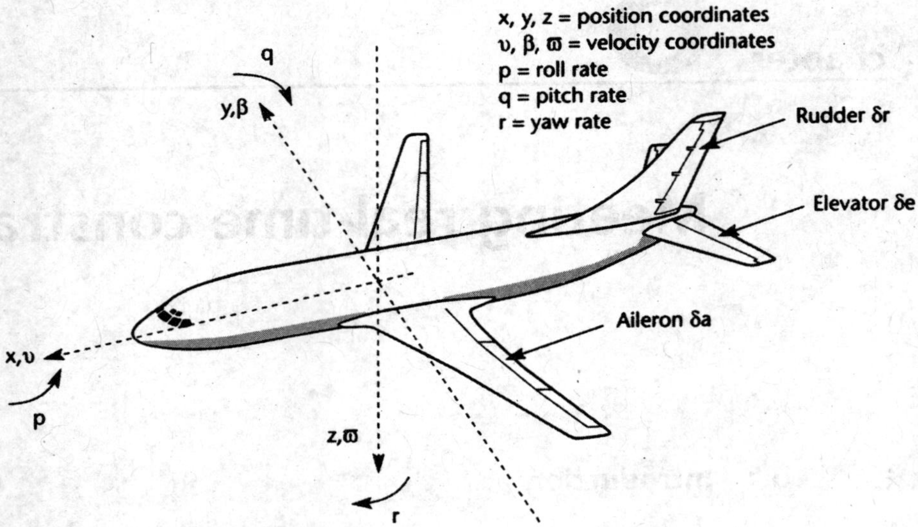

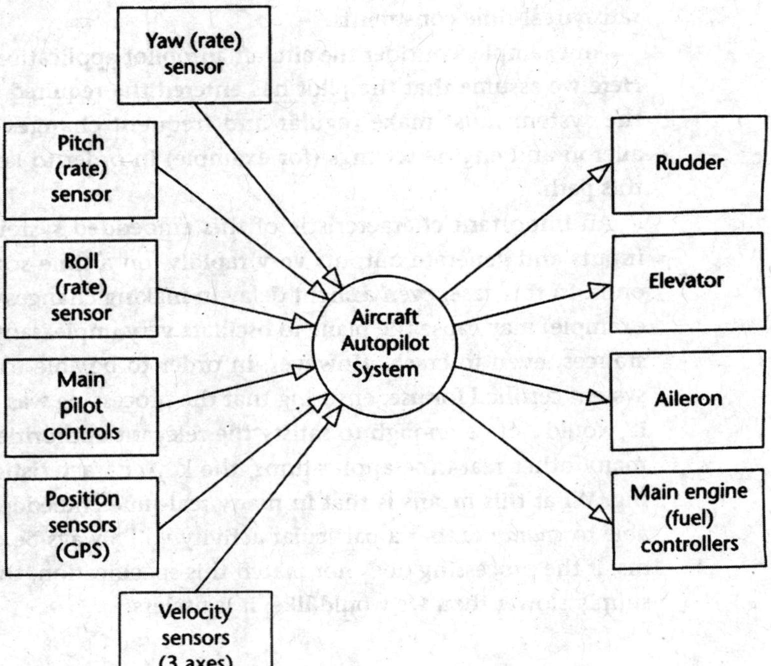

FIGURE 6.1 A high-level schematic view of a simple autopilot system

To date, the code we have developed certainly does not satisfy the real-time requirements of many embedded applications. For example, in Chapter 4, we presented an example in which we counted goats moving into a milking parlour. At the heart of this system was the function shown in annotated form in Listing 6.1.

Listing 6.1 Identifying problems with some simple switch-interface code

```
bit SWITCH_Get_Input(const tByte DEBOUNCE_PERIOD)
   {
   tByte Return_value = SWITCH_NOT_PRESSED;

   if (Switch_pin == 0)
      {
      // Switch is pressed

      // Debounce - just wait...
      DELAY_LOOP_Wait(DEBOUNCE_PERIOD); // POTENTIAL PROBLEM

      // Check switch again
      if (Switch_pin == 0)
         {
         // Wait until the switch is released.
         while (Switch_pin == 0);            // POTENTIAL CATASTROPHE
         Return_value = SWITCH_PRESSED;
         }
      }

   // Now (finally) return switch value
   return Return_value;
   }
```

Listing 6.1 highlights two potential problems with function `SWITCH_Get_Input()`.[21]

The first problem is that we wait for a 'debounce' period in order to confirm that the switch has been pressed:

```
DELAY_LOOP_Wait(DEBOUNCE_PERIOD);
```

Because this delay is implemented using a software loop it may not be very precisely timed. We illustrate how we can set this delay period more accurately using a hardware timer in Section 6.2.

21. There are, in fact, three problems. The third problem is that – while waiting for the switch to be released and (to a lesser extent) while executing the 'debounce delay' – we are wasting processor cycles that could be put to better use. We need to defer consideration of this third problem until Chapter 7, when we will demonstrate that it may be solved using an embedded operating system.

The second problem is even more serious in a system with real-time characteristics. With this code:

```
while (Switch_pin == 0);
```

we cause the system to wait – indefinitely – for the user to release the switch. This means that a damaged switch connection – or a determined user – can bring the system to a halt. Such code is simply unacceptable in production code (and certainly would not achieve certification, in the case of the autopilot system). We will begin to consider how we can solve this second problem in Section 6.6.

6.2 Creating 'hardware delays' using Timer 0 and Timer 1

We have used simple loop delays (similar to that shown below) in earlier chapters:

```
void DELAY_LOOP_Wait(const unsigned int DELAY)
   {
   unsigned int x, y;

   for (x = 0; x <= DELAY; x++)
      {
      for (y = 0; y <= 120; y++);
      }
   }
```

This approach to generating delays is easy to understand and easy to use (on any embedded or desktop processor). However, it is not easy to produce precisely timed delays using this approach, and the loops must be re-tuned if you decide to use a different processor, change the clock frequency, or even change the compiler optimization settings.

If we want to create more accurate delays, then we can do so using one of the 8051's on-chip timers. As we noted in Chapter 2, all members of the 8051 family have at least two 16-bit timer / counters, known as Timer 0 and Timer 1. These timers can be used to generate accurate delays.

To see how these timers operate, we need to explain the features of:

- The TCON SFR;
- The TMOD SFR; and,
- The THx and TLx registers.

We will first consider – in outline – how hardware timers are used to generate accurate delays, then consider each of the above timer components in more detail.

a) Overview

We noted in Chapter 2 that – when the timer hardware is running and appropriately configured – the timers are incremented periodically. In the original 8051 and 8052, the timers were incremented every 12 oscillator cycles:[22] assuming we used a 12 MHz oscillator, the timers were incremented 1 million times per second.

In most cases, we will be concerned with 16-bit timers. Assuming the count starts at 0, then – after 65.535 ms – our 12 MHz 8051 will reach its maximum value (65535) and the timer will then 'overflow'. When it overflows, a hardware flag will be set. We can easily read this flag in software.

This is very useful behaviour. For example, if we start the timer with an initial value of zero and wait until the flag is set, we know that precisely 65.535 ms will have elapsed. More importantly, we can vary the initial value stored in the timer: this allows us to generate shorter, precisely-timed, delays of – say – 50ms or 1ms, as required.

Building on the material discussed above, calculations of hardware delays generally take the following form:

- We calculate the required starting value for the timer.
- We load this value into the timer.
- We start the timer.
- The timer will be incremented, without software intervention, at a rate determined by the oscillator frequency; we wait for the timer to reach its maximum value and 'roll over'.
- The timer signals the end of the delay by changing the value of a flag variable.

As noted above, if we are using a '12-oscillations per instruction' 8051, running at 12 MHz, the longest delay that can be produced with a 16-bit timer is approximately 65 ms. If we need longer delays, we can repeat the steps above.

We will now consider how we can write code to achieve this.

b) The TCON SFR

We first need to introduce the TCON special function register (SFR): see Table 6.1. The various bits in the TCON SFR have the following functions:

TABLE 6.1 The TCON Special Function Register. Note that the grey bits are not connected with either Timer 0 or Timer 1

Bit	7 (MSB)	6	5	4	3	2	1	0 (LSB)
NAME	TF1	TR1	TF0	TR0	IE1	IT1	IE0	IT0

22. We consider some more modern 8051 devices in Section 6.4: these require fewer than 12 oscillator cycles per timer increment.

TR0, TR1 **Timer run control bits**

These bits need to be set to 1 (by the programmer) to run the corresponding timer (TR0 controls Timer 0, TR1 controls Timer 1). If set to 0, the corresponding timer will not run. Default value (after reset) is 0.

TF0, TF1 **Timer overflow flags**

These bits are set to 1 (by the microcontroller) when the corresponding timer overflows. They need to be manually cleared (set to 0) by the programmer. Default value (after reset) is 0.

For completeness we will briefly explain the purpose of the remaining bits in TCON:

IE0, IE1 **Interrupt flags**

Set by hardware when an (external) interrupt is detected on Pin 12 or Pin 13, respectively. These features are not related to Timer 0 or Timer 1 and are not used in this book (these bits can be left at their default value).

IT0, IT1 **Interrupt type control bit**

Used to determine with the external interrupt flags (above) are set in response to a falling edge ('edge triggered') or a low-level ('level triggered') input on the relevant port pins. These features are not related to Timer 0 or Timer 1 and are not used in this book (these bits can be left at their default value).

c) What about interrupts?

The code we use to create delays in this chapter will take the following form:

```
while (TF0 == 0); // Wait until Timer 0 overflows
```

That is, we wait until the timer overflow flag indicates that the timer has reached its maximum value. It should be pointed out that the overflow of the timers can be used to generate an interrupt: this can allow you to perform other activities while the counting goes on. We will not make use of this facility in the delay code presented in this chapter, but we will do so when we create an embedded operating system in Chapter 7.

To disable the generation of interrupts, we can use the C statements:

```
ET0 = 0; // No interupts (Timer 0)
ET1 = 0; // No interupts (Timer 1)
```

d) The TMOD SFR

We also need to introduce the TMOD SFR (Table 6.2).

TABLE 6.2 The TMOD Special Function Register. See text for details

Bit	7 (MSB)	6	5	4	3	2	1	0 (LSB)
NAME	Gate	$C/\overline{T}$	M1	M0	Gate	$C/\overline{T}$	M1	M0
	Timer 1				Timer 0			

The main thing to note is that there are three modes of operation (for each timer), set using the M1 and M0 bits. We will only be concerned in this book with Mode 1 and Mode 2, which operate in the same way for both Timer 0 and Timer 1, as follows:

Mode 1 (M1 = 0; M0 = 1)

16-bit timer/counter (with manual reload)[23]

Mode 2 (M1 = 1; M0 = 0)

8-bit timer/counter (with 8-bit automatic reload)

The remaining bits in TMOD have the following purpose:

GATE **Gating control**

We will not use gating control in this book. We will ensure that this bit is cleared, which means that Timer 0 or Timer 1 will be enabled whenever the corresponding control bit (TR0 or TR1) is set in the TCON SFR.

$C/\overline{T}$ **Counter or timer select bit**

We will not use counter mode in this book. We will ensure that this bit is cleared (for the appropriate timer), so that timer mode is used.

e) The THx and TLx registers

The final components you need to be aware of are the two 8-bit registers associated with each timer: these are known as TL0 and TH0, and TL1 and TH1. Here, 'L' and 'H' refer to 'low' and 'high' bytes, as will become clear shortly.

23. The distinction between 'automatic reload' and 'manual reload' timers has no impact on the hardware delay code we use here: to avoid confusion, we delay a discussion of this topic until Section 7.2b.

In all of the delay examples we use in this book, we will use the timers in Mode 1: that is, as 16-bit timers. If we are using Timer 1 to generate the delays, then the values loaded into TL1 and TH1 at the start of the delay routine will determine the delay duration.

For example, suppose we wish to generate a 15 ms hardware delay. We will assume that we are using a 12 MHz 8051, and that this device requires 12 oscillator cycles to perform each timer increment: the timer is incremented at a 1 MHz rate. A 15 ms delay therefore requires the following number of timer increments:

$$\frac{15ms}{1000ms} \times 1000000 = 15000 \text{ increments.}$$

The timer overflows when it is incremented from its maximum count of 65535. Thus, the initial value we need to load to produce a 15ms delay is:

$$65536 - 15000 = 50536 \text{ (decimal)} = \text{0xC568}$$

We can load this initial value into Timer 1 as follows:

```
TH1 = 0xC5;     // Timer 1 initial value (High Byte)
TL1 = 0x68;     // Timer 1 initial value (Low Byte)
```

We give another illustration of this process in the next section.

6.3 Example: Generating a precise 50 ms delay

To see how this all fits together, we will consider a 'flashing LED' example based on a precise 50 ms hardware delay (Listing 6.2).

Listing 6.2 A complete example using a hardware-based delay. See text for details

```
/*------------------------------------------------------------------*-

   Hardware_Delay_50ms.C (v1.00)

  ------------------------------------------------------------------

   A test program for hardware-based delays.

-*------------------------------------------------------------------*/

#include <reg52.h>
```

```
sbit LED_pin = P1^5;
bit LED_state_G;

void LED_FLASH_Init(void);
void LED_FLASH_Change_State(void);

void DELAY_HARDWARE_One_Second(void);
void DELAY_HARDWARE_50ms(void);

/*...................................................................*/

void main(void)
  {
  LED_FLASH_Init();

  while(1)
     {
     // Change the LED state (OFF to ON, or vice versa)
     LED_FLASH_Change_State();

     // Delay for approx 1000 ms
     DELAY_HARDWARE_One_Second();
     }
  }

/*-------------------------------------------------------------------*-

  LED_FLASH_Init()

  Prepare for LED_Change_State() function - see below.

-*-------------------------------------------------------------------*/
void LED_FLASH_Init(void)
  {
  LED_state_G = 0;
  }

/*-------------------------------------------------------------------*-

  LED_FLASH_Change_State()

  Changes the state of an LED (or pulses a buzzer, etc) on a
  specified port pin.

  Must call at twice the required flash rate: thus, for 1 Hz
```

```
   flash (on for 0.5 seconds, off for 0.5 seconds) must call
   every 0.5 seconds.

-*-----------------------------------------------------------*/
void LED_FLASH_Change_State(void)
   {
   // Change the LED from OFF to ON (or vice versa)
   if (LED_state_G == 1)
      {
      LED_state_G = 0;
      LED_pin = 0;
      }
   else
      {
      LED_state_G = 1;
      LED_pin = 1;
      }
   }

/*-----------------------------------------------------------*-

   DELAY_HARDWARE_One_Second()

   Hardware delay of 1000 ms.

   *** Assumes 12MHz 8051 (12 osc cycles) ***

-*-----------------------------------------------------------*/
void DELAY_HARDWARE_One_Second(void)
   {
   unsigned char d;

   // Call DELAY_HARDWARE_50ms() twenty times
   for (d = 0; d < 20; d++)
      {
      DELAY_HARDWARE_50ms();
      }
   }

/*-----------------------------------------------------------*-

   DELAY_HARDWARE_50ms()

   Hardware delay of 50ms.
```

```
   *** Assumes 12MHz 8051 (12 osc cycles) ***

-*------------------------------------------------------------------*/
void DELAY_HARDWARE_50ms(void)
   {
   // Configure Timer 0 as a 16-bit timer
   TMOD &= 0xF0; // Clear all T0 bits (T1 left unchanged)
   TMOD |= 0x01; // Set required T0 bits (T1 left unchanged)

   ET0 = 0; // No interupts

   // Values for 50 ms delay
   TH0 = 0x3C;  // Timer 0 initial value (High Byte)
   TL0 = 0xB0;  // Timer 0 initial value (Low Byte)

   TF0 = 0;           // Clear overflow flag
   TR0 = 1;           // Start timer 0

   while (TF0 == 0); // Loop until Timer 0 overflows (TF0 == 1)

   TR0 = 0;           // Stop Timer 0
   }

/*------------------------------------------------------------------*-
  ---- END OF FILE -------------------------------------------------
-*------------------------------------------------------------------*/
```

In Listing 6.2, these lines set up Timer 0, in Mode 1 (16-bit timer), without gating:

```
TMOD &= 0xF0; // Clear all T0 bits (T1 left unchanged)
TMOD |= 0x01; // Set required T0 bits (T1 left unchanged)
```

Note the use of the bitwise operators to change the state of SFR bits while leaving others unchanged: this is important as a different part of your program may be using Timer 1 for another purpose.

As we discussed in Section 6.2c the overflow of a timer can be used to generate an interrupt: we have no need for this in the delay code presented here. We therefore disable interrupt generation as follows:

```
ET0 = 0; // No interupts
```

Next, we load the timer registers with the initial timer value:

```
THO = 0x3C; // Timer 0 initial value (High Byte)
TLO = 0xB0; // Timer 0 initial value (Low Byte)
```

In this case, we assume – again – the standard 12 MHz / 12 oscillations-per-instruction microcontroller environment. We require a 50 ms delay, so the timer requires the following number of increments before it overflows:

$$\frac{50ms}{1000ms} \times 1000000 = 50000 \text{ increments}$$

The timer overflows when it is incremented from its maximum count of 65535. Thus, the initial value we need to load to produce a 50 ms delay is:

65536 – 50000 = 15536 (decimal) = 0x3CB0

Then we are ready to clear the timer flag, and start the timer running:

```
TF0 = 0; // Clear overflow flag
TR0 = 1; // Start timer 0
```

We discussed how to use the Keil simulator to 'profile' code in Chapter 3. In this case, executing the program in the hardware simulator confirms that the delays operate as required (Figure 6.2).

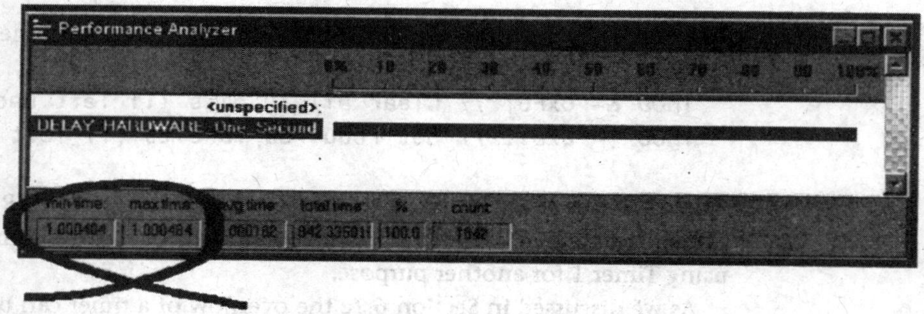

FIGURE 6.2 Executing Listing 6.2 in the hardware simulator

6.4 Example: Creating a portable hardware delay

In previous examples, we have usually assumed that the oscillator frequency will be 12 MHz and that the processor will require 12 oscillations per instruction. Of course, this will not always be the situation and – if your delay code assumes '12 MHz / 12 osc' (or any other combination) – then you may run into problems.

Here are some examples:

- If your application is battery powered, you will generally wish to use as low an operating frequency as possible (refer back to Chapter 2, Section 2.5b, for further details). To do this, you will typically work with late prototypes of your system (first in the simulator and then on hardware) to 'profile' the code and determine the minimum safe operating frequency. If delay code is 'hard wired' it is easy to forget to adjust the timing in these circumstances.
- If you add a serial interface then – for reasons we will discuss in Chapter 9 – you are likely to use an 11.059 MHz crystal. If you assumed a 12 MHz oscillator and forget to adjust delay timing, then the differences can be difficult to detect in bench tests, and any problems may only show up after your product has been released. This can prove very costly.
- System maintenance is always an issue. Operation of your code may be clear to you, but less experienced developers may subsequently assume that your '50 ms delay code' always gives a 50 ms delay (no matter what oscillator they use).

To reduce the likelihood of such problems, the code presented in this example is designed to be as portable as possible. What this means in practice is that the initial timer values are 'automatically' determined for different processor and oscillator combinations, by means of the project header file (`Main.H`: see Chapter 5), and some appropriate use of C pre-processor directives.

The relevant parts of `Main.H` are as follows:

```
// Oscillator / resonator frequency (in Hz) e.g. (11059200UL)
#define OSC_FREQ (12000000UL)

// Number of oscillations per instruction (12, etc)
// 12 - Original 8051 / 8052 and numerous modern versions
//  6 - Various Infineon and Philips devices, etc.
//  4 - Dallas 320, 520 etc
//  1 - Dallas 420, etc.
#define OSC_PER_INST (12)
```

The timer reload values are then determined as follows (please refer to the file `Delay_T0.C`):

```
// Timer preload values for use in simple (hardware) delays
// - Timers are 16-bit, manual reload ('one shot').
//
// NOTE: These values are portable but timings are *approximate*
//       and *must* be checked by hand if accurate timing is
//         required.
//
```

```
// Define Timer 0 / Timer 1 reload values for ~1 msec delay
// NOTE:
// Adjustment made to allow for function call overheard etc.
#define PRELOAD01 (65536 - (tWord)(OSC_FREQ / (OSC_PER_INST *
1020)))
#define PRELOAD01H (PRELOAD01 / 256)
#define PRELOAD01L (PRELOAD01 % 256)

...

// Delay value is *approximately* 1 ms per loop
for (ms = 0; ms < N; ms++)
    {
    TH0 = PRELOAD01H;
    TL0 = PRELOAD01L;

    TF0 = 0;            // Clear overflow flag
    TR0 = 1;            // Start timer 0
    while (TF0 == 0);   // Loop until Timer 0 overflows (TF0 == 1)

    TR0 = 0;            // Stop Timer 0
    }
```

To illustrate how this all fits together, the two key files required in the project are shown in Listing 6.3 and Listing 6.4 in their entirety. As usual, a complete set of files is included on the CD.

Listing 6.3 Part of the generic delay code (Hardware Delay) example

```
/*------------------------------------------------------------------*-

   Main.C (v1.00)

  ------------------------------------------------------------------

   Flashing LED with hardware-based delay (T0).

-*------------------------------------------------------------------*/

#include "Main.H"
#include "Port.H"

#include "Delay_T0.h"
#include "LED_Flash.h"
```

```
void main(void)
   {
   LED_FLASH_Init();

   while(1)
      {
      // Change the LED state (OFF to ON, or vice versa)
      LED_FLASH_Change_State();

      // Delay for *approx* 1000 ms
      DELAY_T0_Wait(1000);
      }
   }

/*------------------------------------------------------------------*-
  ---- END OF FILE -------------------------------------------------
-*------------------------------------------------------------------*/
```

Listing 6.4 Part of the generic delay code (Hardware Delay) example

```
/*------------------------------------------------------------------*-

   Delay_T0.C (v1.00)

  ------------------------------------------------------------------

   Simple hardware delays based on T0.

-*------------------------------------------------------------------*/

#include "Main.H"

// ------ Private constants ----------------------------------------

// Timer preload values for use in simple (hardware) delays
// - Timers are 16-bit, manual reload ('one shot').
//
// NOTE: These values are portable but timings are *approximate*
//       and *must* be checked by hand if accurate timing is
//       required.
//
// Define Timer 0 / Timer 1 reload values for ~1 msec delay
// NOTE: Adjustment made to allow for function call overheard etc.
#define PRELOAD01 (65536 - (tWord)(OSC_FREQ / (OSC_PER_INST * 1020)))
```

```
#define PRELOAD01H (PRELOAD01 / 256)
#define PRELOAD01L (PRELOAD01 % 256)

/*------------------------------------------------------------------*-

  DELAY_T0()

  Function to generate N millisecond delay (approx).

  Uses Timer 0 (easily adapted to Timer 1).

-*------------------------------------------------------------------*/
void DELAY_T0_Wait(const tWord N)
   {
   tWord ms;

   // Configure Timer 0 as a 16-bit timer
   TMOD &= 0xF0; // Clear all T0 bits (T1 left unchanged)
   TMOD |= 0x01; // Set required T0 bits (T1 left unchanged)

   ET0 = 0; // No interupts

   // Delay value is *approximately* 1 ms per loop
   for (ms = 0; ms < N; ms++)
      {
      TH0 = PRELOAD01H;
      TL0 = PRELOAD01L;

      TF0 = 0;           // clear overflow flag
      TR0 = 1;           // start timer 0

      while (TF0 == 0); // Loop until Timer 0 overflows (TF0 == 1)

      TR0 = 0;           // Stop Timer 0
      }
}
/*------------------------------------------------------------------*-
  ---- END OF FILE -------------------------------------------------
-*------------------------------------------------------------------*/
```

The output from this project is shown running in the Keil hardware simulator in Figure 6.3. Note that the delay value obtained is very close to the required value.

FIGURE 6.3 The output from the Hardware Delay example project running in the Keil hardware simulator. Please see Chapter 3 for information about the use of the performance analyzer

6.5 Why not use Timer 2?

In many cases, as we saw in Chapter 2, modern '8051' family devices are based on the slightly later 8052 architecture: such devices include an extra, more flexible timer: this is called – logically – Timer 2.

Timer 2 can be used to generate delays (in a manner nearly identical to that used with Timer 0 and Timer 1 in this chapter). However, this is not an appropriate use for this resource (in most applications). This is because Timer 2 has features which make it particularly well suited to the creation of an operating system, and most 'real' applications will reserve Timer 2 for this purpose.

We will describe an operating system based on Timer 2 in Chapter 7.

6.6 The need for 'timeout' mechanisms

In Section 6.1 we considered some of the weaknesses of the software used to implement the first version of our goat-counting system from Chapter 4. One of the main problems we noted arose from the use of code like this:

```
while (Switch_pin == 0);
```

As we noted above, the problem is that the system will 'hang' if the switch is never released. In our goat-counting system, this might happen – for example – if one of the animals got stuck in the entrance to the milking parlour, and held up the whole herd. In these circumstances, it would be useful if we could have an alarm sound (to alert the farmer) if any goat took longer than – say – 15 seconds to pass through the gate. However, with the first simple implementation of this system, 100% of the processor power is wasted in an idle loop, waiting for the switch to be released. This is clearly not an ideal design.

Such problems are not, of course, limited to switch interfaces. For example, the Philips 8Xc552 is an Extended 8051 device with a number of on-chip peripherals, including an 8-channel, 10-bit analog-to-digital converter (ADC). Philips provide an application note (AN93017) that describes how to use this feature of the micro-controller. This application note includes the following code:

```
// Wait until AD conversion finishes (checking ADCI)
while ((ADCON & ADCI) == 0);
```

Such code is potentially unreliable, because there are circumstances under which our application may 'hang'. This might occur for one or more of the following reasons:

- If the ADC has been incorrectly initialized, we cannot be sure that a data conversion will be carried out.
- If the ADC has been subjected to an excessive input voltage, then it may not operate at all.
- If the variable ADCON or ADCI were not conectly initialized, they may not operate as required.

The Philips example is not intended to illustrate 'production' code. Unfortunately, however, code in this form is common in embedded applications. If the systems you create are to be reliable, you need to be able to guarantee that no function will hang in this way.

There are several ways we can provide such a guarantee. We will consider two of the most popular in the sections that follow:

- The loop timeout (see Section 6.7).
- The hardware timeout (see Section 6.10).

6.7 Creating loop timeouts

A loop timeout may be easily created. The basis of the code structure is a form of loop delay, created as follows:

```
tWord Timeout_loop = 0;

...

while (++Timeout_loop != 0);
```

This loop will keep running until the variable `Timeout_loop` reaches its maximum value (assuming 16-bit integers) of 65535, and then overflows. When this happens, the program will continue. Note that, without some simulation studies or prototyping, we cannot easily determine how long this delay will be. However, we do know that the loop will, eventually, time out.

Such a loop is simply a slightly modified version of the loop-delay code which we have presented previously. However, if we consider again the ADC example discussed in the previous section, we can illustrate how such a loop can be used to provide a timeout facility. Recall that the original code was as follows:

```
// Wait until AD conversion finishes (checking ADCI)
while ((ADCON & ADCI) == 0);
```

Here is a modified version of this code, with a loop timeout:

```
tWord Timeout_loop = 0;

   // Take sample from ADC
   // Wait until conversion finishes (checking ADCI)
   // - simple loop timeout
   while (((ADCON & ADCI) == 0) && (++Timeout_loop != 0));
```

Note that we can vary the duration of the loop timeout by changing the initial value assigned to the loop variable. The file `TimeoutL.H`, reproduced in Listing 6.5 and included on the CD in the directory associated with this chapter, includes a set of constants that give – very approximately – the specified timeout values.

Listing 6.5 The file TimeoutL.H. See text for details

```
/*------------------------------------------------------------------*-

   TimeoutL.H (v1.00)

  ------------------------------------------------------------------

   Simple software (loop) timeout delays for the 8051 family.

   * THESE VALUES ARE NOT PRECISE - YOU MUST ADAPT TO YOUR SYSTEM *

-*------------------------------------------------------------------*/

#ifndef _TIMEOUTL_H
#define _TIMEOUTL_H

// ------ Public constants ------------------------------------------

// Vary this value to change the loop duration
// THESE ARE APPROX VALUES FOR VARIOUS TIMEOUT DELAYS
// ON 8051, 12 MHz, 12 Osc / cycle

// *** MUST BE FINE TUNED FOR YOUR APPLICATION ***

// *** Timings vary with compiler optimisation settings ***

// tWord
#define LOOP_TIMEOUT_INIT_001ms 65435U
#define LOOP_TIMEOUT_INIT_010ms 64535U
#define LOOP_TIMEOUT_INIT_500ms 14535U
// tLong
#define LOOP_TIMEOUT_INIT_10000ms 4294795000UL

#endif

/*------------------------------------------------------------------*-
  ---- END OF FILE -------------------------------------------------
-*------------------------------------------------------------------*/
```

We give an example of how to use this file below.

6.8 Example: Testing loop timeouts

We present a simple example here that may be used – in the simulator – to fine-tune the software timeout loops to match your particular hardware.

Listing 6.6 shows the required code.

Listing 6.6 Testing loop timeouts

```
/*------------------------------------------------------------------*-

   Main.C (v1.00)

  ------------------------------------------------------------------

   Testing timeout loops.

-*------------------------------------------------------------------*/

#include <reg52.H>

#include "TimeoutL.H"

// Typedefs (see Chap 5)
typedef unsigned char tByte;
typedef unsigned int tWord;
typedef unsigned long tLong;

// Function prototypes
void Test_Timeout(void);

/*------------------------------------------------------------------*/
void main(void)
   {
   while(1)
      {
      Test_Timeout();
      }
   }

/*------------------------------------------------------------------*/
void Test_Timeout(void)
   {
   tLong Timeout_loop = LOOP_TIMEOUT_INIT_10000ms;

   // Simple loop timeout...
```

```
    while (++Timeout_loop != 0);
    }

/*------------------------------------------------------------------*-
  ---- END OF FILE -------------------------------------------------
-*------------------------------------------------------------------*/
```

The simulator output is shown in Figure 6.4.

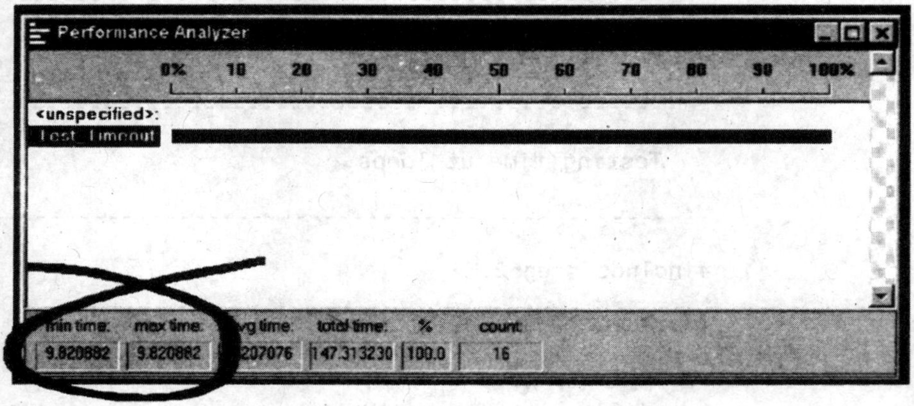

FIGURE 6.4 Testing timeout loops: see text for details

6.9 Example: A more reliable switch interface

In this example, we apply the loop timeout code to the problem of switch debouncing.

In this case, the user is allowed up to 10 seconds to release the switch: if it is not released in this period, the function will 'time out' and return.

The key code is shown in Listing 6.7. Complete files for this project will be found on the CD.

Listing 6.7 Code for a more reliable switch interface. See text for details

```
/*------------------------------------------------------------------*-

   Switch_Wait_TimeoutL.C (v1.00)

  ------------------------------------------------------------------

   Simple library for processing a switch input.

   (Made more reliable by means of a ~10-second timeout.)

-*------------------------------------------------------------------*/
```

```
#include "Main.H"
#include "Port.H"

#include "Switch_wait_TimeoutL.H"
#include "Delay_T0.h"
#include "TimeoutL.H"

/*------------------------------------------------------------------*-

  SWITCH_Init()

  Initialisation function for the switch library.

-*------------------------------------------------------------------*/
void SWITCH_Init(void)
   {
   Switch_pin = 1; // Use this pin for input
   }

/*------------------------------------------------------------------*-

  SWITCH_Get_Input()

  Reads and debounces a mechanical switch as follows:

  1. If switch is not pressed, return SWITCH_NOT_PRESSED.

  2. If switch is pressed, wait for DEBOUNCE_PERIOD (in ms).
     a. If switch is not pressed, return SWITCH_NOT_PRESSED.
     b. If switch is pressed, wait (with timeout) for
        switch to be released. If it times out,
        then return SWITCH_NOT_PRESSED: otherwise, return
        SWITCH_PRESSED.

  See Switch_Wait.H for details of return values.

-*------------------------------------------------------------------*/
bit SWITCH_Get_Input(const tByte DEBOUNCE_PERIOD)
   {
   tByte Return_value = SWITCH_NOT_PRESSED;
   tLong Timeout_loop = LOOP_TIMEOUT_INIT_10000ms;

   if (Switch_pin == 0)
      {
      // Switch is pressed
```

```
      // Debounce - just wait...
      DELAY_T0_Wait(DEBOUNCE_PERIOD);

      // Check switch again
      if (Switch_pin == 0)
         {
         // Wait until the switch is released.
         // (WITH TIMEOUT LOOP - 10 seconds)
         while ((Switch_pin == 0) && (++Timeout_loop != 0));

         // Check for timeout
         if (Timeout_loop == 0)
            {
            Return_value = SWITCH_NOT_PRESSED;
            }
         else
            {
            Return_value = SWITCH_PRESSED;
            }
         }
      }

   // Now (finally) return switch value
   return Return_value;
   }

/*------------------------------------------------------------------*-
  ---- END OF FILE -------------------------------------------------
-*------------------------------------------------------------------*/
```

6.10 Creating hardware timeouts

If we consider the ability to meet real-time requirements by code without timeouts and code with a loop timeout, it is clear that the loop timeout solution is significantly better.

Loop timeouts are particularly well suited to applications involving long timeout delays (typically measured in seconds). Where we require shorter delays, with very precise timing, we can often gain a further improvement in performance through the use of hardware-based timeouts.

As we saw in earlier in this chapter, we can create portable and easy to use delay code for the 8051 family as follows:

```
// Define Timer 0 / Timer 1 preload values for ~1 msec delay
#define PRELOAD_01ms (65536-(tWord)(OSC_FREQ/(OSC_PER_INST*1000)))
#define PRELOAD_01ms_H (PRELOAD_01ms / 256)
#define PRELOAD_01ms_L (PRELOAD_01ms % 256)
//

...

void Hardware_Delay_T0(const tLong MS)
   {
   tLong ms;

   // Configure Timer 0 as a 16-bit timer
   TMOD &= 0xF0; // Clear all T0 bits (T1 left unchanged)
   TMOD |= 0x01; // Set required T0 bits (T1 left unchanged)

   ET0 = 0;  // No interrupts

   // Delay value is *approximately* 1 ms per loop
   for (ms = 0; ms < MS; ms++)
      {
      TH0 = PRELOAD_01ms_H;
      TL0 = PRELOAD_01ms_L;

      TF0 = 0;           // Clear overflow flag
      TR0 = 1;           // Start Timer 0

      while (TF0 == 0); // Loop until Timer 0 overflows

      TR0 = 0;           // Stop Timer 0
      }
   }
```

Creating a hardware timeout involves a simple variation on this technique, and allows precise timeout delays to be easily generated.

For example, in Section 6.6 we considered the process of reading from an ADC in a Philips 8Xc552 microcontroller. This was the original, potentially dangerous, code:

```
// Wait until AD conversion finishes (checking ADCI)
while ((ADCON & ADCI) == 0);
```

Here is a solution with a hardware timeout, providing a delay of 10 ms which will, with reasonable accuracy, apply across the whole 8051 family (without code modifications):

```
// Configure Timer 0 as a 16-bit timer
TMOD &= 0xF0; // Clear all T0 bits (T1 left unchanged)
TMOD |= 0x01; // Set required T0 bits (T1 left unchanged)

ET0 = 0;       // No interrupts

// Simple timeout feature - approx 10 ms
TH0 = PRELOAD_10ms_H; // See Timeout.H for PRELOAD details
TL0 = PRELOAD_10ms_L;
TF0 = 0; // Clear flag
TR0 = 1; // Start timer

while (((ADCON & ADCI) == 0) && !TF0);
```

Various portable PRELOAD_ macros suitable for use in this way are given in the file Timeout.H reproduced in Listing 6.8 and included on the CD. Note that the same PRELOAD_ values may be used with either Timer 0 or Timer 1, as required.

Listing 6.8 The file TimeoutH.H

```
/*------------------------------------------------------------------*-

   TimeoutH.H (v1.00)

  ------------------------------------------------------------------

   Simple timeout delays for the 8051 family based on T0/T1.

   Timer must be correctly configured to use these values:
   See Chapter 6 for details.

-*------------------------------------------------------------------*/

#ifndef _TIMEOUTH_H
#define _TIMEOUTH_H

// ------ Public constants ------------------------------------------

// Timer T_ values for use in simple (hardware) timeouts
// - Timers are 16-bit, manual reload ('one shot').
//
// NOTE: These macros are portable but timings are *approximate*
```

```
//      and *must* be checked by hand if accurate timing is
//      required.
//
// Define initial Timer 0 / Timer 1 values for ~50 µs delay
#define T_50micros (65536-(tWord)((OSC_FREQ / 26000)/(OSC_PER_INST)))
#define T_50micros_H (T_50micros / 256)
#define T_50micros_L (T_50micros % 256)

// Define initial Timer 0 / Timer 1 values for ~500 µs delay
#define T_500micros (65536 - (tWord)(OSC_FREQ / (OSC_PER_INST * 2000)))
#define T_500micros_H (T_500micros / 256)
#define T_500micros_L (T_500micros % 256)

// Define initial Timer 0 / Timer 1 values for ~1 msec delay
#define T_01ms (65536 - (tWord)(OSC_FREQ / (OSC_PER_INST * 1000)))
#define T_01ms_H (T_01ms / 256)
#define T_01ms_L (T_01ms % 256)
//
// Define initial Timer 0 / Timer 1 values for ~5 msec delay
#define T_05ms (65536 - (tWord)(OSC_FREQ / (OSC_PER_INST * 200)))
#define T_05ms_H (T_05ms / 256)
#define T_05ms_L (T_05ms % 256)
//
// Define initial Timer 0 / Timer 1 values for ~10 msec delay
#define T_10ms (65536 - (tWord)(OSC_FREQ / (OSC_PER_INST * 100)))
#define T_10ms_H (T_10ms / 256)
#define T_10ms_L (T_10ms % 256)
//
// Define initial Timer 0 / Timer 1 values for ~15 msec delay
#define T_15ms (65536 - (tWord)(OSC_FREQ / (OSC_PER_INST * 67)))
#define T_15ms_H (T_15ms / 256)
#define T_15ms_L (T_15ms % 256)
//
// Define initial Timer 0 / Timer 1 values for ~20 msec delay
#define T_20ms (65536 - (tWord)(OSC_FREQ / (OSC_PER_INST * 50)))
#define T_20ms_H (T_20ms / 256)
#define T_20ms_L (T_20ms % 256)
//
// Define initial Timer 0 / Timer 1 values for ~50 msec delay
```

```
#define T_50ms (65536 - (tWord)(OSC_FREQ / (OSC_PER_INST * 20)))
#define T_50ms_H (T_50ms / 256)
#define T_50ms_L (T_50ms % 256)

#endif

/*------------------------------------------------------------------*-
  ---- END OF FILE -------------------------------------------------
-*------------------------------------------------------------------*/
```

6.11 Example: Testing a hardware timeout

Listing 6.9 shows a simple program for testing hardware-based timeout mechanisms.

Please note that, to avoid undue repetition, only part of this source file is reproduced here: the complete file is included on the CD.

Listing 6.9 Testing hardware-based timeout loops (incomplete listing). See text for detail

```
/*------------------------------------------------------------------*-

   Main.C (v1.00)

  ------------------------------------------------------------------

   Testing hardware timeouts.

-*------------------------------------------------------------------*/

#include "Main.H"
#include "TimeoutH.H"

// Function prototypes
void Test_50micros(void);
void Test_500micros(void);
void Test_1ms(void);
void Test_5ms(void);
void Test_10ms(void);
void Test_15ms(void);
void Test_20ms(void);
void Test_50ms(void);
```

```
// TIMEOUT code variable & TIMEOUT code (dummy here)
#define TIMEOUT 0xFF
tByte Error_code_G;

/*------------------------------------------------------------------*/
void main(void)
   {
   while(1)
      {
      Test_50micros();
      Test_500micros();
      Test_1ms();
      Test_5ms();
      Test_10ms();
      Test_15ms();
      Test_20ms();
      Test_50ms();
      }
   }

/*------------------------------------------------------------------*/
void Test_50micros(void)
   {
   // Configure Timer 0 as a 16-bit timer
   TMOD &= 0xF0; // Clear all T0 bits (T1 left unchanged)
   TMOD |= 0x01; // Set required T0 bits (T1 left unchanged)

   ET0 = 0;       // No interrupts

   // Simple timeout feature - approx 50 µs
   TH0 = T_50micros_H; // See TimeoutH.H for T_ details
   TL0 = T_50micros_L;
   TF0 = 0; // Clear flag
   TR0 = 1; // Start timer

   while (!TF0);

   TR0 = 0;

   // Normally need to report timeout TIMEOUTs
   // (this test is for demo purposes here)
   if (TF0 == 1)
      {
```

```
        // Operation timed out
        Error_code_G = TIMEOUT;
        }
    }

/*------------------------------------------------------------------*/

. . .

// Other functions very similar [OMITTED HERE]
// see CD for details

/*------------------------------------------------------------------*-
  ---- END OF FILE -------------------------------------------------
-*------------------------------------------------------------------*/
```

The output from Listing 6.9 is shown in Figure 6.5.

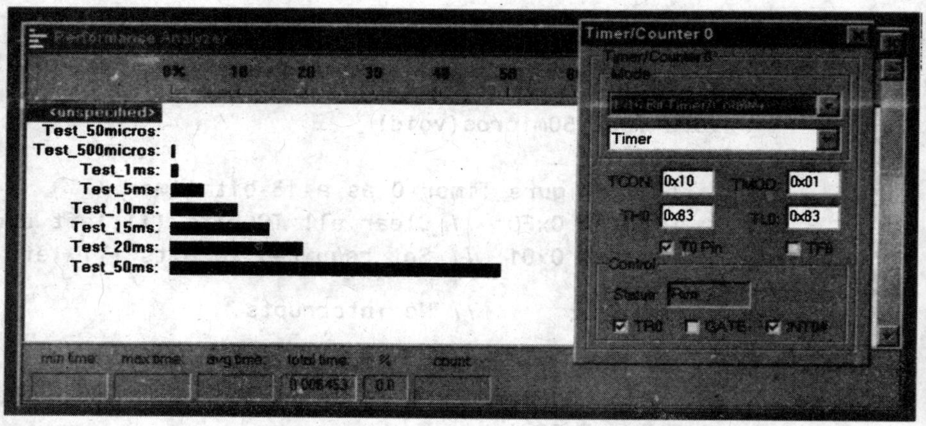

FIGURE 6.5 Testing hardware-based timeout mechanisms. See text for details

6.12 Conclusions

The delay and timeout considered in this chapter are widely used in embedded applications.

In Chapter 7, we go on to consider another key software component in many embedded applications: the operating system.

chapter 7

Creating an embedded operating system

7.1 Introduction

The Super Loop architecture illustrated in Listing 7.1 is used in many embedded applications and has formed the basis of all of the example code which we have considered in previous chapters. From the developer's perspective, the main advantages of this architecture are that it is easy to understand, and that it consumes virtually no system memory or CPU resources.

Despite these advantages, Super Loops are not an appropriate basis for all embedded applications. A particular limitation with this architecture is that it is very difficult to execute function X() at precise intervals of time: as we will see, this is a very significant drawback.

Listing 7.1 In this chapter, we will consider an alternative to this simple Super Loop architecture

```
void main(void)
   {
   // Prepare run function X
   X_Init();

   while(1) // 'for ever' (Super Loop)
      {
      X();  // Run function X
      }
   }
```

FIGURE 7.1 Using an audio museum guide. Please see text for details

For example, consider an embedded application that is now in widespread use: an audio guide (Figure 7.1). Such applications are used in museums and galleries throughout the world, in order to describe the numbered exhibits to visitors. The guide can typically be used in two ways. First, the visitor can select 'auto pilot': this will then cause the guide to describe a sequence of exhibits in order, in the following manner:

Item 345 was painted by Selvio Guaranteen early in the 16th century. At this time, Guaranteen, who is generally known as a member of the Slafordic School, was ...

Now turn to your left, and locate Item 346, a small painting which was until recently also thought to have been painted by Guarateen but which is now ... .

Alternatively, the visitor can use the device in 'manual' mode. In this case, the user will be free to wander at leisure around the exhibition and, when he or she finds an item of interest, they will type in the exhibit number on the electronic guide: they will then hear the relevant commentary.

No matter what technique we use, the basic processing required in this application will be the same: we need to generate a long stream of speech from a store of data in memory. This will typically involve using a digital-to-analog converter to generate an analog signal at a rate of at least 5000 samples per second (Figure 7.2).

The need to call the same function repeatedly, at precise intervals, is by no means restricted to this museum system (or similar systems such as MP3 players). For example, consider a collection of requirements assembled from a range of different embedded projects (in no particular order):

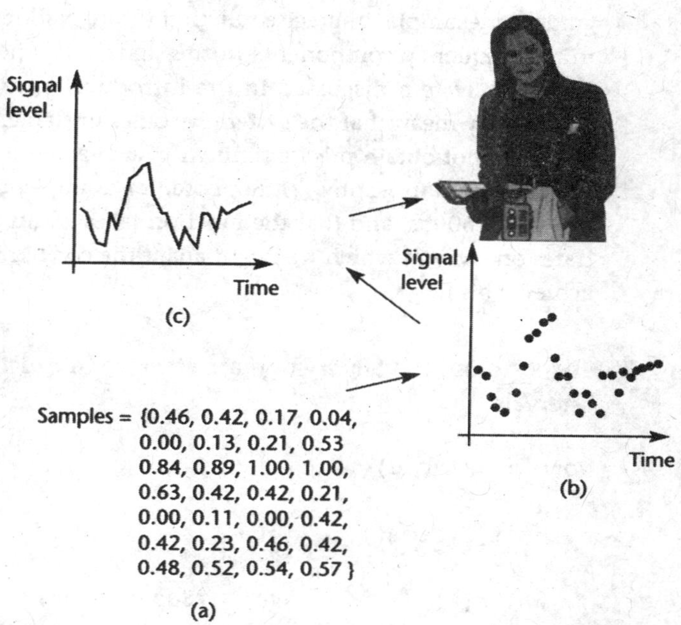

FIGURE 7.2 The generation of speech for the museum guide. (a) The raw speech data, stored in ROM. (b) The result of playing these data through a digital-to-analog converter, generating one sample every 0.2 ms. (c) The (low-pass) filtered and amplified version of the converter output signal

- The current speed of the vehicle must be measured at 0.5 second intervals.
- The display must be refreshed 40 times every second.
- The calculated new throttle setting must be applied every 0.5 seconds.
- A time-frequency transform must be performed 20 times every second.
- The engine vibration data must be sampled 1000 times per second.
- The frequency-domain data must be classified 20 times every second.
- The keypad must be scanned every 200 ms.
- The master (control) node must communicate with all other nodes (sensor nodes and sounder nodes) once per second.
- The new throttle setting must be calculated every 0.5 seconds.
- The sensors must be sampled once per second.

In practice, many embedded systems must be able to support this type of 'periodic function': that is, activities that are performed repeatedly, every millisecond or every ten milliseconds. In most cases, the process must take place at precisely the specified interval if the device is to operate as required. In the case of the museum guide, for example, imprecise function timing will result in unpleasant distortions to the frequency components in the signal. In other cases – such as the aircraft autopilot system discussed in the introduction to Chapter 6 – lack of precise timing may mean that the system becomes unstable.

We cannot obtain precise timing for such activities using the Super Loop architecture shown in Listing 7.1. Suppose, for example, that we need to start function X() every 60 ms, and that the function takes 10 ms to complete. Listing 7.2 illustrates one way in which we might adapt the code in Listing 7.1 in order to try and achieve this.

Listing 7.2 Trying to use the Super Loop architecture to execute functions at regular intervals

```
void main(void)
   {
   Init_System();

   while(1) // 'for ever' (Super Loop)
      {
      X();           // Call the function (10 ms duration)
      Delay_50ms(); // Delay for 50 ms
      }
   }
```

You may recall that we used this basic architecture in our 'Hello, Embedded World' program in Chapter 3. For the purposes of an introductory example, or in situations – such as the simple central-heating controller outlined in Chapter 1 – this approach is often adequate.

However, in the many circumstances where more accurate timing is needed, the architecture shown in Listing 7.2 will only prove adequate if the following conditions are satisfied:

- We know the precise duration of function X(), and,
- This duration never varies.

In practical applications, determining the precise function duration is rarely straightforward. Suppose we have a very simple function that does not interact with the outside world but, instead, performs some internal calculations. Even under these rather restricted circumstances, changes to compiler optimization settings – even changes to an apparently unrelated part of the program – can alter the speed at which the function executes. This can make fine-tuning the timing very tedious and error-prone.

The second condition is even more problematic. Often in an embedded system functions will be required to interact with the outside world in a complex way. In these circumstances the function duration will vary according to outside activities in a manner over which the programmer has very little control.

Finally, it should also be noted that the code shown in Listing 7.2 is very inefficient, because most of the processor time is wasted in a delay loop.

7.2 The basis of a simple embedded OS

To obtain periodic function executions – and avoid wasting processor cycles – we can use **interrupts**.

As we saw in Chapter 2, an interrupt is a hardware mechanism used to notify a processor that an 'event' has taken place. Timer overflows are a particularly effective and widely-used source of interrupts in embedded applications. For example, the 8051 microcontrollers discussed in this book all have an on-chip timer which can be set to generate an interrupt (a 'tick') at regular and precise intervals of, say, 1 millisecond. This interrupt can be used to call an appropriate function periodically.

While the process of handling interrupts may seem rather complicated, creating interrupt service routines (ISRs) in a high-level language is a straightforward process, as illustrated in Listing 7.3.

Listing 7.3 The framework of an application using a timer ISR to call functions on a periodic basis

```
/*------------------------------------------------------------------*-

   Main.c

  ------------------------------------------------------------------

   Simple timer ISR demonstration program.

-*------------------------------------------------------------------*/

#include <Reg52.H>

#define INTERRUPT_Timer_2_Overflow 5
```

```
// Function prototype
// NOTE:
// ISR is not explictly called and does not require a prototype
void Timer_2_Init(void);

/* ------------------------------------------------------------ */

void main(void)
   {
   Timer_2_Init();  // Set up Timer 2

   EA = 1;          // Globally enable interrupts

   while(1);        // An empty Super Loop
   }

/* ------------------------------------------------------------ */

void Timer_2_Init(void)
   {
   // Timer 2 is configured as a 16-bit timer,
   // which is automatically reloaded when it overflows
   //
   // This code (generic 8051/52) assumes a 12 MHz system osc.
   // The Timer 2 resolution is then 1.000 µs
   //
   // Reload value is FC18 (hex) = 64536 (decimal)
   // Timer (16-bit) overflows when it reaches 65536 (decimal)
   // Thus, with these setting, timer will overflow every 1 ms
   T2CON   = 0x04;  // Load Timer 2 control register

   TH2     = 0xFC;  // Load Timer 2 high byte
   RCAP2H  = 0xFC;  // Load Timer 2 reload capt. reg. high byte
   TL2     = 0x18;  // Load Timer 2 low byte
   RCAP2L  = 0x18;  // Load Timer 2 reload capt. reg. low byte

   // Timer 2 interrupt is enabled, and ISR will be called
   // whenever the timer overflows - see below.
   ET2     = 1;

   // Start Timer 2 running
   TR2   = 1;
   }

/* ------------------------------------------------------------ */
```

```
void X(void) interrupt INTERRUPT_Timer_2_Overflow
   {
   // This ISR is called every 1 ms

   // Place required code here...
   }

/*------------------------------------------------------------------*-
  ---- END OF FILE -------------------------------------------------
-*------------------------------------------------------------------*/
```

The result of running the program shown in Listing 7.3 in the Keil hardware simulator is shown in Figure 7.3.

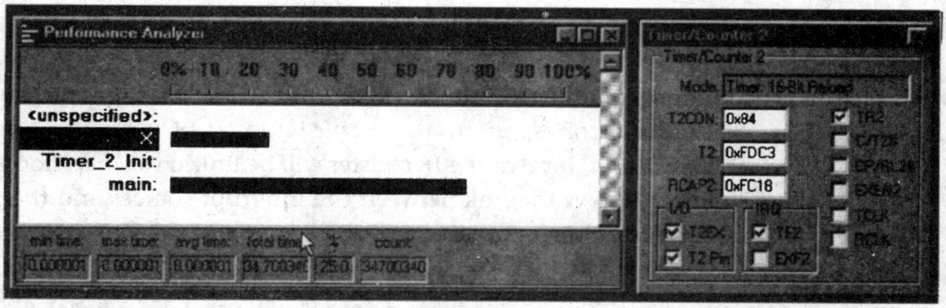

FIGURE 7.3 The result of running the program shown in Listing 7.3 in the Keil hardware simulator

Much of Listing 7.3 should be familiar. The code to set up Timer 2 in the function `Timer_2_Init()` is the same as the delay code discussed in Chapter 6, the two main differences being that, in this case:

1 The timer will generate an interrupt when it overflows, and

2 The timer will be automatically reloaded, and will immediately begin counting again.

We discuss both of these differences in the following sub-sections.

a) The interrupt service routine (ISR)

The interrupt generated by the overflow of Timer 2, invokes the ISR called, here, `X()`.

```
/* ------------------------------------------------------------ */
void X(void) interrupt INTERRUPT_Timer_2_Overflow
   {
   // This ISR is called every 1 ms

   // Place required code here...
   }
```

The link between this function and the timer overflow is made using the Keil keyword `interrupt` (included after the function header in the function definition):

```
void X(void) interrupt INTERRUPT_Timer_2_Overflow
```

plus the following `#define` directive:

```
#define INTERRUPT_Timer_2_Overflow 5
```

To understand where the '5' comes from, note that the interrupt numbers used in ISRs directly correspond to the enable bit index of the interrupt source in the 8051 IE SFR. That is, bit 0 of the IE register will be linked to a function using 'interrupt 0'. Table 7.1 shows the link between the interrupt sources and the required interrupt numbers for the original 8051/8052.

TABLE 7.1 8051 interrupt sources. Please note that many 8051s have further interrupt sources: refer to the manufacturer's documentation for details of the required interrupt numbers

Interrupt source	Address	IE Index
Power On Reset	0x00	–
External Interrupt 0	0x03	0
Timer 0 Overflow	0x0B	1
External Interrupt 1	0x13	2
Timer 1 Overflow	0x1B	3
UART Receive/Transmit	0x23	4
Timer 2 Overflow	0x2B	5

Overall, the use of interrupts linked to timer overflows is a safe and powerful technique.

b) Automatic timer reloads

In the hardware delay code we considered in Chapter 6, we used a code structure like this:

```
// Preload values for 50 ms delay
TH0 = 0x3C;        // Timer 0 initial value (High Byte)
TL0 = 0xB0;        // Timer 0 initial value (Low Byte)

TF0 = 0;           // Clear overflow flag
TR0 = 1;           // Start timer 0

while (TF0 == 0); // Loop until Timer 0 overflows (TF0 == 1)

TR0 = 0;           // Stop Timer 0
```

In this case, we load the counter registers with an appropriate initial value, run the timer and wait until it overflows: we then stop the timer. This is appropriate behaviour for a delay function.

For our operating system, we have slightly different requirements:

- We require a series of interrupts, generated for a long period, at a precisely-determined intervals.
- We would like to generate these interrupts without imposing a significant load on the CPU.

Timer 2 matches these requirements precisely.[24] When Timer 2 overflows, it is automatically reloaded, and immediately begins counting again. In this case, the timer is reloaded using the contents of the 'capture' registers (note that the names of these registers vary slightly between chip manufacturers):

```
RCAP2H = 0xFC;   // Load Timer 2 reload capt. reg. high byte
RCAP2L = 0x18;   // Load Timer 2 reload capt. reg. low byte
```

This automatic reload facility ensures that the timer keeps generating the required ticks, at precise 1 ms intervals, with very little software load, and without any intervention from the user's program.

24. As we discussed in Chapter 2, Timer 2 was a component added (by Intel) when the 8052 architecture was introduced shortly after the launch of the 8051. Most – but not all – current '8051s' include this component.

7.3 Introducing sEOS

The techniques used in Listing 7.3 can be adapted very easily to create the simple embedded operating system that we require. For ease of reference, we will refer to this operating system as 'sEOS' in this book. We examine the operation and use of sEOS here.

a) Complete code listing

To illustrate the use and operation of sEOS, we will re-implement the following example using this operating system:

```
void main(void)
   {
   Init_System();

   while(1) // 'for ever' (Super Loop)
      {
      X();            // Call the function (10 ms duration)
      Delay_50ms(); // Delay for 50 ms
      }
   }
```

In this case, the sEOS code required to provide the same behaviour is given (in part) in Listing 7.4 to Listing 7.6. (As in previous example, all of the files for this project are included on the CD: to avoid undue repetition, only the key files are presented here.)

Listing 7.4 Part of a demonstration of sEOS running a dummy task

```
/*------------------------------------------------------------------*-

   Main.c (v1.00)

  ------------------------------------------------------------------

   Demonstration of sEOS running a dummy task.

-*------------------------------------------------------------------*/

#include "Main.H"
```

```
#include "Port.H"
#include "Simple_EOS.H"

#include "X.H"

/* ------------------------------------------------------------------ */

void main(void)
   {
   // Prepare for dummy task
   X_Init();

   // Set up simple EOS (60 ms tick interval)
   sEOS_Init_Timer2(60);

   while(1) // Super Loop
      {
      // Enter idle mode to save power
      sEOS_Go_To_Sleep();
      }
   }

/*------------------------------------------------------------------*-
  ---- END OF FILE -------------------------------------------------
-*------------------------------------------------------------------*/
```

Listing 7.5 Part of a demonstration of sEOS running a dummy task

```
/*------------------------------------------------------------------*-

   Simple_EOS.C (v1.00)

  ------------------------------------------------------------------

   Main file for Simple Embedded Operating System (sEOS) for 8051.

   Demonstration version with dummy task X().

-*------------------------------------------------------------------*/

#include "Main.H"
#include "Simple_EOS.H"

// Header for dummy task
#include "X.H"
```

```
/*------------------------------------------------------------------*-

  sEOS_ISR()

  Invoked periodically by Timer 2 overflow:
  see sEOS_Init_Timer2() for timing details.

-*------------------------------------------------------------------*/
void sEOS_ISR() interrupt INTERRUPT_Timer_2_Overflow
   {
   // Must manually reset the T2 flag
   TF2 = 0;

   //===== USER CODE - Begin ==================================

   // Call dummy task here
   X();

   //===== USER CODE - End ====================================
   }

/*------------------------------------------------------------------*-

  sEOS_Init_Timer2()

  Sets up Timer 2 to drive the simple EOS.

  Parameter gives tick interval in MILLISECONDS.

  Max tick interval is ~60ms (12 MHz oscillator).

  Note: Precise tick intervals are only possible with certain
  oscillator / tick interval combinations.  If timing is
  important, you should check the timing calculations manually.

-*------------------------------------------------------------------*/
void sEOS_Init_Timer2(const tByte TICK_MS)
   {
   tLong Inc;
   tWord Reload_16;
   tByte Reload_08H, Reload_08L;

   // Timer 2 is configured as a 16-bit timer,
   // which is automatically reloaded when it overflows
   T2CON   = 0x04;   // Load Timer 2 control register
```

```
   // Number of timer increments required (max 65536)
   Inc = ((tLong)TICK_MS * (OSC_FREQ/1000)) / (tLong)OSC_PER_INST;

   // 16-bit reload value
   Reload_16 = (tWord) (65536UL - Inc);

   // 8-bit reload values (High & Low)
   Reload_08H = (tByte)(Reload_16 / 256);
   Reload_08L = (tByte)(Reload_16 % 256);

   // Used for manually checking timing (in simulator)
   //P2 = Reload_08H;
   //P3 = Reload_08L;

   TH2     = Reload_08H;  // Load T2 high byte
   RCAP2H  = Reload_08H;  // Load T2 reload capt. reg. high byte
   TL2     = Reload_08L;  // Load T2 low byte
   RCAP2L  = Reload_08L;  // Load T2 reload capt. reg. low byte

   // Timer 2 interrupt is enabled, and ISR will be called
   // whenever the timer overflows.
   ET2     = 1;

   // Start Timer 2 running
   TR2   = 1;

   EA = 1;            // Globally enable interrupts
   }

/*------------------------------------------------------------------*-

  sEOS_Go_To_Sleep()

  This operating system enters 'idle mode' between clock ticks
  to save power.  The next clock tick will return the
  processor to the normal operating state.

-*------------------------------------------------------------------*/
void sEOS_Go_To_Sleep(void)
   {
   PCON |= 0x01;    // Enter idle mode (generic 8051 version)
   }
```

```
/*------------------------------------------------------------------*-
  ---- END OF FILE -------------------------------------------------
-*------------------------------------------------------------------*/
```

Listing 7.6 Part of a demonstration of sEOS running a dummy task

```
/*------------------------------------------------------------------*-

   X.C (v1.00)

   -----------------------------------------------------------------

   Dummy task to introduce sEOS.

-*------------------------------------------------------------------*/

#include "X.H"

/*------------------------------------------------------------------*-

  X_Init()

  Dummy task init function.

-*------------------------------------------------------------------*/
void X_Init(void)
   {
   // Dummy task init...
   }

/*------------------------------------------------------------------*-

  X()

  Dummy task called from sEOS ISR.

-*------------------------------------------------------------------*/
void X(void)
   {
   // Dummy task...
   }

/*------------------------------------------------------------------*-
  ---- END OF FILE -------------------------------------------------
-*------------------------------------------------------------------*/
```

This program uses all of the features discussed in Section 7.2, but arranges the code in a slightly different way, in order to make it easy to adapt for use *in different projects*.

b) Tasks, functions and scheduling

Before we consider the implementation of this simple embedded operating system, we should first say something about the terminology used to describe such systems.

In discussions about embedded systems, you will frequently hear and read about 'task design', 'task execution times' and 'multi-tasking' systems. In this context, the term 'task' is usually used to refer to a **function that is executed on a periodic basis.** In the case of sEOS, we are able to control the execution times of a single task. This process is often referred to as 'scheduling the task'. The task will be implemented as (or called from) an interrupt service routine: this ISR will, in turn, be invoked by the overflow of a timer.

Note that the task will often call (other) functions in order to meet the needs of the application. For example, in the design of a controller for a domestic washing machine presented in Chapter 8, we will identify one task required by the system, and ten functions to be called from this task.

c) Setting the tick interval

Let us now consider the operation of sEOS in more detail. One of the key features of this OS is the way that the tick interval is set. In the function `main()`, we can see that the control of this interval has been largely automated:

```
// Set up simple EOS (60 ms tick interval)
sEOS_Init_Timer2(60);
```

In this example, a tick interval of 60 ms is used: this means that the ISR (the 'update' function) at the heart of sEOS will be invoked every 60 ms:

```
/*------------------------------------------------------------------*-

  sEOS_ISR()

  Invoked periodically by Timer 2 overflow:
  see sEOS_Init_Timer2() for timing details.

-*------------------------------------------------------------------*/
void sEOS_ISR() interrupt INTERRUPT_Timer_2_Overflow
   {
   ...
   }
```

The 'automatic' tick interval control is achieved using the C pre-processor, and the information included in the project header file (`Main.H`):

```
// Oscillator / resonator frequency (in Hz) e.g. (11059200UL)
#define OSC_FREQ (12000000UL)

// Number of oscillations per instruction (12, etc)
...
#define OSC_PER_INST (12)
```

This information is then used to calculate the required timer reload values in `Simple_EOS.C` as follows:

```
    // Number of timer increments required (max 65536)
    Inc = ((tLong)TICK_MS * (OSC_FREQ/1000)) / (tLong)OSC_PER_INST;

    // 16-bit reload value
    Reload_16 = (tWord) (65536UL - Inc);

    // 8-bit reload values (High & Low)
    Reload_08H = (tByte)(Reload_16 / 256);
    Reload_08L = (tByte)(Reload_16 % 256);
. . .
    TH2     = Reload_08H;   // Load T2 high byte
    RCAP2H  = Reload_08H;   // Load T2 reload capt. reg. high byte
    TL2     = Reload_08L;   // Load T2 low byte
    RCAP2L  = Reload_08L;   // Load T2 reload capt. reg. low byte
```

It is very important to understand that, if using a 12 MHz oscillator, then accurate timing can usually be obtained over a range of tick intervals from 1 ms to 60 ms (approximately). However, if using other clock frequencies (such as the popular 11.0592 MHz),[25] precise timing can only be obtained at a much more limited range of tick intervals. If you are developing an application where precise timing is required, you must check the timing calculations by hand. This code in `Simple_EOS.C` – used in the simulator – can help you check the timing:

```
// Used for manually checking timing (in simulator)
P2 = Reload_08H;
P3 = Reload_08L;
```

25. In applications involving the serial interface, 11.0592 MHz is widely used, as we will see in Chapter 8. This 'odd' frequency is used because it gives rise to acurate baud rate values (e.g. 9600 baud). If you require both accurate baud rates and asscurate EOS timing, use an 11.0592 MHz crystal and a tick rate of 5, 10, 15, ... 60 or 65 ms. Such 'divide by 5' tick rates are precise with an 11.0592 MHz crystal. (As an exercise, you might like to confirm this for yourself.)

d) Saving power

One of the problems noted with many 'Super Loop' applications is that that the processor wasted a large number of CPU cycles in a delay loop:

```
void main(void)
   {
   Init_System();

   while(1) // 'for ever' (Super Loop)
      {
      X();              // Perform the task (10 ms duration)
      Delay_50ms();     // Delay for 50 ms
      }
   }
```

We noted in Chapter 2 that 8051 devices have an 'idle' mode where power consumption may be reduced by a factor of 10 (approximately). Using sEOS, we can reduce the power consumption of the application by having the processor enter idle mode when it finishes executing the ISR (Figure 7.4).

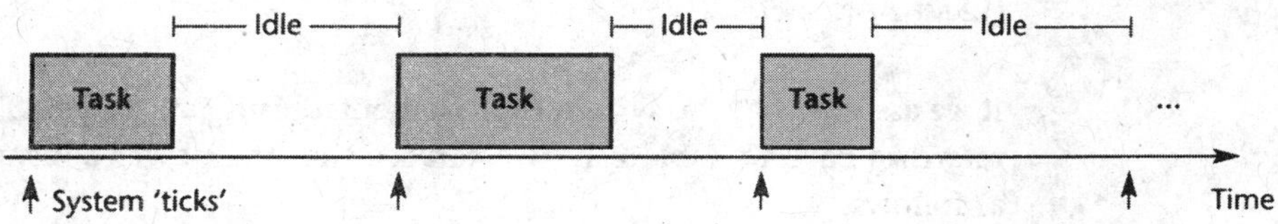

FIGURE 7.4 Saving power with sEOS. See text for details

This is achieved through the function sEOS_Go_To_Sleep():

```
/*------------------------------------------------------------------*-

  sEOS_Go_To_Sleep()

  This operating system enters 'idle mode' between clock ticks
  to save power. The next clock tick will return the processor
  to the normal operating state.

-*------------------------------------------------------------------*/
void sEOS_Go_To_Sleep(void)
   {
   PCON |= 0x01;    // Enter idle mode (generic 8051 version)
   }
```

Note that the processor will automatically return to 'Normal' mode when the timer next overflows (generating an interrupt).

Overall, this application is 'asleep' for 99.9% of the time, meaning that the total load imposed by this operating system is around 0.1% of the available CPU capacity (Figure 7.5).

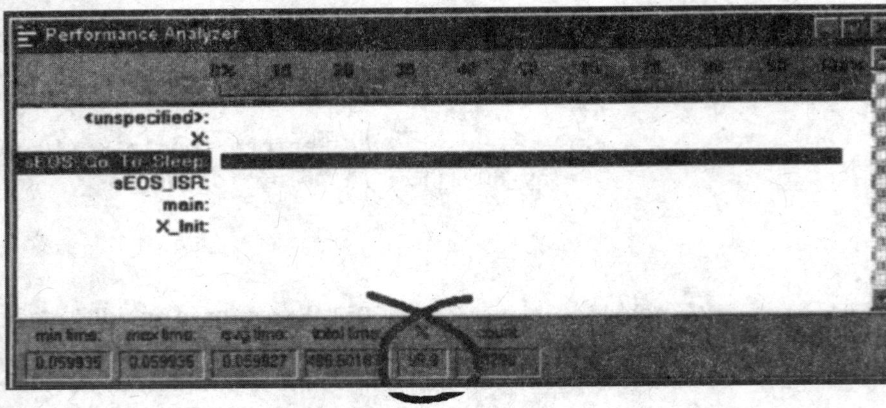

FIGURE 7.5 The sEOS example is in idle mode for 99.9% of the time, meaning that the total load imposed by this operating system is around 0.1% of the available CPU capacity [12 MHz / 12 osc]

If we assume that the system is implemented using an Atmel AT89S53 chip, then – referring back to Table 2.1 – we can see that the power consumption figures are as follows:

Device	Normal	Idle	Power Down
Atmel 89S53	11 mA	2 mA	60 uA

In this case, we would expect the average current consumption to be given by:

$$\text{Average current consumption} = \frac{2 \times 99.9 + 11 \times 0.1}{100} = 2.009 \text{ mA}$$

If the system runs at 5V, the average power consumption will then be: 10.045 mW.

Note that this is the power consumption of the processor itself: if you add LEDs or other devices to the system, then the power consumption will inevitably increase. In these circumstances, theoretical calculations will only be a guide, and will you need to take some measurements from a prototype system to determine the true figure.

e) Using sEOS in your own projects

When using sEOS in your own applications, you will need to include a copy of the files `Simple_EOS.C` and `Simple_EOS.H` in your project: the .C file will then need to be edited – in the area indicated below – in order to match your requirements:

```
void sEOS_ISR() interrupt INTERRUPT_Timer_2_Overflow
   {
   // Must manually reset the T2 flag
   TF2 = 0;

   //===== USER CODE - Begin ==================================

   // ADD YOUR FUNCTION CALLS HERE...

   //===== USER CODE - End ====================================
   }
```

7.4 Using Timer 0 or Timer 1

The example code above used Timer 2 as the source of ticks for the operating system. In most cases, this is good choice: however, if Timer 2 is not available on your 8051 device, or is in use for some other purpose, Timer 0 or Timer 1 can be used in its place.

Like Timer 2, Timer 0 and Timer 1 also have an auto-reload capability. However, Timer 2 has this facility when used in 16-bit mode whereas Timer 0 and Timer 1 can only be reloaded automatically when operating in 8-bit mode. In typical 8051 applications, an 8-bit timer can only be used to generate interrupts at intervals of around 0.25 ms (or less). This can be useful for some applications where very rapid processing is required. However, in most cases, this short tick interval will simply increase the processor load imposed by the operating system.

To illustrate the increased load imposed by short tick intervals, Figure 7.6 repeats the example shown in Figure 7.5, this time using a 0.25 ms tick interval. Note that by using the shorter tick interval, the percentage of 'sleep' time has fallen from 99.9% to 74.5%: this reflects the fact that the scheduler ISR is called more frequently.

Although the auto-reload modes of Timer 0 and Timer 1 are less useful than the equivalent mode in Timer 2, Timer 0 and Timer 1 can also be used in 'manual reload' mode. Manual-reload mode means that – when it overflows – the timer must be stopped, loaded with the required count value and then restarted. With this approach it is almost impossible to guarantee precise tick intervals. However, the level of timing accuracy obtained is adequate for many applications.

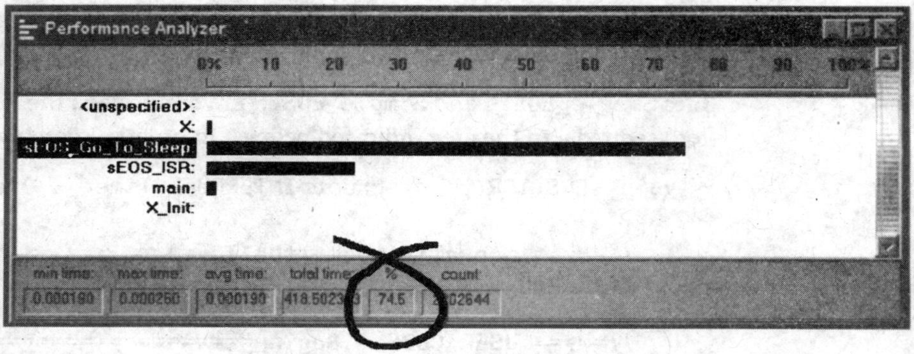

FIGURE 7.6 The impact of a 0.25ms tick interval [12 Mhz / 12 osc 8051]. See text for details

Listing 7.7 shows the key source code from an operating system based on Timer 0, with manual reloads. The code may be easily adapted to work with Timer 1 if required.

Listing 7.7 Driving sEOS using Timer 0. See text for details.

```
/*------------------------------------------------------------------*-

   Simple_EOS.C (v1.00)

  ------------------------------------------------------------------

   Main file for Simple Embedded Operating System (sEOS) for 8051.

   *** This version uses T0 (easily adapted for T1) ***

   Demonstration version with dummy task X().

-*------------------------------------------------------------------*/

#include "Main.H"
#include "Simple_EOS.H"

// Header for dummy task
#include "X.H"

// ------ Private variable definitions -----------------------
static tByte Reload_08H;
static tByte Reload_08L;

// ------ Private function prototypes ------------------------
static void sEOS_Manual_Timer0_Reload(void);
```

```
/*------------------------------------------------------------------*-

  sEOS_ISR()

  Invoked periodically by Timer 0 overflow:
  see sEOS_Init_Timer0() for timing details.

-*------------------------------------------------------------------*/
void sEOS_ISR() interrupt INTERRUPT_Timer_0_Overflow
   {
   // Flag cleared automatically but must reload the timer
   sEOS_Manual_Timer0_Reload();
   //===== USER CODE - Begin ===================================

   // Call dummy task here
   X();

   //===== USER CODE - End =====================================
   }

/*------------------------------------------------------------------*-

  sEOS_Init_Timer0()

  Sets up Timer 0 to drive the simple EOS.

  Parameter gives tick interval in MILLISECONDS.

  Max tick interval is ~60ms (12 MHz oscillator).

  Note: Precise tick intervals are only possible with certain
  oscillator / tick interval combinations. If timing is important,
  you should check the timing calculations manually.

-*------------------------------------------------------------------*/
void sEOS_Init_Timer0(const tByte TICK_MS)
   {
   tLong Inc;
   tWord Reload_16;

   // Using Timer 0, 16-bit *** manual reload ***
   TMOD &= 0xF0; // Clear all T0 bits (T1 left unchanged)
   TMOD |= 0x01; // Set required T0 bits (T1 left unchanged)

   // Number of timer increments required (max 65536)
   Inc = ((tLong)TICK_MS * (OSC_FREQ/1000)) / (tLong)OSC_PER_INST;
```

```
   // 16-bit reload value
   Reload_16 = (tWord) (65536UL - Inc);

   // 8-bit reload values (High & Low)
   Reload_08H = (tByte)(Reload_16 / 256);
   Reload_08L = (tByte)(Reload_16 % 256);

   // Used for manually checking timing (in simulator)
   //P2 = Reload_08H;
   //P3 = Reload_08L;

   TL0  = Reload_08L;
   TH0  = Reload_08H;

   // Timer 0 interrupt is enabled, and ISR will be called
   // whenever the timer overflows.
   ET0 = 1;

   // Start Timer 0 running
   TR0 = 1;

   EA = 1;              // Globally enable interrupts
   }

/*------------------------------------------------------------------*-

  sEOS_Manual_Timer0_Reload()

  This OS uses a (manually reloaded) 16-bit timer.
  The manual reload means that all timings are approximate.

  THIS OS IS NOT SUITABLE FOR APPLICATIONS WHERE
  ACCURATE TIMING IS REQUIRED!!!

  Timer reload is carried out in this function.

-*------------------------------------------------------------------*/
void sEOS_Manual_Timer0_Reload()
   {
   // Stop Timer 0
   TR0 = 0;

   // See 'init' function for calculations
   TL0  = Reload_08L;
   TH0  = Reload_08H;
```

```
    //  Start Timer 0
    TR0   = 1;
    }

/*------------------------------------------------------------------*-

  sEOS_Go_To_Sleep()

  This operating system enters 'idle mode' between clock ticks
  to save power. The next clock tick will return the processor
  to the normal operating state.

-*------------------------------------------------------------------*/
void sEOS_Go_To_Sleep(void)
    {
    PCON |= 0x01;     // Enter idle mode (generic 8051 version)
    }

/*------------------------------------------------------------------*-
  ---- END OF FILE --------------------------------------------------
-*------------------------------------------------------------------*/
```

Figure 7.7 shows this example running in the simulator.

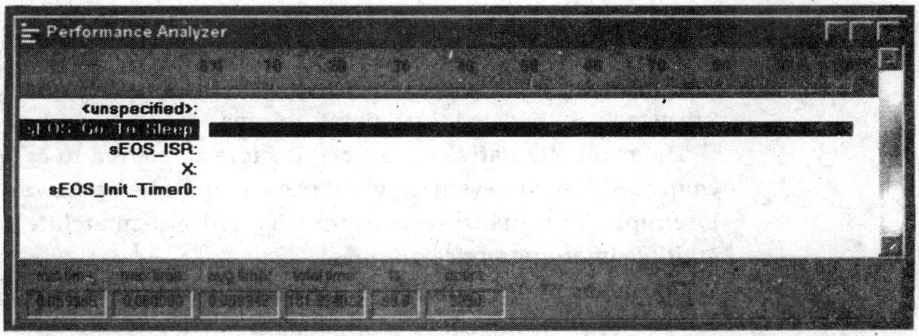

FIGURE 7.7 Driving sEOS using Timer 0

A complete set of files for this project will be found on the CD.

7.5 Is this approach portable?

The presence of an on-chip timer which can be used to generate interrupts in this way is by no means restricted to the 8051 family: almost all processors intended for use in embedded applications have timers which can be used in a manner very similar to that described in this chapter.

For example, similar timers are included on other 8-bit microcontrollers (e.g. Microchip PIC family, the Motorola HC08 family), and also on 16-bit devices (e.g. the Infineon C167 family) as well as on 32-bit processors (e.g. the ARM family, the Motorola MPC500 family).[26]

7.6 Alternative system architectures

The very simple operating system discussed in this chapter has two key features:

- A time-triggered architecture.
- A co-operative scheduling algorithm.

To explain what these phrases mean, and consider some alternative approaches, we will examine how tasks in this system are started, and how they come to an end.

a) Starting tasks

The 'time-triggered' nature of this system means that functions are started (or 'triggered') at pre-determined points in time.

The main alternative to this architecture is referred to as 'event-triggered'. In embedded systems, event-triggered behaviour is often achieved through the use of interrupts. To support these, event-triggered system architectures often provide multiple interrupt service routines.

To understand the difference between event- and time-triggered architectures, we will first consider an analogy. Suppose that a hospital doctor must look after the needs of ten seriously-ill patients overnight, with the support of some nursing staff. The doctor might consider two ways of performing this task:

- The doctor might arrange for one of the nursing staff to waken her if there is a significant problem with one of the patients. This is the 'event triggered' solution.
- The doctor might set her alarm clock to ring every hour. When the alarm goes off, she will get up and visit each of the patients, in turn, to check that they are well and, if necessary, prescribe treatment. This is the 'time triggered' solution.

26. For sources of further information about the use of the embedded operating system described here on other processors, please refer to Chapter 11.

For most doctors, the event-triggered approach will seem the most attractive, because they are likely to get a few hours of sleep during the course of the night. By contrast, with the time-triggered approach, the doctor will inevitably suffer sleep deprivation.

However, in the case of many embedded systems – which do not need sleep – the time-triggered approach has many advantages. Indeed, within industrial sectors where safety is an obvious concern, such as the aerospace industry and the automotive industry, time-triggered techniques are widely used because it is accepted, both by the system developers (and certification authorities), that they help improve reliability and safety.

The main reason that time-triggered approaches are preferred in safety-related applications is that they result in systems which have very *predictable* behaviour. If we revisit the hospital analogy, we can begin to see why this is so.

Suppose that our 'event triggered' doctor is sleeping peacefully. An apparently minor problem develops with one of the patients, and the nursing staff decide not to awaken the doctor but to deal with the problem themselves. After another two hours, when four patients have 'minor' problems, the nurses decide that they will have to wake the doctor after all. As soon as the doctor sees the patients, she recognizes that two of them have a severe complications, and she has to begin surgery. Before she can complete the surgery on the first patient, the second patient is very close to death.

Consider the same example with the 'time triggered' doctor. In this case, because the patient visits take place at hourly intervals, the doctor sees each patient before serious complications arise, and arranges appropriate treatment. **Another way of viewing this is that the workload is spread out evenly throughout the night.** As a result, all of the patients survive the night without difficulty.

In embedded applications, the (rather macabre) hospital situation is mirrored in the event-driven application by the occurrence of several events (that is, several interrupts) at the same time. This might indicate, for example, that two different faults had been detected simultaneously in an aircraft, or simply that two switches had been pressed at the same time on a keypad.

To see why the simultaneous occurrence of two interrupts causes a problem, consider what happens in the 8051 architecture in these circumstances. Like many microcontrollers, the original 8051 architecture supports two different interrupt priority levels: Low and High. If two interrupts (we will call them Interrupt 1 and Interrupt 2) occur in rapid succession, the system will behave as follows:

- **If Interrupt 1 is a low-priority interrupt and Interrupt 2 is a high-priority interrupt.**

The interrupt service routine (ISR) invoked by a low-priority interrupt can be interrupted by a high-priority interrupt. In this case, the low-priority ISR will be paused, to allow the high-priority ISR to be executed, after which the operation of the low-priority ISR will be completed. In most cases, the system will operate correctly (**provided that the two ISRs do not interfere with one another**).

- **If Interrupt 1 is a low-priority interrupt and Interrupt 2 is also a low-priority interrupt.**

The ISR invoked by a low-priority interrupt cannot be interrupted by another low-priority interrupt. **As a result the response to the second interrupt will be at the very least delayed; under some circumstances it will be ignored altogether.**

- **If Interrupt 1 is a high-priority interrupt and Interrupt 2 is a low-priority interrupt.**

The interrupt service routine (ISR) invoked by a high-priority interrupt cannot be interrupted by a low-priority interrupt. **As a result the response to the second interrupt will be at the very least delayed; under some circumstances it will be ignored altogether.**

- **If Interrupt 1 is a high-priority interrupt and Interrupt 2 is also a high-priority interrupt.**

The interrupt service routine (ISR) invoked by a high-priority interrupt cannot be interrupted by another high-priority interrupt. **As a result the response to the second interrupt will be at the very least delayed; under some circumstances it will be ignored altogether.**

Note carefully what this means! There is a common misconception among the developers of embedded applications that interrupt events will never be lost. This simply is not true. If you have multiple sources of interrupts that may appear at 'random' time intervals, interrupt responses can be missed: indeed, where there are several active interrupt sources, it is practically impossible to create code that will deal correctly with all possible combinations of interrupts.

It is the need to deal with the simultaneous occurrence of more than one event that both adds to the system complexity and reduces the ability to predict the behaviour of an event-triggered system under all circumstances. By contrast, in a time-triggered embedded application, the designer is able to ensure that only single events must be handled at a time, in a carefully controlled sequence.

b) Stopping tasks

As we noted at the start of this section, sEOS has a time-triggered, co-operatively scheduled, architecture. We have discussed the meaning of 'time triggered'. Now we turn our attention to the co-operative nature of this system.

When we say that an operating system is co-operative, we mean that a task, once started, will run until it is complete: that is, the OS will never interrupt an active task. This is a 'single task' approach to operating system design. The alternative is a 'pre-emptive' or 'time sliced' approach. In a pre-emptive system, tasks will typically run for – say – a millisecond. The OS will then pause this task, and run another task for a millisecond, and so on. From the perspective of the user, the pre-emptive OS appears to be running multiple tasks at the same time.

Co-operative scheduling is simpler and is generally considered to be more predictable than pre-emptive scheduling. To understand why this is, consider that we wish to run two tasks on a pre-emptive system, and that both tasks require access to the same port. Suppose that one task is reading from this port, and that the scheduler performs a 'context switch', causing the second task to access the same port: under these circumstances, unless we take action to prevent it, data may be lost or corrupted.

This problem arises frequently in multi-tasking environments where we have what are known as 'critical sections' of code. Such critical sections are code segments that – once started – must run to completion, without interruption. Examples of critical sections include:

- Code which modifies or reads variables, particularly global variables used for inter-task communication. In general, this is the most common form of critical section, since inter-task communication is often a key requirement.
- Code which interfaces to hardware, such as ports, analog-to-digital converters (ADCs), and so on. What happens, for example, if the same ADC is used simultaneously by more than one task?
- Code which calls common functions. What happens, for example, if the same function is called simultaneously by more than one task?

In a co-operative system, these problems do not arise, since only one task is ever active at a time.

To deal with critical sections of code in a pre-emptive system, we have two main possibilities:

- 'Pause' the scheduling by disabling the scheduler interrupt before beginning the critical section; re-enable the scheduler interrupt when we leave the critical section, or;
- Use a 'lock' (or some other form of 'semaphore mechanism') to achieve a similar result.

The first solution means that, when we start accessing the shared resource (say Port X), we disable the scheduler. This solves the immediate problem since (say) Task A will be allowed to run without interruption until it has finished with Port X. However, this 'solution' is less than perfect. For one thing, by disabling the scheduler, we will no longer be keeping track of the elapsed time and all timing functions will begin to drift – in this case by a period up to the duration of Task A every time we access Port X. This simply is not acceptable.

The use of locks is a better solution and appears, at first inspection, easy to implement. Before entering the critical section of code, we 'lock' the associated resource; when we have finished with the resource we 'unlock' it. While locked, no other process may enter the critical section.[27]

This is one way we might try to achieve this:

1. Task A checks the 'lock' for Port X it wishes to access.
2. If the section is locked, Task A waits.
3. When the port is unlocked, Task A sets the lock and then uses the port.
4. When Task A has finished with the port, it leaves the critical section and unlocks the port.

Implementing this algorithm in code also seems straightforward, as illustrated in Listing 7.8.

27. Of course, this is only a partial solution to the problem caused by multi-tasking. If the purpose of Task A is to read from an ADC, and Task B has locked the ADC when the Task A is invoked, then Task A cannot carry out its required activity. Use of locks, or any other mechanism, will not solve this problem; however, they may prevent the system from crashing.

Listing 7.8 Attempting to implement a simple locking mechanism in a pre-emptive scheduler. See text for details

```
#define UNLOCKED    0
#define LOCKED      1

bit Lock;   // Global lock flag

// . . .

// Ready to enter critical section
// - wait for lock to become clear
// (FOR SIMPLICITY, NO TIMEOUT CAPABILITY IS SHOWN)
while(Lock == LOCKED);

// Lock is clear
// Enter critical section
```

```
// Set the lock
Lock = LOCKED;

// CRITICAL CODE HERE //

// Ready to leave critical section
// Release the lock
Lock = UNLOCKED;

// . . .
```

However, the above code cannot be guaranteed to work correctly under all circumstances.

Consider the part of the code labelled 'A' in Listing 7.8. If our system is fully pre-emptive, then Task A may be at this point when the scheduler performs a context switch and allows (say) Task B access to the CPU. If Task B also requires access the Port X, we can then have a situation as follows:

- Task A has checked the lock for Port X and found that the port is not locked; Task A has, however, not yet changed the lock flag.
- Task B is then 'switched in'. Task B checks the lock flag and it is still clear. Task B sets the lock flag and begins to use Port X.
- Task A is 'switched in' again. As far as Task A is concerned, the port is not locked; this task therefore sets the flag, and starts to use the port, unaware that Task B is already doing so.

As we can see, this simple lock code violates the principal of *mutual exclusion*: that is, it allows more than one task to access a critical code section. The problem arises because it is possible for the context switch to occur after a task has checked the lock flag but before the task changes the lock flag. **In other words, the lock 'check and set code' (designed to control access to a critical section of code), is itself a critical section.**

This problem can be solved. For example, because it takes little time to 'check and set' the lock code, we can disable interrupts for this period. However, this is not in itself a complete solution: because there is a chance that an interrupt may have occurred even in the short period of 'check and set', we then need to check the relevant interrupt flag(s) and – if necessary – call the relevant ISR(s). This can be done, but it adds substantially to the complexity of the operating environment.

c) Reliability matters

As we have discussed, the simple, predictable, nature of time-triggered, co-operatively scheduled, applications makes this approach the usual choice in safety-related applications, where reliability is a crucial design requirement. However, the need for reliability is not restricted to systems such as fly-by-wire aircraft and drive-by-wire passenger cars: even at the lowest level, an alarm clock that fails to sound on time, or a video recorder that operates intermittently may not have safety implications but, equally, will not have high sales figures.

In addition to increasing reliability, the use of time-triggered techniques can help to reduce both CPU loads and memory usage: as a result, even the smallest of embedded applications can benefit from the use of this form of system architecture.

7.7 Important design considerations when using sEOS

Following on from the discussions in Section 7.6, we consider here two important factors which must be taken into account when using sEOS in your own projects.

a) Worst-case task execution time

We noted in Section 7.6 that sEOS has a time-triggered architecture. This has important implications for the designer of the system. In particular, the designer must ensure that the execution time for a task can never exceed the tick interval (Figure 7.8).

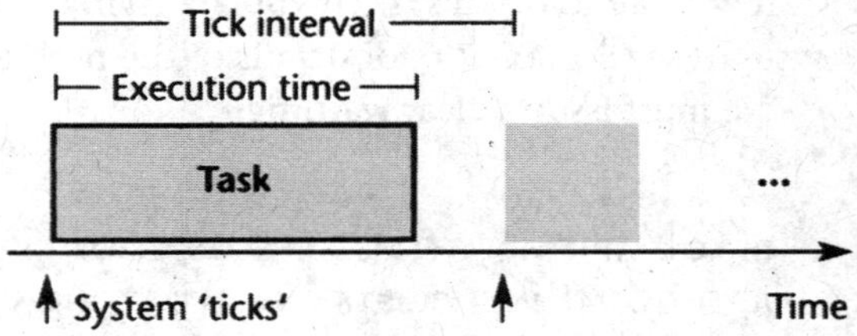

FIGURE 7.8 The operating system described in the chapter will only be reliable if the execution time of the task (run from the ISR) never exceeds the system tick interval

For example, suppose the following situation applies:

- The operating system has a 10 ms tick interval.
- A task runs for 22 milliseconds.

In these circumstances, at least one 'tick' will be lost and the system may fail to operate as required (see Figure 7.9).

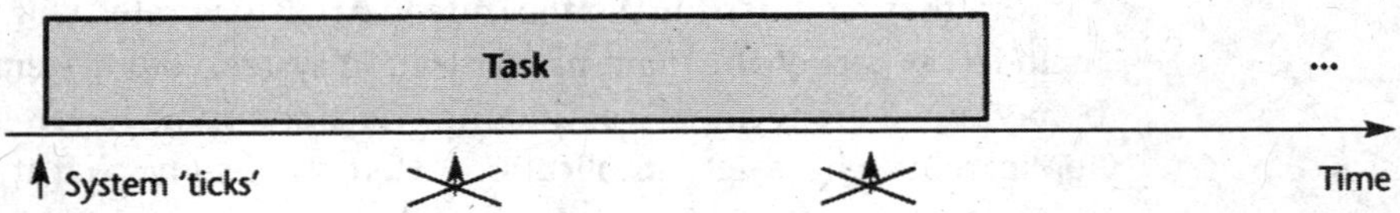

FIGURE 7.9 Executing a 22 ms task using an OS with a 10 ms tick interval. See text for details

These problems can be solved with due care at the design stage. For example, we have shown (first in Chapter 3) how simulations can be used to determine task durations. We have also considered (in Chapter 6) several different timeout mechanisms that can help us to meet 'worst-case execution time' conditions.

We make some suggestions for further improvements to this operating system in Chapter 11: these can help to greatly improve the performance of this system in the presence of 'long tasks'.

b) The 'One Interrupt per Microcontroller' rule

As we discussed in Section 7.6a, sEOS has a time-triggered architecture. The sEOS initialization function enables the generation of interrupts associated with the overflow of one of the microcontroller timers. To ensure correct operation of the system, it is essential that – with the exception of the single timer interrupt driving the OS – all interrupts are disabled.

If you fail to do this, then you are trying to operate sEOS as an 'event-triggered' system (see Section 7.6 for details of the problems this can cause).

We must issue a clear warning:

> IF YOU ATTEMPT TO USE THE OS CODE PRESENTED IN THIS CHAPTER WITH ADDITIONAL INTERRUPTS ENABLED, YOUR SYSTEM CANNOT BE GUARANTEED TO OPERATE AT ALL: AT BEST, YOU ARE LIKELY TO OBTAIN VERY UNPREDICTABLE – AND UNRELIABLE – SYSTEM BEHAVIOUR.

7.8 Example: Milk pasteurization

We will now consider the use of sEOS in a practical embedded application.

The system discussed in this example is intended to monitor the rate of liquid (milk) flow through a pasteurization[28] system. The monitoring is required primarily because too high a flow rate can result in incomplete sterilization of the product, and a consequent reduction in shelf life.

Note that facilities for the measurement of flow rates will probably already be included as part of the main pasteurization system: our system will reproduce this behaviour. This form of 'redundancy' is a common requirement in embedded applications with safety implications. Here we assume that it is unlikely that one device for measuring flow rates may fail, and very unlikely that both will fail simultaneously. As a consequence, adding the redundant sensor from this study will be likely to improve the overall reliability of the system.

a) Measuring the flow rates

To measure the rate of flow, we will be measuring the frequency of a stream of pulses. This is a common requirement: for example, many industrial systems require measurement of rotational speed. This is often carried out using a sensor of the type illustrated in Figure 7.10.

As the figure illustrates, the rotating shaft gives rise to a pulse train.

In the case of the milk production system, we assume that a similar sensor is used (Figure 7.11). This (optical) sensor will not exhibit 'switch bounce' (see Chapter 4). However, some older pasteurization systems still employ mechanical

28. The French chemist Louis Pasteur demonstrated that the spoilage of perishable products could be prevented by destroying the microbes through a heat treatment and then protecting the (sterilized) material from subsequent contamination. Pasteur applied this theory to the preservation of beverages and foodstuffs. His process is now most widely associated with milk production.

switches: these pulse streams will exhibit switch bounce. To make this system as flexible as possible, we will incorporate debounce behaviour (in software) in our system. This will have no impact on the measurement of pulses from the optical sensor, but will allow our system to be applied more widely.

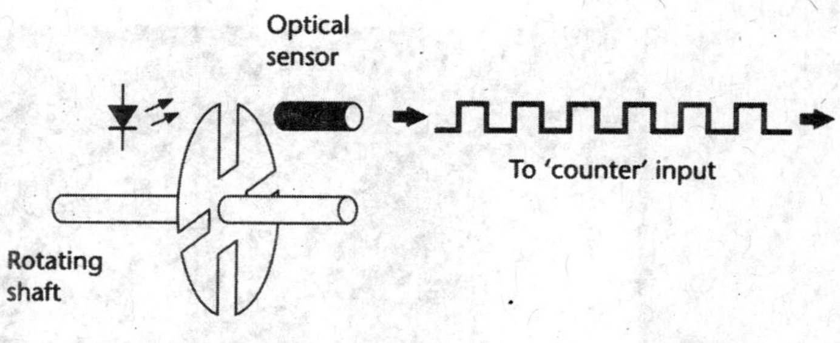

FIGURE 7.10 Counting pulses from an optical encoder in order to measure the speed of rotation of a shaft

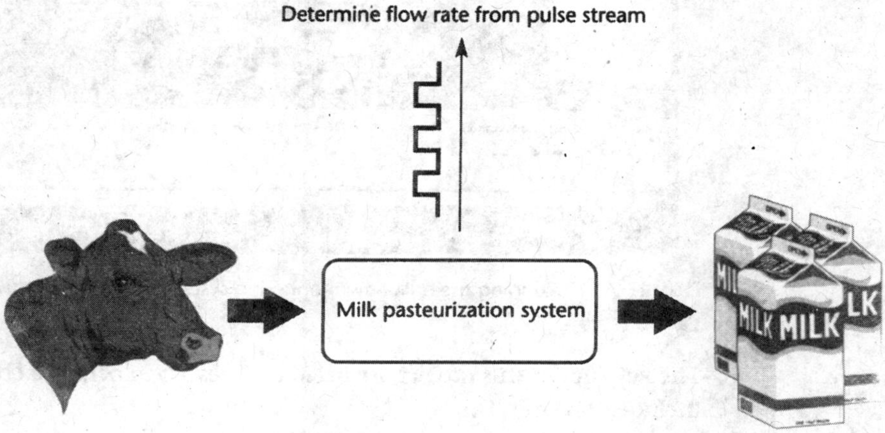

FIGURE 7.11 A schematic representation of the milk pasteurization system considered in the present example

b) Output from the program

The output from this program will take two forms:

- A bargraph display, giving the operator an instant visual representation of the flow rate.
- An audible alarm, which will sound when the flow rate falls below an acceptable level.

Please see Section 7.8d for relevant code listings.

c) Running the program

The code for the project is on the CD, in the directory '/Pont/Ch07_05 – Milk' (please refer to Chapter 3 for further information about the CD).

Figure 7.12 shows the project running in the Keil hardware simulator.

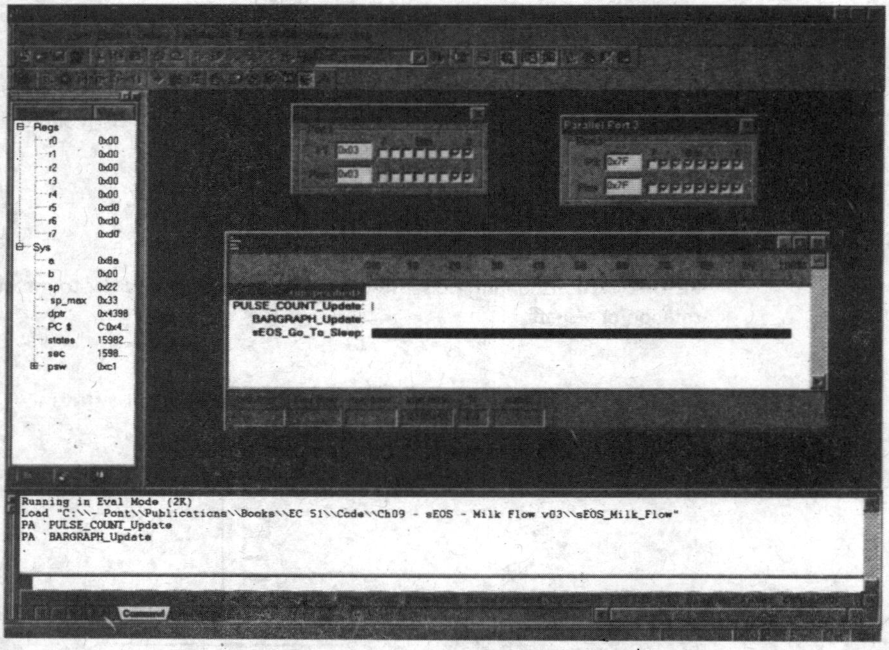

FIGURE 7.12 Running the milk-flow monitoring system in the Keil hardware simulator

The key files in this project are listed and described below: a complete set of files is included on the CD.

d) Software

The key files associated with this project are listed here.

When examining this code, please note in particular:

- The efficient code for counting the pulses: no delay code is required.
- The techniques used to generate the bargraph display.

Listing 7.9 Part of the software for the milk pasteurization system

```
/*------------------------------------------------------------------*-

  Port.H (v1.00)

  ------------------------------------------------------------------

  Port Header file for the milk pasteurization example (Chapter 7)

-*------------------------------------------------------------------*/

// ------ Pulse_Count.C -----------------------------------------------

// Connect pulse input to this pin - debounced in software
sbit  Sw_pin = P3^0;

// Connect alarm to this pin (set if pulse is below threshold)
sbit Alarm_pin = P3^7;

// ------ Bargraph.C --------------------------------------------------

// Bargraph display on these pins
// The 8 port pins may be distributed over several ports if
required
sbit Pin0 = P1^0;
sbit Pin1 = P1^1;
sbit Pin2 = P1^2;
sbit Pin3 = P1^3;
sbit Pin4 = P1^4;
sbit Pin5 = P1^5;
sbit Pin6 = P1^6;
sbit Pin7 = P1^7;

/*------------------------------------------------------------------*-
  ---- END OF FILE -------------------------------------------------
-*------------------------------------------------------------------*/
```

Listing 7.10 Part of the software for the milk pasteurization system

```
/*------------------------------------------------------------------*-

  Main.c (v1.00)

  ------------------------------------------------------------------
```

```
    Milk pasteurization example.

-*------------------------------------------------------------------*/

#include "Main.H"
#include "Port.H"
#include "Simple_EOS.H"
#include "Bargraph.H"

#include "Pulse_Count.H"

/* ---------------------------------------------------------------- */

void main(void)
   {
   PULSE_COUNT_Init();
   BARGRAPH_Init();

   // Set up simple EOS (30ms tick interval)
   sEOS_Init_Timer2(30);

   while(1) // Super Loop
     {
     // Enter idle mode to save power
     sEOS_Go_To_Sleep();
     }
   }

/*------------------------------------------------------------------*-
  ---- END OF FILE -------------------------------------------------
-*------------------------------------------------------------------*/
```

Listing 7.11 Part of the software for the milk pasteurization system

```
/*------------------------------------------------------------------*-

   Simple_EOS.C (v1.00)

  ------------------------------------------------------------------

   Main file for Simple Embedded Operating System (sEOS) for 8051.

   -- This version for milk-flow-rate monitoring.

-*------------------------------------------------------------------*/
```

```
#include "Main.H"
#include "Simple_EOS.H"

#include "Pulse_count.H"

/*------------------------------------------------------------------*-

  sEOS_ISR()

  Invoked periodically by Timer 2 overflow:
  see sEOS_Init_Timer2() for timing details.

-*------------------------------------------------------------------*/
void sEOS_ISR() interrupt INTERRUPT_Timer_2_Overflow
   {
   // Must manually reset the T2 flag
   TF2 = 0;

   //===== USER CODE - Begin ==================================

   // Call 'Update' function here
   PULSE_COUNT_Update();

   //===== USER CODE - End ====================================
   }

/*------------------------------------------------------------------*-

  sEOS_Init_Timer2()

  Sets up Timer 2 to drive the simple EOS.

  Parameter gives tick interval in MILLISECONDS.

  Max tick interval is ~60ms (12 MHz oscillator).

  Note: Precise tick intervals are only possible with certain
  oscillator / tick interval combinations. If timing is important,
  you should check the timing calculations manually.

-*------------------------------------------------------------------*/
void sEOS_Init_Timer2(const tByte TICK_MS)
   {
   tLong Inc;
   tWord Reload_16;
```

```
   tByte Reload_08H, Reload_08L;

   // Timer 2 is configured as a 16-bit timer,
   // which is automatically reloaded when it overflows
   T2CON   = 0x04;   // Load Timer 2 control register

   // Number of timer increments required (max 65536)
   Inc = ((tLong)TICK_MS * (OSC_FREQ/1000)) / (tLong)OSC_PER_INST;

   // 16-bit reload value
   Reload_16 = (tWord) (65536UL - Inc);

   // 8-bit reload values (High & Low)
   Reload_08H = (tByte)(Reload_16 / 256);
   Reload_08L = (tByte)(Reload_16 % 256);

   // Used for manually checking timing (in simulator)
   //P2 = Reload_08H;
   //P3 = Reload_08L;

   TH2    = Reload_08H; // Load T2 high byte
   RCAP2H = Reload_08H; // Load T2 reload capt. reg. high byte
   TL2    = Reload_08L; // Load T2 low byte
   RCAP2L = Reload_08L; // Load T2 reload capt. reg. low byte

   // Timer 2 interrupt is enabled, and ISR will be called
   // whenever the timer overflows.
   ET2     = 1;

   // Start Timer 2 running
   TR2   = 1;

   EA = 1;              // Globally enable interrupts
   }

/*------------------------------------------------------------------*-

  sEOS_Go_To_Sleep()

  This operating system enters 'idle mode' between clock ticks
  to save power. The next clock tick will return the processor
  to the normal operating state.

-*------------------------------------------------------------------*/
```

```
void sEOS_Go_To_Sleep(void)
   {
   PCON |= 0x01;    // Enter idle mode (generic 8051 version)
   }

/*------------------------------------------------------------------*-
  ---- END OF FILE -------------------------------------------------
-*------------------------------------------------------------------*/
```

Listing 7.12 Part of the software for the milk pasteurization system

```
/*------------------------------------------------------------------*-

   Pulse_Count.C (v1.00)

  ------------------------------------------------------------------

   Count pulses from a mechanical switch or similar device.
                                           ___
   Responds to falling edge of pulse:        |___

-*------------------------------------------------------------------*/

#include "Main.H"
#include "Port.H"

#include "Bargraph.H"
#include "Pulse_Count.H"

// ------ Private function prototypes ------------------------------
void PULSE_COUNT_Check_Below_Threshold(const tByte);

// ------ Public variable declarations -----------------------------
// The data to be displayed
extern tBargraph Data_G;

// ------ Public variable definitions ------------------------------
// Set only after falling edge is detected
bit Falling_edge_G;

// ------ Private variable definitions -----------------------------
// The results of successive tests of the pulse signal
// (NOTE: Can't have arrays of bits...)
static bit Test4, Test3, Test2, Test1, Test0;
```

```
static tByte Total_G = 0;
static tWord Calls_G = 0;

// ------ Private constants ----------------------------------

// Allows changed of logic without hardware changes
#define HI_LEVEL (0)
#define LO_LEVEL (1)

/*------------------------------------------------------------------*-

  PULSE_COUNT_Init()

  Initialisation function for the switch library.

-*------------------------------------------------------------------*/
void PULSE_COUNT_Init(void)
   {
   Sw_pin = 1; // Use this pin for input

   // The tests (see text)
   Test4 = LO_LEVEL;
   Test3 = LO_LEVEL;
   Test2 = LO_LEVEL;
   Test1 = LO_LEVEL;
   Test0 = LO_LEVEL;
   }

/*------------------------------------------------------------------*-

  PULSE_COUNT_Check_Below_Threshold()

  Checks to see if pulse count is below a specified
  threshold value.  If it is, sounds an alarm.

-*------------------------------------------------------------------*/
void PULSE_COUNT_Check_Below_Threshold(const tByte THRESHOLD)
   {
   if (Data_G < THRESHOLD)
      {
      Alarm_pin = 0;
      }
   else
      {
      Alarm_pin = 1;
```

```
      }
   }

/*------------------------------------------------------------------*-

   PULSE_COUNT_Update()

   This is the main switch function.

   It should be called every 30 ms
   (to allow for typical 20 ms debounce time).

-*------------------------------------------------------------------*/
void PULSE_COUNT_Update(void)
   {
   // Clear timer flag
   TF2 = 0;

   // Shuffle the test results
   Test4 = Test3;
   Test3 = Test2;
   Test2 = Test1;
   Test1 = Test0;

   // Get latest test result
   Test0 = Sw_pin;

   // Required result:
   // Test4 == HI_LEVEL
   // Test3 == HI_LEVEL
   // Test1 == LO_LEVEL
   // Test0 == LO_LEVEL

   if ((Test4 == HI_LEVEL) &&
       (Test3 == HI_LEVEL) &&
       (Test1 == LO_LEVEL) &&
       (Test0 == LO_LEVEL))
      {
      // Falling edge detected
      Falling_edge_G = 1;
      }
   else
      {
      // Default
```

```
      Falling_edge_G = 0;
      }

   // Calculate average every 45 calls to this task
   // - maximum count over this period is 9 pulses
   //   if (++Calls_G < 45)

   // 450 used here for test purposes (in simulator)
   // [Because there is a limit to how fast you can
   // simulate pulses by hand...]
   if (++Calls_G < 450)
      {
      Total_G += (int) Falling_edge_G;
      }
   else
      {
      // Update the display
      Data_G = Total_G; // Max is 9
      Total_G = 0;
      Calls_G = 0;
      PULSE_COUNT_Check_Below_Threshold(3);
      BARGRAPH_Update();
      }
   }

/*------------------------------------------------------------------*-
  ---- END OF FILE -------------------------------------------------
-*------------------------------------------------------------------*/
```

Listing 7.13 Part of the software for the milk pasteurization system

```
/*------------------------------------------------------------------*-

   Bargraph.h (v1.00)

  ------------------------------------------------------------------

   - See Bargraph.c for details.

-*------------------------------------------------------------------*/

#include "Main.h"
```

```
// ------ Public data type declarations ---------------------

typedef tByte tBargraph;

// ------ Public function prototypes -----------------------

void BARGRAPH_Init(void);
void BARGRAPH_Update(void);

// ------ Public constants ---------------------------------

#define BARGRAPH_MAX (9)
#define BARGRAPH_MIN (0)

/*------------------------------------------------------------------*-
  ---- END OF FILE -------------------------------------------------
-*------------------------------------------------------------------*/
```

Listing 7.14 Part of the software for the milk pasteurization system

```
/*------------------------------------------------------------------*-

   Bargraph.c (v1.00)

  ------------------------------------------------------------------

   Simple bargraph library.

-*------------------------------------------------------------------*/

#include "Main.h"
#include "Port.h"

#include "Bargraph.h"

// ------ Public variable declarations ----------------------

// The data to be displayed
tBargraph Data_G;

// ------ Private constants ---------------------------------

#define BARGRAPH_ON (1)
#define BARGRAPH_OFF (0)

// ------ Private variables ---------------------------------

// These variables store the thresholds
```

```
// used to update the display
static tBargraph M9_1_G;
static tBargraph M9_2_G;
static tBargraph M9_3_G;
static tBargraph M9_4_G;
static tBargraph M9_5_G;
static tBargraph M9_6_G;
static tBargraph M9_7_G;
static tBargraph M9_8_G;

/*------------------------------------------------------------------*-

  BARGRAPH_Init()

  Prepare for the bargraph display.

-*------------------------------------------------------------------*/
void BARGRAPH_Init(void)
   {
   Pin0 = BARGRAPH_OFF;
   Pin1 = BARGRAPH_OFF;
   Pin2 = BARGRAPH_OFF;
   Pin3 = BARGRAPH_OFF;
   Pin4 = BARGRAPH_OFF;
   Pin5 = BARGRAPH_OFF;
   Pin6 = BARGRAPH_OFF;
   Pin7 = BARGRAPH_OFF;

   // Use a linear scale to display data
   // Remember: *9* possible output states
   // - do all calculations ONCE
   M9_1_G = (BARGRAPH_MAX - BARGRAPH_MIN) / 9;
   M9_2_G = M9_1_G * 2;
   M9_3_G = M9_1_G * 3;
   M9_4_G = M9_1_G * 4;
   M9_5_G = M9_1_G * 5;
   M9_6_G = M9_1_G * 6;
   M9_7_G = M9_1_G * 7;
   M9_8_G = M9_1_G * 8;
   }

/*------------------------------------------------------------------*-
```

```
   BARGRAPH_Update()

   Update the bargraph display.

-*------------------------------------------------------------------*/
void BARGRAPH_Update(void)
   {
   tBargraph Data = Data_G - BARGRAPH_MIN;

   Pin0 = ((Data >= M9_1_G) == BARGRAPH_ON);
   Pin1 = ((Data >= M9_2_G) == BARGRAPH_ON);
   Pin2 = ((Data >= M9_3_G) == BARGRAPH_ON);
   Pin3 = ((Data >= M9_4_G) == BARGRAPH_ON);
   Pin4 = ((Data >= M9_5_G) == BARGRAPH_ON);
   Pin5 = ((Data >= M9_6_G) == BARGRAPH_ON);
   Pin6 = ((Data >= M9_7_G) == BARGRAPH_ON);
   Pin7 = ((Data >= M9_8_G) == BARGRAPH_ON);
   }

/*------------------------------------------------------------------*-
  ---- END OF FILE -------------------------------------------------
-*------------------------------------------------------------------*/
```

7.9 Conclusions

The operating system ('sEOS') introduced in this chapter imposes a very low processor load but is nonetheless flexible and useful.

The simple nature of sEOS also provides other benefits. For example, it means that developers themselves can, very rapidly, port the OS onto a new microcontroller environment. It also means that the architecture may be readily adapted to meet the needs of a particular application.

However, perhaps the most important side effect of this form of simple OS is that – unlike a traditional 'real-time operating system' – it becomes part of the application itself (Figure 7.13). In our experience, this tight integration of OS and application means that developers quickly understand, and claim ownership of, the OS code. This is important, since it avoids a 'not invented here' or 'blame it on the OS' philosophy, which can arise when developers must interface their code to a large and complex real-time operating system, the features and behaviour of which they may never fully understand.

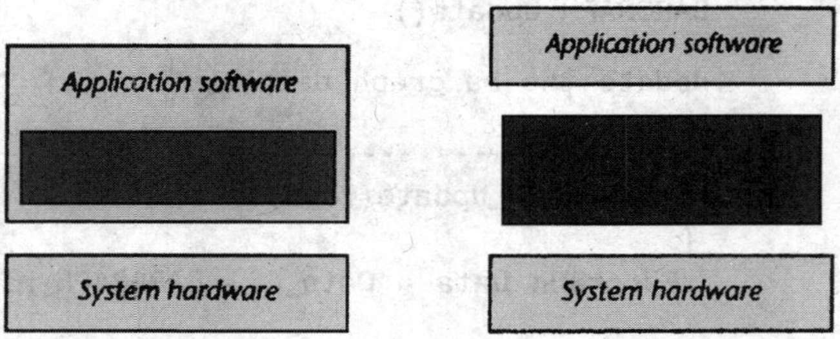

FIGURE 7.13 A simple OS (of the type discussed in this book) becomes part of the developer's application, rather than being seen as a 'separate system that has nothing to do with us'

Finally, as we conclude this chapter, we should note that it is possible to create other, more flexible, operating systems for the 8051 and other processors by building on the techniques presented here: we consider some of the possibilities in Chapter 11.

chapter 8

Multi-state systems and function sequences

8.1 Introduction

In Chapter 6, we considered the design of a simple aircraft autopilot system. We assumed that the pilot would enter the required course heading and that the autopilot would then monitor the aircraft position and orientation, and – where necessary – make changes to the rudder, elevator, aileron and engine settings in order to keep the aircraft following this path.

Like the various embedded systems we considered in Chapter 7, this system involves periodic function calls. In the case of the autopilot, the various sensor inputs would be measured at pre-determined intervals (typically every 10 ms). The autopilot would then calculate the required system outputs, and make appropriate adjustments to the relevant actuators (Figure 8.1).

As we saw in Chapter 7, the ability to execute tasks on a periodic basis can be provided very effectively using a simple operating system like sEOS. On its own, however, periodic execution of functions would not allow us to meet all the requirements of the autopilot application. In particular, it would not allow us to execute the sequence of operations that would be required if we wanted to have the aircraft follow a preset course, carry out an automated landing or even retract its undercarriage. This requires us to execute a sequence of functions, in a predetermined order.

In most cases, it is helpful to model such systems as a series of states: in each state, we may read system inputs and / or generate appropriate system outputs.

This architecture is common not only in autopilot systems, but also in automatic car wash systems, industrial robots and traffic lights, all the way through to domestic dishwashers and microwave ovens.

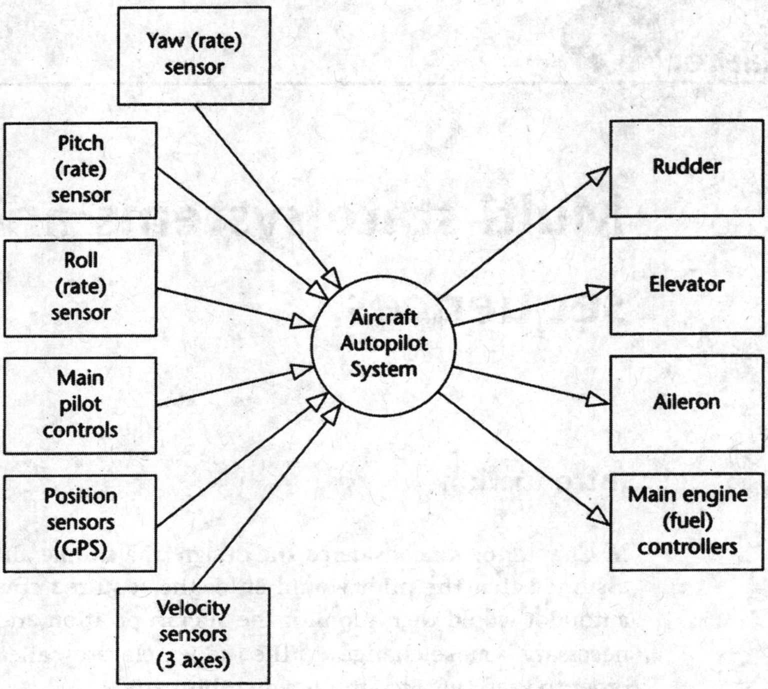

FIGURE 8.1 An overview of a simple autopilot system showing the main sensors to be monitored (left) and the actuators to be controlled (right)

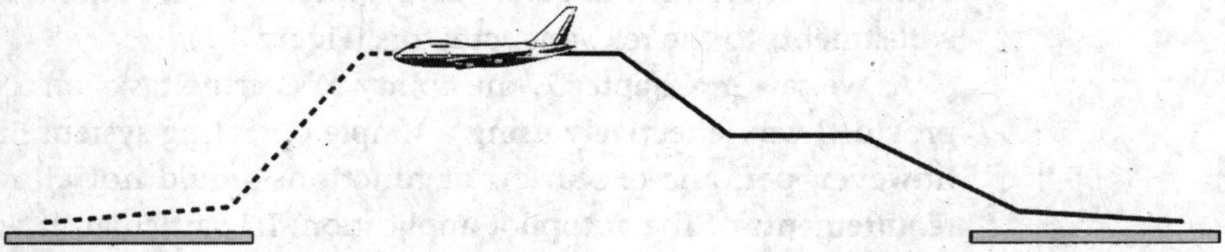

FIGURE 8.2 A high-level schematic view of a simple autopilot system in use

The common characteristics of such systems are that:

- They involve a series of system states.
- In each state, one or more functions may be called.
- There will be rules defining the transitions between states.
- As the system moves between states, one or more functions may be called.

The different nature of the rules used to control the transitions between states allows us to identify two broad categories of multi-state systems:

- **Multi-State (Timed)**

  In a multi-state (timed) system, the transition between states will depend **only** on the passage of time.

  For example, the system might begin in State A, repeatedly executing `FunctionA()`, for ten seconds. It might then move into State B and remain there for five seconds, repeatedly executing `FunctionB()`. It might then move back into State A, *ad infinituum*.

  A basic traffic-light control system might follow this pattern.

- **Multi-State (Input/Timed)**

  This is a more common form of system, in which the transition between states (and behaviour in each state) will depend both on the passage of time **and** on system inputs.

  For example, the system might only move between State A and State B if a particular input is received within X seconds of a system output being generated.

  The autopilot system discussed at the start of this chapter might follow this pattern, as might a control system for a washing machine, or an intruder alarm system.

For completeness, we will mention one further possibility:

- **Multi-State (Input)**

  This is a comparatively rare form of system, in which the transition between states (and behaviour in each state) depends **only** on the system inputs.

  For example, the system might only move between State A and State B if a particular input is received. It will remain indefinitely in State A if this input is not received.

  Such systems have no concept of time, and – therefore – no way of implementing timeout or similar behaviours. We will not consider such systems in this book.

In this chapter, we will consider how the Multi-State (Time) and Multi-State (Input/Time) architectures can be implemented in C.

8.2 Implementing a Multi-State (Timed) system

We can describe the time-driven, Multi-State architecture as follows:

- The system will operate in two or more states.
- Each state may be associated with one or more function calls.
- Transitions between states will be controlled by the passage of time.
- Transitions between states may also involve function calls.

Please note that, in order to ease subsequent maintenance tasks, the system states should not be arbitrarily named, but should – where possible – reflect a physical state observable by the user and / or developer. For example, a telephone system with the set of states {'State 1', 'State 2', 'State 3'} may prove more difficult to maintain than one with states {'Charging', 'In use', 'Ringing'}.

Please also note that the system states will usually be represented by means of a switch statement in the operating system ISR.

We illustrate this architecture in the two examples that follow.

8.3 Example: Traffic light sequencing

Suppose we wish to create a system for driving three traffic light bulbs in a traffic system for use in Europe. The conventional 'red', 'amber' (orange) and 'green' bulbs will be used, with European sequencing (Figure 8.3).

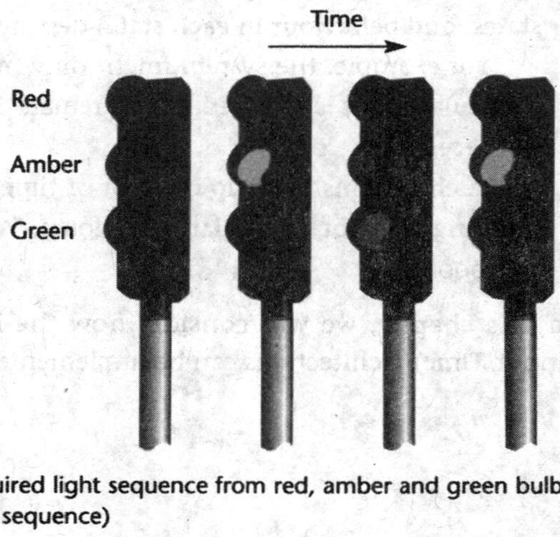

FIGURE 8.3 The required light sequence from red, amber and green bulbs in a traffic-light application (European sequence)

a) Basic system architecture

A basic version of the traffic-light sequencer requires no inputs from the environment and will perform well by executing a sequence of pre-determined manoeuvres. It is a classic example of a Multi-State (Timed) system.

b) The system states

In this case, the various states are easily identified:

- Red
- Red-Amber
- Green
- Amber

In the code, we will represent these states as follows:

```
// Possible system states
typedef enum {RED, RED_AND_AMBER, GREEN, AMBER} eLight_State;
```

We will store the time to be spent in each state using appropriate constants:

```
// Times in each of the (four) possible light states
// (Times are in seconds)
//
#define RED_DURATION 20
#define RED_AND_AMBER_DURATION 5
#define GREEN_DURATION 30
#define AMBER_DURATION 5
```

In this simple case, we do not require function calls from (or between) system states: the required behaviour will be implemented directly through control of the (three) port pins which – in the final system – would be connected to appropriate bulbs.

For example:

```
case RED:
     {
     Red_light = ON;
     Amber_light = OFF;
     Green_light = OFF;
```

c) Complete implementation

Listing 8.1 to Listing 8.3 show how we can use sEOS to implement the complete traffic-light sequencer.

Listing 8.1 Part of an example showing traffic-light sequencing using a simple EOS

```
/*------------------------------------------------------------------*-

  Main.c (v1.00)

  ------------------------------------------------------------------

  Traffic light example.

-*------------------------------------------------------------------*/
#include "Main.H"
#include "Port.H"
#include "Simple_EOS.H"

#include "T_Lights.H"

/* ---------------------------------------------------------------- */

void main(void)
   {
   // Prepare to run traffic sequence
   TRAFFIC_LIGHTS_Init(RED);

   // Set up simple EOS (50 ms ticks)
   sEOS_Init_Timer2(50);

   while(1) // Super Loop
   {
     // Enter idle mode to save power
     sEOS_Go_To_Sleep();
     }
   }

/*------------------------------------------------------------------*-
  ---- END OF FILE -------------------------------------------------
-*------------------------------------------------------------------*/
```

Listing 8.2 Part of an example showing traffic-light sequencing using a simple EOS

```
/*------------------------------------------------------------------*-

   T_Lights.H (v1.00)

  ------------------------------------------------------------------

   - See T_Lights.C for details.

-*------------------------------------------------------------------*/

#ifndef _T_LIGHTS_H
#define _T_LIGHTS_H

// ------ Public data type declarations -----------------------------

// Possible system states
typedef enum {RED, RED_AND_AMBER, GREEN, AMBER} eLight_State;

// ------ Public function prototypes --------------------------------

void TRAFFIC_LIGHTS_Init(const eLight_State);
void TRAFFIC_LIGHTS_Update(void);

#endif

/*------------------------------------------------------------------*-
  ---- END OF FILE -------------------------------------------------
-*------------------------------------------------------------------*/
```

Listing 8.3 Part of an example showing traffic-light sequencing using a simple EOS

```
/*------------------------------------------------------------------*-

   T_lights.C (v1.00)

  ------------------------------------------------------------------

   Traffic light control program (Test Version 1.0)

-*------------------------------------------------------------------*/

#include "Main.H"
#include "Port.H"
```

```
#include "T_lights.H"

// ------ Private constants -------------------------------

// Easy to change logic here
#define ON 0
#define OFF 1

// Times in each of the (four) possible light states
// (Times are in seconds)
#define RED_DURATION 20
#define RED_AND_AMBER_DURATION 5
#define GREEN_DURATION 30
#define AMBER_DURATION 5

// ------ Private variables -------------------------------

// The state of the system
static eLight_State Light_state_G;

// The time in that state
static tLong Time_in_state;

// Used by sEOS
static tByte Call_count_G = 0;

/*------------------------------------------------------------*-

  TRAFFIC_LIGHTS_Init()

  Prepare for traffic light activity.

-*------------------------------------------------------------*/
void TRAFFIC_LIGHTS_Init(const eLight_State START_STATE)
   {
   Light_state_G = START_STATE; // Decide on initial state
   }

/*------------------------------------------------------------*-
  TRAFFIC_LIGHTS_Update()

  Must be called once per second.

-*------------------------------------------------------------*/
void TRAFFIC_LIGHTS_Update(void)
```

```
{
switch (Light_state_G)
   {
   case RED:
      {
      Red_light = ON;
      Amber_light = OFF;
      Green_light = OFF;

      if (++Time_in_state == RED_DURATION)
         {
         Light_state_G = RED_AND_AMBER;
         Time_in_state = 0;
         }

      break;
      }

   case RED_AND_AMBER:
      {
      Red_light = ON;
      Amber_light = ON;
      Green_light = OFF;

      if (++Time_in_state == RED_AND_AMBER_DURATION)
         {
         Light_state_G = GREEN;
         Time_in_state = 0;
         }

      break;
      }

   case GREEN:
      {
      Red_light = OFF;
      Amber_light = OFF;
      Green_light = ON;

      if (++Time_in_state == GREEN_DURATION)
         {
         Light_state_G = AMBER;
         Time_in_state = 0;
         }
```

```
            break;
            }

         case AMBER:
            {
            Red_light = OFF;
            Amber_light = ON;
            Green_light = OFF;

            if (++Time_in_state == AMBER_DURATION)
               {
               Light_state_G = RED;
               Time_in_state = 0;
               }

            break;
            }
         }
      }

/*------------------------------------------------------------------*-
  ---- END OF FILE -------------------------------------------------
-*------------------------------------------------------------------*/
```

8.4 Example: Animatronic dinosaur

The scheduling of traffic lights is a common example. In this second example, we will consider a more complicated system.

The Natural History Museum in London recently installed a robotic dinosaur among the fossils in their Dinosaur Gallery.[29] This large exhibit models a tyrannosaurus rex guarding a recent kill: the robot is large, very loud and moves quickly. It has proved to be very popular with visitors.

We will consider here the software architecture that could be used in the implementation of such a system.

a) Basic system architecture

This system requires no inputs from the environment and will perform well by executing a sequence of pre-determined manoeuvres. It is a good example of a Multi-State (Timed) system.

29. There is a video showing the dinosaur in action on the museum website: www.nhm.ac.uk

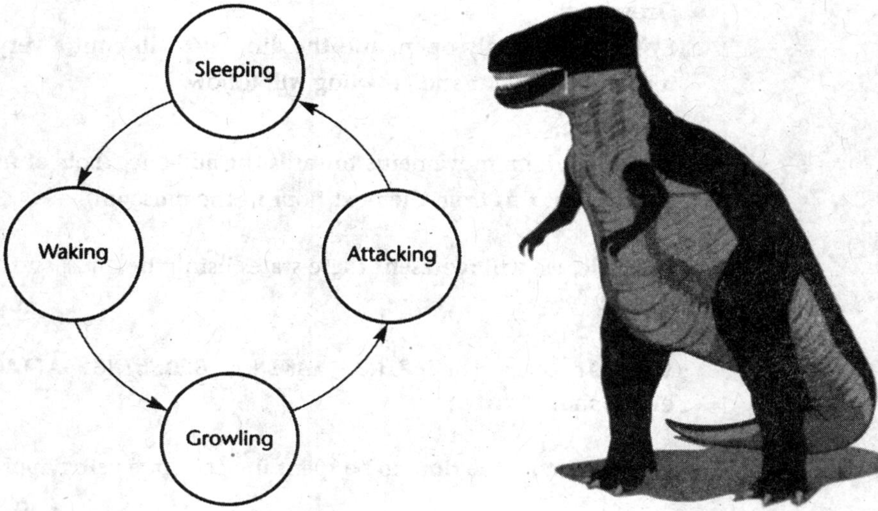

FIGURE 8.4 This example considers the software architecture required to control an animatronic dinosaur. See text for details

We will assume that the sequence of manoeuvres will take a few minutes to execute, and will run approximately every ten minutes.

To implement a complete system, we would probably prepare a number of slightly different programs, and execute a program 'at random'. This would make the display more interesting for people who choose to watch the show more than once. This option is not implemented in the example code here: however, the approach used to implement different washing machine programs could be employed here if you wish to explore this example further (see Section 8.6).

b) The system states

We will assume that the following system states are to be implemented:

- **Sleeping:**
  The dinosaur will be largely motionless, but will be obviously 'breathing'. Irregular snoring noises, or slight movements during this time will add interest for the audience.
- **Waking:**
  The dinosaur will begin to wake up. Eyelids will begin to flicker. Breathing will become more rapid.

- **Growling:**
  Eyes will suddenly open, and the dinosaur will emit a very loud growl. Some further movement and growling will follow.
- **Attacking:**
  Rapid 'random' movements towards the audience. Lots of noise (you should be able to hear this from the next floor in the museum).

In the code, we will represent these states using the `enum` and `typedef` keywords, as follows:

```
typedef enum {SLEEPING, WAKING, GROWLING, ATTACKING}
eDinosaur_State;
```

We will also store the time to be spent in each state using appropriate contants:

```
// Times in each of the (four) possible states
// (Times are in seconds)
#define SLEEPING_DURATION 255
#define WAKING_DURATION 60
#define GROWLING_DURATION 40
#define ATTACKING_DURATION 120
```

Appropriate functions will also be created to implement the key behaviours:

```
// ------ Private function prototypes ----------------------
void DINOSAUR_Perform_Sleep_Movements(void);
void DINOSAUR_Perform_Waking_Movements(void);
void DINOSAUR_Growl(void);
void DINOSAUR_Perform_Attack_Movements(void);
```

We will not be concerned with the implementation of these functions in this introductory book (Chapter 11 provides suggestions for further reading if you want to explore this example in more depth).

c) Complete implementation

Listing 8.4 shows how we can use sEOS to implement the complete dinosaur behaviour.

Note that we assume the dinosaur 'update' function will be called from the sEOS ISR once per second: refer to the CD for complete code details.

Listing 8.4 Part of an example showing control of an animatronic dinosaur using a simple EOS

```
/*------------------------------------------------------------------*-

   Dinosaur.C (v1.00)

  ------------------------------------------------------------------

   Demonstration of multi-state (timed) architecture:
   Dinosaur control system.

-*------------------------------------------------------------------*/

#include "Main.h"
#include "Port.h"

#include "Dinosaur.h"

// ------ Private data type declarations ---------------------
// Possible system states
typedef
enum {SLEEPING, WAKING, GROWLING, ATTACKING} eDinosaur_State;

// ------ Private function prototypes -----------------------
void DINOSAUR_Perform_Sleep_Movements(void);
void DINOSAUR_Perform_Waking_Movements(void);
void DINOSAUR_Growl(void);
void DINOSAUR_Perform_Attack_Movements(void);

// ------ Private constants ---------------------------------
// Times in each of the (four) possible states
// (Times are in seconds)
#define SLEEPING_DURATION 255
#define WAKING_DURATION 60
#define GROWLING_DURATION 40
#define ATTACKING_DURATION 120

// ------ Private variables ---------------------------------
// The current state of the system
static eDinosaur_State Dinosaur_state_G;

// The time in the state
static tByte Time_in_state_G;
```

```
// Used by sEOS
static tByte Call_count_G = 0;

/*------------------------------------------------------------------*-

  DINOSAUR_Init()
  Prepare for the dinosaur activity.

-*------------------------------------------------------------------*/
void DINOSAUR_Init(void)
   {
   // Initial dinosaur state
   Dinosaur_state_G = SLEEPING;
   }

/*------------------------------------------------------------------*-

  DINOSAUR_Update()

  Must be scheduled once per second (from the sEOS ISR).

-*------------------------------------------------------------------*/
void DINOSAUR_Update(void)
   {
   switch (Dinosaur_state_G)
      {
      case SLEEPING:
         {
         // Call relevant function
         DINOSAUR_Perform_Sleep_Movements();

         if (++Time_in_state_G == SLEEPING_DURATION)
            {
            Dinosaur_state_G = WAKING;
            Time_in_state_G = 0;
            }

         break;
         }

      case WAKING:
         {
         // Call relevant function
         DINOSAUR_Perform_Waking_Movements();
```

```
         if (++Time_in_state_G == WAKING_DURATION)
            {
            Dinosaur_state_G = GROWLING;
            Time_in_state_G = 0;
            }

         break;
         }

      case GROWLING:
         {
         // Call relevant function
         DINOSAUR_Growl();

         if (++Time_in_state_G == GROWLING_DURATION)
            {
            Dinosaur_state_G = ATTACKING;
            Time_in_state_G = 0;
            }

         break;
         }

      case ATTACKING:
         {
         // Call relevant function
         DINOSAUR_Perform_Attack_Movements();

         if (++Time_in_state_G == ATTACKING_DURATION)
            {
            Dinosaur_state_G = SLEEPING;
            Time_in_state_G = 0;
            }

         break;
         }
      }
   }

/*------------------------------------------------------------*/
void DINOSAUR_Perform_Sleep_Movements(void)
   {
   // Demo only...
   P1 = (tByte) Dinosaur_state_G;
```

```
   P2 = Time_in_state_G;
   }

/*--------------------------------------------------------------*/
void DINOSAUR_Perform_Waking_Movements(void)
   {
   // Demo only…
   P1 = (tByte) Dinosaur_state_G;
   P2 = Time_in_state_G;
   }

/*--------------------------------------------------------------*/
void DINOSAUR_Growl(void)
   {
   // Demo only…
   P1 = (tByte) Dinosaur_state_G;
   P2 = Time_in_state_G;
   }

/*--------------------------------------------------------------*/
void DINOSAUR_Perform_Attack_Movements(void)
   {
   // Demo only...
   P1 = (tByte) Dinosaur_state_G;
   P2 = Time_in_state_G;
   }

/*--------------------------------------------------------------*-
  ---- END OF FILE -------------------------------------------------
-*--------------------------------------------------------------*/
```

8.5 Implementing a Multi-State (Input/Timed) system

As we noted in Section 8.1, the general Multi-State software architecture has two common forms. Here we consider how we can create a Multi-State system driven both by time and system inputs.

a) Basic design

We can describe the time-and-inout-driven Multi-State architecture as follows:

- The system will operate in two or more states.
- Each state may be associated with one or more function calls.
- Transitions between states may be controlled by the passage of time, by system inputs or by a combination of time and inputs.
- Transitions between states may also involve function calls.

b) Implementing state timeouts

We introduced timeout mechanisms in Chapter 6. As we noted in Chapter 7, such mechanisms play a key role in applications using sEOS.

When working with Multi-State systems, timeout mechanisms are still important: however, in this case we sometimes require what might be described as a 'state timeout' mechanism.

For example, consider the following – informal – system requirements:

- The pump should be run for 10 seconds. If, during this time, no liquid is detected in the outflow tank, then the pump should be switched off and 'low water' warning should be sounded. If liquid is detected, the pump should be run for a further 45 seconds, or until the 'high water' sensor is activated (whichever is first).
- After the front door is opened, the correct password must be entered on the control panel within 30 seconds or the alarm will sound.
- The 'down flap' signal will be issued. If, after 5 ms, no flap movement is detected, it should be concluded that the flap hydraulics are damaged. Th system should then alert the user and enter manual mode.

To meet this type of requirement, we will do two things:

- Keep track of the time in each system state.
- If the time exceeds a pre-determined error value, then we should move to a ferent state.

We illustrate this procedure in the next example.

8.6 Example: Controller for a washing machine

In this example we consider the design of a controller for a domest machine (Figure 8.5).

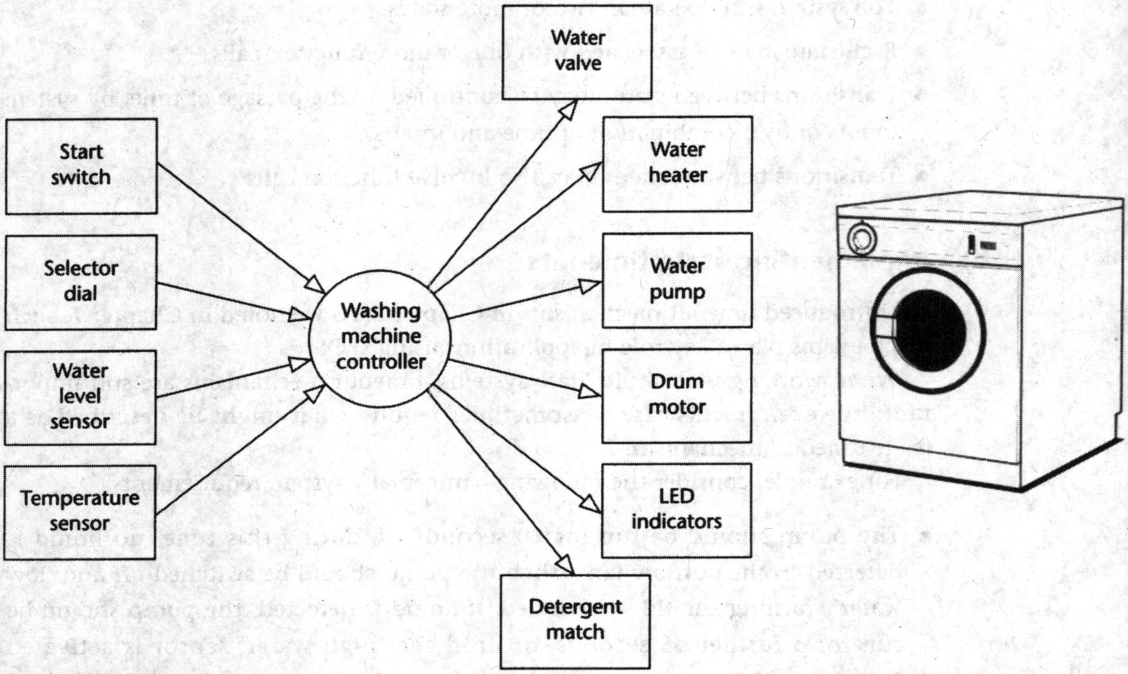

FIGURE 8.5 The outline design – in the form of a context diagram (left) – for the control system to be used in a domestic washing machine (right)

Here is a brief description of the way in which we expect the system to operate:

1 The user selects a wash program (e.g. 'Wool', 'Cotton') on the selector dial.

2 The user presses the 'Start' switch.

3 The door lock is engaged.

4 The water valve is opened to allow water into the wash drum.

5 If the wash program involves detergent, the detergent hatch is opened. When the detergent has been released, the detergent hatch is closed.

6 When the 'full water level' is sensed, the water valve is closed.

7 If the wash program involves warm water, the water heater is switched on. When the water reaches the correct temperature, the water heater is switched off.

8 The washer motor is turned on to rotate the drum. The motor then goes through a series of movements, both forward and reverse (at various speeds) to wash the clothes. (The precise set of movements carried out depends on the wash program that the user has selected.) At the end of the wash cycle, the motor is stopped.

9 The pump is switched on to drain the drum. When the drum is empty, the pump is switched off.

The description is simplified for the purposes of this example, but it will be adequate for our purposes here.

a) Functions

Based on the above description we will try to identify some of the functions that will be required to implement this system. A provisional list might be as shown in Figure 8.6.

• Read_Selector_Dial()	• Control_Detergent_Hatch()
• Read_Start_Switch()	• Control_Door_Lock()
• Read_Water_Level()	• Control_Motor()
• Read_Water_Temperature()	• Control_Pump()
	• Control_Water_Heater()
	• Control_Water_Valve()

FIGURE 8.6 A provisional list of functions that could be used to develop a washing-machine control system

b) System architecture

The washing machine software will be a based on a 'Multi-State' task. It will be driven by both elapsed time and system inputs.

c) Code listing

Listings for key files are given in this section.

When reviewing this code, please note the key differences between this architecture and that of the earlier traffic-light and dinosaur examples. In the earlier examples, the system was 'blind': it performed a sequence of actions, without reference to the system environment. In this case, the system is much more responsive. Typical behaviour involves starting a pump and waiting – for a finite time – for the drum to fill. If the behaviour has not completed within this period then we assume that an error has occurred.

Please note, again, that this behaviour is by no means unique to 'white goods' (such as washing machines). For example, the sequence of events used to raise the landing gear in a passenger aircraft will be controlled in a similar manner. In this case, basic tests (such as 'WoW' – 'Weight on Wheels') will be used to determine whether the aircraft is on the ground or in the air: these tests will be completed before the operation begins. Feedback from various door and landing-gear sensors will then be used to ensure that each phase of the manoeuvre completes correctly.

Listing 8.5 Part of the framework for a simple washing machine controller

```
/*-------------------------------------------------------------------*-

   Washer.C (v1.00)

  -------------------------------------------------------------------

   Multi-state framework for washing-machine controller.

-*-------------------------------------------------------------------*/

#include "Main.H"
#include "Port.H"

#include "Washer.H"

// ------ Private data type declarations ----------------------------

// Possible system states
typedef enum {INIT, START, FILL_DRUM, HEAT_WATER,
              WASH_01, WASH_02, ERROR} eSystem_state;

// ------ Private function prototypes -------------------------------

tByte WASHER_Read_Selector_Dial(void);
bit WASHER_Read_Start_Switch(void);
bit WASHER_Read_Water_Level(void);
bit WASHER_Read_Water_Temperature(void);

void WASHER_Control_Detergent_Hatch(bit);
void WASHER_Control_Door_Lock(bit);
void WASHER_Control_Motor(bit);
void WASHER_Control_Pump(bit);
void WASHER_Control_Water_Heater(bit);
void WASHER_Control_Water_Valve(bit);
```

```
// ------ Private constants ----------------------------------

#define OFF 0
#define ON 1

#define MAX_FILL_DURATION (tLong) 1000
#define MAX_WATER_HEAT_DURATION (tLong) 1000

#define WASH_01_DURATION 30000

// ------ Private variables ----------------------------------

static eSystem_state System_state_G;

static tWord Time_in_state_G;

static tByte Program_G;

// Ten different programs are supported
// Each one may or may not use detergent
static tByte Detergent_G[10] = {1,1,1,0,0,1,0,1,1,0};

// Each one may or may not use hot water
static tByte Hot_Water_G[10] = {1,1,1,0,0,1,0,1,1,0};

/* --------------------------------------------------------- */
void WASHER_Init(void)
   {
   System_state_G = INIT;
   }

/* --------------------------------------------------------- */
void WASHER_Update(void)
   {
   // Call once per second
   switch (System_state_G)
      {
      case INIT:
         {
         // For demo purposes only
         Debug_port = (tByte) System_state_G;

         // Set up initial state
         // Motor is off
         WASHER_Control_Motor(OFF);
```

```
            // Pump is off
            WASHER_Control_Pump(OFF);

            // Heater is off
            WASHER_Control_Water_Heater(OFF);

            // Valve is closed
            WASHER_Control_Water_Valve(OFF);

            // Wait (indefinitely) until START is pressed
            if (WASHER_Read_Start_Switch() != 1)
               {
               return;
               }

            // Start switch pressed...
            // Read the selector dial
            Program_G = WASHER_Read_Selector_Dial();

            // Change state
            System_state_G = START;
            break;
            }

         case START:
            {
            // For demo purposes only
            Debug_port = (tByte) System_state_G;

            // Lock the door
            WASHER_Control_Door_Lock(ON);

            // Start filling the drum
            WASHER_Control_Water_Valve(ON);

            // Release the detergent (if any)
            if (Detergent_G[Program_G] == 1)
               {
               WASHER_Control_Detergent_Hatch(ON);
               }

            // Ready to go to next state
            System_state_G = FILL_DRUM;
            Time_in_state_G = 0;
```

```
      break;
      }

   case FILL_DRUM:
      {
      // For demo purposes only
      Debug_port = (tByte) System_state_G;

      // Remain in this state until drum is full
      // NOTE: Timeout facility included here
      if (++Time_in_state_G >= MAX_FILL_DURATION)
         {
         // Should have filled the drum by now...
         System_state_G = ERROR;
         }

      // Check the water level
      if (WASHER_Read_Water_Level() == 1)
         {
         // Drum is full

         // Does the program require hot water?
         if (Hot_Water_G[Program_G] == 1)
            {
            WASHER_Control_Water_Heater(ON);

            // Ready to go to next state
            System_state_G = HEAT_WATER;
            Time_in_state_G = 0;
            }
         else
            {
            // Using cold water only
            // Ready to go to next state
            System_state_G = WASH_01;
            Time_in_state_G = 0;
            }
         }
      break;
      }
```

```
case HEAT_WATER:
   {
   // For demo purposes only
   Debug_port = (tByte) System_state_G;

   // Remain in this state until water is hot
   // NOTE: Timeout facility included here
   if (++Time_in_state_G >= MAX_WATER_HEAT_DURATION)
      {
      // Should have warmed the water by now...
      System_state_G = ERROR;
      }

   // Check the water temperature
   if (WASHER_Read_Water_Temperature() == 1)
      {
      // Water is at required temperature
      // Ready to go to next state
      System_state_G = WASH_01;
      Time_in_state_G = 0;
      }

   break;
   }

case WASH_01:
   {
   // For demo purposes only
   Debug_port = (tByte) System_state_G;

   // All wash program involve WASH_01
   // Drum is slowly rotated to ensure clothes are fully wet
   WASHER_Control_Motor(ON);

   if (++Time_in_state_G >= WASH_01_DURATION)
      {
      System_state_G = WASH_02;
      Time_in_state_G = 0;
      }

   break;
   }

// REMAINING WASH PHASES OMITTED HERE ...
```

```
      case WASH_02:
         {
         // For demo purposes only
         Debug_port = (tByte) System_state_G;

         break;
         }

      case ERROR:
         {
         // For demo purposes only
         Debug_port = (tByte) System_state_G;

         break;
         }
      }
   }

/* --------------------------------------------------------- */
tByte WASHER_Read_Selector_Dial(void)
   {
   // User code here...

   return 0;
   }

/* --------------------------------------------------------- */
bit WASHER_Read_Start_Switch(void)
   {
   // Simplified for demo ...

   if (Start_pin == 0)
      {
      // Start switch pressed
      return 1;
      }
   else
      {
      return 0;
      }
   }

/* --------------------------------------------------------- */
```

```
bit WASHER_Read_Water_Level(void)
   {
   // User code here...
   return 1;
   }

/* ------------------------------------------------------------------ */
bit WASHER_Read_Water_Temperature(void)
   {
   // User code here...

   return 1;
   }

/* ------------------------------------------------------------------ */
void WASHER_Control_Detergent_Hatch(bit State)
   {
   bit Tmp = State;
   // User code here...
   }

/* ------------------------------------------------------------------ */
void WASHER_Control_Door_Lock(bit State)
   {
   bit Tmp = State;
   // User code here...
   }

/* ------------------------------------------------------------------ */
void WASHER_Control_Motor(bit State)
   {
   bit Tmp = State;
   // User code here...
   }

/* ------------------------------------------------------------------ */
void WASHER_Control_Pump(bit State)
   {
   bit Tmp = State;
   // User code here...
   }

/* ------------------------------------------------------------------ */
```

```
void WASHER_Control_Water_Heater(bit State)
   {
   bit Tmp = State;
   // User code here...
   }

/* ------------------------------------------------------------ */
void WASHER_Control_Water_Valve(bit State)
   {
   bit Tmp = State;
   // User code here...
   }

/*------------------------------------------------------------*-
  ---- END OF FILE --------------------------------------------
-*------------------------------------------------------------*/
```

8.7 Conclusions

This chapter has discussed the implementation of Multi-State (Tmed) and Multi-State (Input/Timed) systems. Used in conjunction with an operating system like that presented in Chapter 7, this flexible system architecture is in widespread use in embedded applications.

In Chapter 9, we move on to look at the use of the 8051's serial interface.

chapter 9

Using the serial interface

9.1 Introduction

In Chapter 2, we introduced the 8051 microcontroller and saw that it had the following features:

- 32 I/O pins.
- At least two timers.
- An interrupt system.
- A serial interface supporting the RS-232 standard.

In previous chapters, we have used the I/O pins for input and output, and the timers for generating accurate delays. We have also used the timers – and the interrupt system – to create a simple embedded operating system. In this chapter, we complete our discussion of 8051 features by examining the serial interface.

9.2 What is RS-232?

In 1997 the Telecommunications Industry Association released what is formally known as TIA-232 Version F, a serial communication protocol which has been universally referred to as 'RS-232' since its first 'Recommended Standard' appeared in the 1960s. Similar standards (V.28) are published by the International Telecommunications Union (ITU) and by CCITT (The Consultative Committee International Telegraph and Telephone).

The 'RS-232' standard includes details of:

- The protocol to be used for data transmission.
- The voltages to be used on the signal lines.
- The connectors to be used to link equipment together.

Overall, the standard is comprehensive and widely used, at data transfer rates of up to around 115 or 330 kbits / second (115 / 330 k baud). Data transfer can be over distances of 15 metres or more.

Note that RS-232 is a peer-to-peer communication standard. Unlike – for example – the RS-485 standard, RS-232 is intended to link only two devices together.

9.3 Does RS-232 still matter?

On the desktop, standards such as USB are rapidly replacing RS-232 as 'desirable' protocols. Nonetheless – for embedded development – RS-232 remains important.

Some important applications of RS-232 in embedded systems include the following:

- To program on-chip flash memory (for testing or low-volume production), several 8051 devices use the serial port. This can also be an important means of performing code upgrades to devices in the field.
- Many developers use RS-232 during system development, in order to communicate between desktop PCs (on which code is developed) and prototype boards (on which the code is tested). For example, since most embedded devices have no screen or keyboard available, it is useful to be able to send data to and from a desktop PC to clarify program operation.
- Many embedded data acquisition and control systems receive instructions from and / or transfer data to desktop PCs over an RS-232 link.
- Even very recent components, such as Global Positioning System (GPS) sensors, have RS-232 interfaces.

9.4 The basic RS-232 protocol

RS-232 is a byte-oriented protocol. That is, it is intended to be used to send single 8-bit blocks of data. To transmit a byte of data over an RS-232 link, we generally encode the information as follows:

- We send a 'Start' bit.
- We send the data (8 bits).
- We send a 'Stop' bit (or bits).

We consider each of these stages below.

Quiescent state

When no data are being sent on an RS-232 'transmit' line, the line is held at a Logic 1 level.

Start bit

To indicate the start of a data transmission we pull the 'transmit' line low.

Data

Data are often encoded in ASCII (American Standard Code for Information Interchange), in 7-bit form. The bits are sent least-significant bit first. If we are sending 7-bit data, the 8th data bit is often used as a simple 'parity check bit', in order to provide a rudimentary error detection facility.

Note that none of the code presented here uses parity bits: we use all 8 bits for data transfer.

Stop bit(s)

The stop bits consist of a Logic 1 output. These can be 1 or – less commonly – 1.5 or 2 pulses wide.

Note that we will use a single stop bit in all code examples.

9.5 Asynchronous data transmission and baud rates

RS-232 uses an asynchronous protocol. This means that no clock signal is sent with the data. Instead, both ends of the communication link have an internal clock, running at the same rate. The data (in the case of RS-232, the 'Start' bit) is then used to synchronize the clocks, if necessary, to ensure successful data transfer.

RS-232 generally operates at one of a (restricted) range of baud rates. Typically these are: 75, 110, 300, 1200, 2400, 4800, 9600, 14400, 19200, 28800, 33600, 56000, 115000 and (rarely) 330000 baud. Of these, 9600 baud is a very 'safe' choice, as it is very widely supported.

9.6 Flow control

RS-232 is often used with some form of flow control. This is a protocol, implemented through software or hardware, that allows a receiver of data to tell the transmitter to pause the data flow. This might be necessary, for example, if we were sending data to a PC, and the PC had filled a RAM buffer: the PC would then tell our embedded application to pause the data transfer until the buffer contents had been stored on disk.

Although hardware handshaking can be used, this requires extra signal lines. The most common flow control technique is 'Xon / Xoff' control. This requires a half- or full-duplex communication link, and can operate as follows:

1. Transmitter sends a byte of data.
2. The receiver is able to receive more data: it does nothing.
3. The transmitter sends another byte of data.
4. Steps 1–3 continue until the receiver cannot accept any more data: it then sends a 'Control s' (Xoff) character back to the transmitter.
5. The transmitter receives the 'Xoff' command and pauses the data transmission.
6. When the receiver node is ready for more data, it sends a 'Control q' (Xon) character to the transmitter.
7. The transmitter resumes the data transmission.
8. The process continues from Step 1.

We illustrate this process in a code library presented in Section 9.12.

9.7 The software architecture

Suppose we wish to transfer data to a PC at a standard 9600 baud; that is, 9600 bits per second. As we discussed above, transmitting each byte of data, plus stop and start bits, involves the transmission of 10 bits of information (assuming a single stop bit is used). As a result, each byte takes approximately 1 ms to transmit.

This has important implications in all applications, not least those using an embedded operating system like sEOS. If, for example, we wish to send this information to the PC:

```
Current core temperature is 36.678 degrees
```

then the task sending these 42 characters will take more than 40 milliseconds to complete. This may be an unacceptably long duration if we need to operate with a high tick rate of, say 10 ms or less (Figure 9.1).

FIGURE 9.1 A schematic representation of the problems caused by sending a long character string on an embedded system with a simple operating system. In this case, sending the message takes 42 ms while the OS tick interval is 10 ms. Please refer back to Chapter 7 for further details

Perhaps the most obvious way of addressing this issue is to increase the baud rate; however, this is not always possible, and – even with very high baud rates – long messages or irregular bursts of data can still cause difficulties.

A complete solution involves a change in the system architecture. Rather than sending all of the data at once, we can simply store the data we want to send to the PC in a buffer (Figure 9.2). Every ten milliseconds (say) we check the buffer and send the next character (if there is one ready to send). In this way, all of the required 43 characters of data will be sent to the PC within 0.5 seconds. This is often (more than) adequate. However, if necessary, we can reduce this time by checking the buffer every millisecond. Note that because we do not have to wait for each character to be sent, the process of sending data from the buffer will be very fast (typically a fraction of a millisecond).

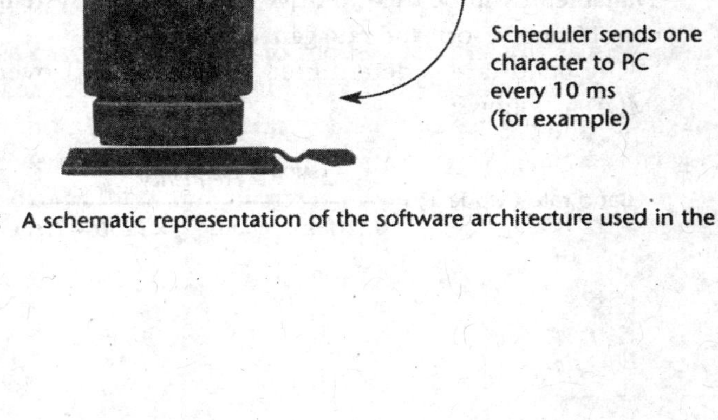

FIGURE 9.2 A schematic representation of the software architecture used in the RS-232 library

9.8 Using the on-chip UART for RS-232 communications

Having decided on the basic architecture for the RS-232 library, we need to consider in more detail how the on-chip serial port is used.

This port is full duplex, meaning it can transmit and receive simultaneously. It is also receive-buffered, meaning it can commence reception of a second byte before a previously received byte has been read from the receive register. (However, if the first byte still has not been read by the time reception of the second byte is complete, one of the bytes will be lost.)

The serial port can operate in four modes (one synchronous mode, three asynchronous modes). In this chapter, we are primarily interested in Mode 1. In this mode, 10 bits are transmitted (through TxD) or received (through RxD): a start bit (0), 8 data bits (least-significant bit first), and a stop bit (1).

Note that the serial interface may also provide interrupt requests when transmission or reception of a byte has been completed. However, for reasons discussed in Chapter 7, none of the 'time-triggered' code used in this chapter will generate interrupts.

a) Serial port registers

The serial port control and status register is the special function register SCON. This register contains the mode selection bits (and the serial port flags, TI and RI).

SBUF is the receive and transmit buffer for the serial interface. Writing to SBUF loads the transmit register and initiates transmission. Reading from SBUF accesses a physically separate receive register.

b) Baud rate generation using Timer 1

There are several different ways to generate the baud rate clock for the serial port depending on the mode in which it is operating.

As noted above, we are primarily concerned here with the use of the serial port in Mode 1. In this mode the baud rate is determined by the overflow rate of Timer 1 or Timer 2. For reasons discussed in Chapter 7, we assume that, if Timer 2 is available, it will be used to drive the operating system. Therefore we focus on the use of Timer 1 for baud rate generation.

The baud rate is determined by the Timer 1 overflow rate and the value of SMOD as follows:

$$\text{Baud rate (Mode 1)} = \frac{2^{SMOD} \times Frequency_{oscillator}}{32 \times Instructions_{cycle} \times (256 - TH1)}$$

Where:

> *SMOD* is the 'double baud rate' bit in the PCON register;
>
> $Frequency_{oscillator}$ is the oscillator / resonator frequency (in Hz);
>
> $Instructions_{cycle}$ is the number of machine instructions per oscillator cycle (e.g. 12 or 6)
>
> *TH1* is the reload value for Timer 1

Note that Timer 1 is used in 8-bit auto-reload mode and that interrupt generation should be disabled.

> It is very important to appreciate that it is not generally possible to produce standard baud rates (e.g. 9600) using Timer 1 (or Timer 2), unless you use an 11.0592 MHz crystal oscillator.

To see why this is so, we will assume SMOD = 0 (it works equally well with SMOD = 1), that there are 12 instructions per cycle and that we require a baud rate of 9600. The above equation becomes:

$$9600 = \frac{11059200}{32 \times 12 \times (256 - TH1)}$$

This becomes:

$$\frac{11059200}{9600 \times 384} = 256 - TH1$$

Or:

$$256 - TH1 = 3$$

Thus, if we set TH1 to 253 (0xFD) we get a *precise* 9600 baud rate.

If – for example – we repeat this with a 12 MHz oscillator, we get:

$$\frac{12000000}{9600 \times 384} = 256 - TH1$$

Or:

$$256 - TH1 = 3.255208333333$$

Thus, the required value of *TH1* is 252.7447916667.

The nearest integer value is 253. This means that our actual baud rate will be approximately 10417 baud – more than 8% higher than the required (9600) rate.

> Remember: this is an asynchronous protocol, and **relies for correct operation on the fact that both ends of the connection are working at the same baud rate**. In practice, you can work with a difference in baud variations of $\pm$2.5%.
>
> Despite this margin, it is always good policy to get the baud rate as close as possible to the standard value because, in the field, there may be significant temperature variations between the oscillator in the PC and that in the embedded system. This will lead to a 'drift' in baud rates on PC and microcontroller, even if they were precisely the same to start with: as a result, if the baud rates were initially mismatched, then communication with the PC may fail completely during normal use. This type of 'inexplicable fault' has caused many developers sleepless nights ('I don't understand it! It works fine in all the tests in the lab!').

c) Other techniques for generating standard baud rates

The frequency 11.0592 MHz may be ideal for generating precise baud rates, but it is not an ideal frequency for driving an embedded operating system of the type presented in Chapter 7.

One good solution to this problem is to use an 8051 device with a programmable baud-rate generator. This allows you to use an oscillator frequency compatible with the operating system (e.g. 24 MHz), and generate precise baud rates.

The Infineon C515C and C517A are examples of 8051 devices with programmable baud-rate generators.

9.9 Memory requirements

The buffered architecture discussed in this chapter is an effective way of managing the transmission of messages and data to a desktop PC.

The biggest problem caused by this approach is the memory load. The root of this difficulty is that fact that, as we discussed in above, the architecture used (to transmit data to the PC) involves a buffer to which the user writes as required; this buffer is then emptied, one character at a time, by a sEOS task.[30]

The buffer itself is very simple (in the code we will describe here):

30. Note that while both the 'transmit' and (where available) 'receive' channels have associated buffers, the transmit buffer is usually larger than the receive buffer, since – in most cases – the direction of data flow is from the microcontroller to the PC. As a result, we focus on the transmit buffer here. However, similar concerns – and solutions – apply to the receive buffer in circumstances where the main direction of information flow is from the PC to the microcontroller.

```
// The transmit buffer length (MAX IS 127; MIN is 1)
#define PC_LINK_TRAN_BUFFER_LENGTH 100

static tByte Tran_buffer[PC_LINK_TRAN_BUFFER_LENGTH];
```

If you run out of memory, then there are several options:

- You can reduce the buffer size. This may mean that the functions in your application must break down the data they send into smaller blocks. Typically, the main implication is that shorter strings must be used.
- You can increase the baud rate, and adapt the code so that the system sends more than one byte of data in every time the RS-232 'update' function is called.
- If using on-chip memory only, you can choose an 8051 device with additional on-chip RAM: for example, Dallas and Infineon produce a number of such devices.

9.10 Example: Displaying elapsed time on a PC

This example illustrates how to link a Standard 8051 device to a PC.

Please note that the crystal used is 11.0592 MHz, for reasons discussed in Section 9.8.

The software is 'write only': data is transferred from the microcontroller to the PC but not vice versa. To illustrate this, the software displays elapsed time on the PC via a terminal emulator program.

In Figure 9.3, we illustrate this software running on the Keil hardware simulator.

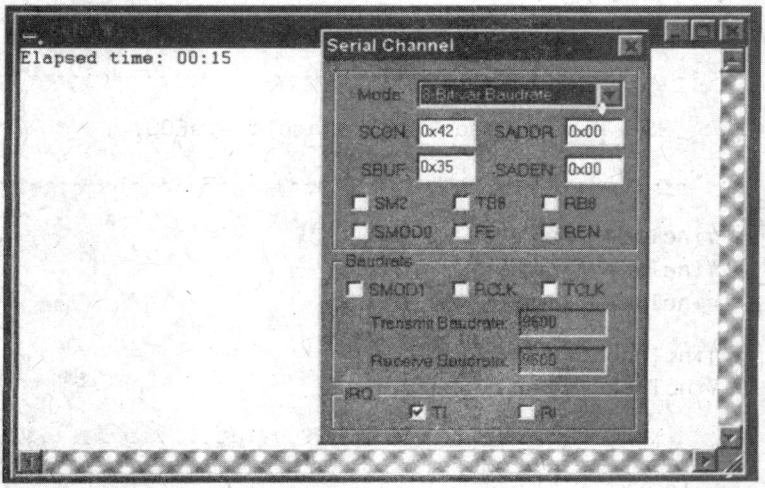

FIGURE 9.3 Output from a simple 'output only' PC-link library, running under the Keil hardware simulator. See text for details

Listing 9.1 Part of the code for a project displaying elapsed time over an RS-232 link

```
/*------------------------------------------------------------------*

   Port.H (v1.00)

  ------------------------------------------------------------------

  'Port Header' (see Chap 5) for the project TIME (see Chap 9)

-*------------------------------------------------------------------*

#ifndef _PORT_H
#define _PORT_H

// ------ PC_0.C -----------------------------------------------------

// Pins 3.0 and 3.1 used for RS-232 interface

#endif

/*------------------------------------------------------------------*
  ---- END OF FILE -------------------------------------------------
-*------------------------------------------------------------------*/
```

Listing 9.2 Part of the code for a project displaying elapsed time over an RS-232 link

```
/*------------------------------------------------------------------*

   Main.c (v1.00)

  ------------------------------------------------------------------

   RS-232 (Elapsed Time) example - sEOS.

-*------------------------------------------------------------------*/

#include "Main.H"
#include "Port.H"
#include "Simple_EOS.H"

#include "PC_O_T1.h"
#include "Elap_232.h"

/* ---------------------------------------------------------------- */

void main(void)
```

```
   {
   // Set baud rate to 9600
   PC_LINK_O_Init_T1(9600);

   // Prepare for elapsed time measurement
   Elapsed_Time_RS232_Init();

   // Set up simple EOS (5ms tick)
   sEOS_Init_Timer2(5);

   while(1) // Super Loop
      {
      sEOS_Go_To_Sleep(); // Enter idle mode to save power
      }
   }

/*------------------------------------------------------------------*-
  ---- END OF FILE -------------------------------------------------
-*------------------------------------------------------------------*/
```

Listing 9.3 Part of the code for a project displaying elapsed time over an RS-232 link

```
/*------------------------------------------------------------------*-

   Elap_232.C (v1.00)

  ------------------------------------------------------------------

   Simple library function for keeping track of elapsed time
   Demo version to display time on PC screen via RS232 link.

-*------------------------------------------------------------------*/

#include "Main.h"
#include "Elap_232.h"
#include "PC_O.h"

// ------ Public variable definitions ------------------------------

tByte Hou_G;
tByte Min_G;
tByte Sec_G;

// ------ Public variable declarations -----------------------------

// See Char_Map.c
```

```
extern const char code CHAR_MAP_G[10];

/*------------------------------------------------------------------*

  Elapsed_Time_RS232_Init()

  Init function for simple library displaying elapsed time on PC
  via RS-232 link.

-*------------------------------------------------------------------*
void Elapsed_Time_RS232_Init(void)
   {
   Hou_G = 0;
   Min_G = 0;
   Sec_G = 0;
   }

/*------------------------------------------------------------------*

  Elapsed_Time_RS232_Update()

  Function for displaying elapsed time on PC Screen.

  *** Must be called once per second ***

-*------------------------------------------------------------------*/
void Elapsed_Time_RS232_Update(void)
   {
   char Time_Str[30] = "\rElapsed time: ";

   if (++Sec_G == 60)
      {
      Sec_G = 0;

      if (++Min_G == 60)
         {
         Min_G = 0;

         if (++Hou_G == 24)
            {
            Hou_G = 0;
            }
         }
      }

   Time_Str[15] = CHAR_MAP_G[Hou_G / 10];
   Time_Str[16] = CHAR_MAP_G[Hou_G % 10];
```

```
   Time_Str[18] = CHAR_MAP_G[Min_G / 10];
   Time_Str[19] = CHAR_MAP_G[Min_G % 10];

   Time_Str[21] = CHAR_MAP_G[Sec_G / 10];
   Time_Str[22] = CHAR_MAP_G[Sec_G % 10];

   // We don't display seconds in this version.
   // We simply use the seconds data to turn on and off the colon
   // (between hours and minutes)
   if ((Sec_G % 2) == 0)
      {
      Time_Str[17] = ':';
      Time_Str[20] = ':';
      }
   else
      {
      Time_Str[17] = ' ';
      Time_Str[20] = ' ';
      }

   PC_LINK_O_Write_String_To_Buffer(Time_Str);
   }

/*------------------------------------------------------------------*-
  ---- END OF FILE -------------------------------------------------
-*------------------------------------------------------------------*/
```

Listing 9.4 Part of the code for a project displaying elapsed time over an RS-232 link

```
/*------------------------------------------------------------------*-

   PC_O_T1.C (v1.00)

  ------------------------------------------------------------------

   Simple write-only PC link library Version A (generic)
   [Sends data to PC - cannot receive data from PC]

   Uses the UART, and Pin 3.1 (Tx)

   See text for details (Chapter 9).

-*------------------------------------------------------------------*/

#include "Main.h"
#include "PC_O_T1.h"
```

```
// ------ Public variable declarations -----------------------

extern tByte Out_written_index_G;
extern tByte Out_waiting_index_G;

/*------------------------------------------------------------*-

  PC_LINK_O_Init_T1()

  This version uses T1 for baud rate generation.

  Uses 8051 (internal) UART hardware

-*------------------------------------------------------------*/
void PC_LINK_O_Init_T1(const tWord BAUD_RATE)
   {
   PCON &= 0x7F; // Set SMOD bit to 0 (don't double baud rates)

   //  Receiver disabled
   //  8-bit data, 1 start bit, 1 stop bit, variable baud rate
   //  (asynchronous)
   SCON = 0x42;

   TMOD |= 0x20; // T1 in mode 2, 8-bit auto reload

   TH1 = (256 - (tByte)((((tLong)OSC_FREQ / 100) * 3125)
            / ((tLong) BAUD_RATE * OSC_PER_INST * 1000)));

   TL1 = TH1;
   TR1 = 1; // Run the timer
   TI = 1;  // Send first character (dummy)

   // Set up the buffers for reading and writing
   Out_written_index_G = 0;
   Out_waiting_index_G = 0;

   // Interrupt *NOT* enabled
   ES = 0;
   }

/*------------------------------------------------------------*-
  ---- END OF FILE -------------------------------------------
-*------------------------------------------------------------*/
```

Listing 9.5 Part of the code for a project displaying elapsed time over an RS-232 link

```
/*------------------------------------------------------------------*-

   PC_O.C (v1.00)

   ------------------------------------------------------------------

   Core files for simple write-only PC link library for 8051
   family
   [Sends data to PC - cannot receive data from PC]

   Uses the UART, and Pin 3.1 (Tx)

   See text for details (Chapter 9).

-*------------------------------------------------------------------*/

#include "Main.h"
#include "PC_O.h"
#include "Elap_232.h"

// ------ Public variable definitions ------------------------------

tByte Out_written_index_G;   // Index of data that has been sent
tByte Out_waiting_index_G;   // Index of data not yet sent

// ------ Private constants ----------------------------------------

// The transmit buffer length
#define TRAN_BUFFER_LENGTH 20

// ------ Private variables ----------------------------------------

static tByte Tran_buffer[TRAN_BUFFER_LENGTH];

static tByte Time_count_G = 0;

/*------------------------------------------------------------------*-

  PC_LINK_O_Update()

  Sends next character from the software transmit buffer

  NOTE: Output-only library (Cannot receive chars)
```

```
    Uses on-chip UART hardware.

-*------------------------------------------------------------------*/
void PC_LINK_O_Update(void)
   {
   // Deal with transmit bytes here
   //
   // Are there any data ready to send?
   if (Out_written_index_G < Out_waiting_index_G)
      {
      PC_LINK_O_Send_Char(Tran_buffer[Out_written_index_G]);

      Out_written_index_G++;
      }
   else
      {
      // No data to send - just reset the buffer index
      Out_waiting_index_G = 0;
      Out_written_index_G = 0;
      }
   }

/*------------------------------------------------------------------*-

  PC_LINK_O_Write_String_To_Buffer()

  Copies a (null terminated) string to the character buffer.
  (The contents of the buffer are then passed over the serial
  link)

-*------------------------------------------------------------------*/
void PC_LINK_O_Write_String_To_Buffer(const char* const STR_PTR)
   {
   tByte i = 0;

   while (STR_PTR[i] != '\0')
      {
      PC_LINK_O_Write_Char_To_Buffer(STR_PTR[i]);
      i++;
      }
   }

/*------------------------------------------------------------------*-

  PC_LINK_O_Write_Char_To_Buffer()
```

```
   Stores a character in the 'write' buffer, ready for
   later transmission

-*---------------------------------------------------------------*/
void PC_LINK_O_Write_Char_To_Buffer(const char CHARACTER)
   {
   // Write to the buffer *only* if there is space
   // (No error reporting in this simple library...)
   if (Out_waiting_index_G < TRAN_BUFFER_LENGTH)
      {
      Tran_buffer[Out_waiting_index_G] = CHARACTER;
      Out_waiting_index_G++;
      }
   }

/*---------------------------------------------------------------*-

   PC_LINK_O_Send_Char()

   Uses on-chip UART hardware.

-*---------------------------------------------------------------*/
void PC_LINK_O_Send_Char(const char CHARACTER)
   {
   tLong Timeout1 = 0;

   if (CHARACTER == '\n')
      {
      Timeout1 = 0;
      while ((++Timeout1) && (TI == 0));

      if (Timeout1 == 0)
         {
         // UART did not respond - error
         // No error reporting in this simple library...
         return;
         }

      TI = 0;
      SBUF = 0x0D; // Output CR
      }
```

```
   Timeout1 = 0;
   while ((++Timeout1) && (TI == 0));

   if (Timeout1 == 0)
      {
      // UART did not respond - error
      // No error reporting in this simple library...
      return;
      }

   TI = 0;

   SBUF = CHARACTER;
   }

/*------------------------------------------------------------------*-
  ---- END OF FILE -------------------------------------------------
-*------------------------------------------------------------------*/
```

Listing 9.6 Part of the code for a project displaying elapsed time over an RS-232 link

```
/*------------------------------------------------------------------*-

   Simple_EOS.C (v1.00)

  ------------------------------------------------------------------

   Main file for Simple Embedded Operating System (sEOS) for 8051.

   - This version for project TIME (Chap 9).

-*------------------------------------------------------------------*/

#include "Main.H"
#include "Simple_EOS.H"

#include "PC_O.H"
#include "Elap_232.H"

// ------ Private variable definitions ----------------------
static tByte Call_count_G = 0;

/*------------------------------------------------------------------*-

  sEOS_ISR()
```

```
   Invoked periodically by Timer 2 overflow:
   see sEOS_Init_Timer2() for timing details.

-*-------------------------------------------------------------*/
void sEOS_ISR() interrupt INTERRUPT_Timer_2_Overflow
   {
   // Must manually reset the T2 flag
   TF2 = 0
   //===== USER CODE - Begin ==================================
   // Call RS-232 update function every 5ms
   PC_LINK_O_Update();

   // This ISR is called every 5 ms
   // - only want to update time every second
   if (++Call_count_G == 200)
      {
      // Time to update time
      Call_count_G = 0;

      // Call time update function
      Elapsed_Time_RS232_Update();
      }
   //===== USER CODE - End ====================================
   }

/*-------------------------------------------------------------*-

   sEOS_Init_Timer2()

   Sets up Timer 2 to drive the simple EOS.

   Parameter gives tick interval in MILLISECONDS.

   Max tick interval is ~60ms (12 MHz oscillator).

   Note: Precise tick intervals are only possible with certain
   oscillator / tick interval combinations. If timing is important,
   you should check the timing calculations manually.

-*-------------------------------------------------------------*/
void sEOS_Init_Timer2(const tByte TICK_MS)
   {
   tLong Inc;
```

```
   tWord Reload_16;
   tByte Reload_08H, Reload_08L;

   // Timer 2 is configured as a 16-bit timer,
   // which is automatically reloaded when it overflows
   T2CON   = 0x04;   // Load Timer 2 control register

   // Number of timer increments required (max 65536)
   Inc = ((tLong)TICK_MS *  (OSC_FREQ/1000))  /
   (tLong)OSC_PER_INST;

   // 16-bit reload value
   Reload_16 = (tWord) (65536UL - Inc);

   // 8-bit reload values (High & Low)
   Reload_08H = (tByte)(Reload_16 / 256);
   Reload_08L = (tByte)(Reload_16 % 256);

   // Used for manually checking timing (in simulator)
   //P2 = Reload_08H;
   //P3 = Reload_08L;

   TH2    = Reload_08H;      // Load Timer 2 high byte
   RCAP2H = Reload_08H;      // Load Timer 2 reload capt. reg. high
                                byte
   TL2    = Reload_08L;      // Load Timer 2 low byte
   RCAP2L = Reload_08L;      // Load Timer 2 reload capt. reg. low
                                byte

   // Timer 2 interrupt is enabled, and ISR will be called
   // whenever the timer overflows.
   ET2 = 1;

   // Start Timer 2 running
   TR2 = 1;

   EA = 1;            // Globally enable interrupts
   }

/*------------------------------------------------------------*-

  sEOS_Go_To_Sleep()

  This operating system enters 'idle mode' between clock ticks
  to save power. The next clock tick will return the processor
  to the normal operating state.
```

```
-*------------------------------------------------------------------*/
void sEOS_Go_To_Sleep(void)
   {
   PCON |= 0x01;     // Enter idle mode (generic 8051 version)
   }

/*------------------------------------------------------------------*-
  ---- END OF FILE ------------------------------------------------
-*------------------------------------------------------------------*/
```

9.11 The Serial-Menu architecture

In Chapter 4, we discussed the fact that mechanical switches are a very common part of the user interface for embedded applications. Another common interface feature is the Serial Menu.

The Serial Menu architecture involves the use of a desktop PC (or similar) on which a list of menu options will be displayed. This menu will allow the user to execute code on an embedded system, which may be located some distance away.

The embedded menu architecture is particularly common in data acquisition and control applications. We give an example of both types of application in the sections that follow.

9.12 Example: Data acquisition

In this section, we give an example of a simple data-acquisition system with a Serial Menu architecture.

In this case, using the menu, the user can determine the state of the input pins on Port 1 or Port 2, as required (Figure 9.4).

The code required to generate this behaviour is given in Listing 9.7 to Listing 9.11.

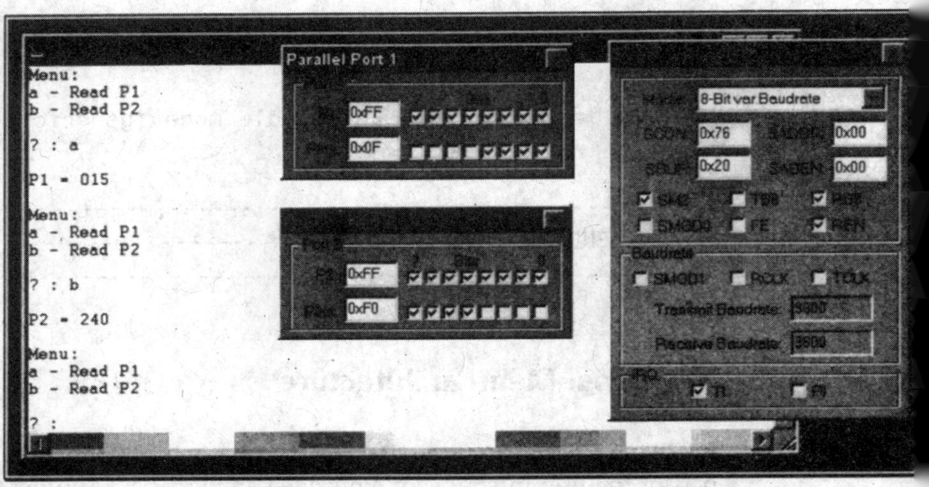

FIGURE 9.4 Running a data-acquisition example in the simulator. See text for details

Listing 9.7 Part of a data-acquisition example.

```
/*--------------------------------------------------------------------*

   Main.c (v1.00)

   -------------------------------------------------------------------

   Data acquisition example.

-*--------------------------------------------------------------------*/

#include "Main.h"
#include "Simple_EOS.H"

#include "PC_IO_T1.h"

/* ............................................................... */
/* ............................................................... */

void main(void)
   {
   // Set baud rate to 9600: generic 8051 version
   PC_LINK_IO_Init_T1(9600);

   // Set up sEOS (5ms tick)
   sEOS_Init_Timer2(5);
```

```
    while(1) // Super Loop
      {
      sEOS_Go_To_Sleep(); // Enter idle mode to save power
      }
    }

/*------------------------------------------------------------------*-
  ---- END OF FILE -------------------------------------------------
-*------------------------------------------------------------------*/
```

Listing 9.8 Part of a data-acquisition example

```
/*------------------------------------------------------------------*-

   Menu_Data.C (v1.00)

  ------------------------------------------------------------------

   Simple framework for menu-driven data acquisition.

   Use 'Hyperterminal' (under Windows 95, 98, 2000) or similar
   terminal emulator program on other operating systems.

   Terminal options:

   - Data bits    = 8
   - Parity       = None
   - Stop bits    = 1
   - Flow control = Xon / Xoff

-*------------------------------------------------------------------*/

#include "Main.H"
#include "Port.H"

#include "Menu_Data.h"
#include "PC_IO.h"

// ------ Public variable declarations -----------------------------
// See Char_Map.c
extern const char code CHAR_MAP_G[10];

// ------ Private variables ----------------------------------------
static bit First_time_only_G;

/*------------------------------------------------------------------*-
```

```
   MENU_Command_Processor()

   This function is the main menu 'command processor' function.

   Schedule this (say) once every 10 ms (approx.).

-*------------------------------------------------------------------*/
void MENU_Command_Processor(void)
   {
   char Ch;

   if (First_time_only_G == 0)
      {
      First_time_only_G = 1;
      MENU_Show_Menu();
      }

   // Check for user inputs
   PC_LINK_IO_Update();

   Ch = PC_LINK_IO_Get_Char_From_Buffer();

   if (Ch != PC_LINK_IO_NO_CHAR)
      {
      MENU_Perform_Task(Ch);
      MENU_Show_Menu();
      }
   }

/*------------------------------------------------------------------*-

   MENU_Show_Menu()

   Display menu options on PC screen (via serial link)
   - edit as required to meet the needs of your application.

-*------------------------------------------------------------------*/
void MENU_Show_Menu(void)
   {
   PC_LINK_IO_Write_String_To_Buffer("Menu:\n");
   PC_LINK_IO_Write_String_To_Buffer("a - Read P1\n");
   PC_LINK_IO_Write_String_To_Buffer("b - Read P2\n\n");
   PC_LINK_IO_Write_String_To_Buffer("? : ");
   }

/*------------------------------------------------------------------*-
```

```
  MENU_Perform_Task()

  Perform the required user task
  - edit as required to match the needs of your application.

-*------------------------------------------------------------*/
void MENU_Perform_Task(char c)
   {
   // Echo the menu option
   PC_LINK_IO_Write_Char_To_Buffer(c);
   PC_LINK_IO_Write_Char_To_Buffer('\n');

   // Perform the task
   switch (c)
      {
      case 'a':
      case 'A':
         {
         Get_Data_From_Port1();
         break;
         }

      case 'b':
      case 'B':
         {
         Get_Data_From_Port2();
         break;
         }
      }
   }

/*------------------------------------------------------------*-

  Get_Data_From_Port1()

-*------------------------------------------------------------*/
void Get_Data_From_Port1(void)
   {
   tByte Port1 = Data_Port1;
   char String[11] = "\nP1 = XXX\n\n";
```

```
    String[6] = CHAR_MAP_G[Port1 / 100];
    String[7] = CHAR_MAP_G[(Port1 / 10) % 10];
    String[8] = CHAR_MAP_G[Port1 % 10];

    PC_LINK_IO_Write_String_To_Buffer(String);
    }

/*------------------------------------------------------------------*-

   Get_Data_From_Port2()

-*------------------------------------------------------------------*/
void Get_Data_From_Port2(void)
    {
    tByte Port2 = Data_Port2;
    char String[11] = '\nP2 = XXX\n\n';

    String[6] = CHAR_MAP_G[Port2 / 100];
    String[7] = CHAR_MAP_G[(Port2 / 10) % 10];
    String[8] = CHAR_MAP_G[Port2 % 10];

    PC_LINK_IO_Write_String_To_Buffer(String);
    }

/*------------------------------------------------------------------*-
   ---- END OF FILE -------------------------------------------------
-*------------------------------------------------------------------*/
```

Listing 9.9 Part of a data-acquisition example

```
/*------------------------------------------------------------------*-

    PC_IO_T1.C (v1.00)

  ----------------------------------------------------------------

    PC link library. Bidirectional. T1 used for baud rate generation.

    Uses the UART, and Pins 3.1 (Tx) and 3.0 (Rx)

    See text for details (Chapter 9).

-*------------------------------------------------------------------*/

#include "Main.h"
#include "PC_IO_T1.h"
```

```
// ------ Public variable declarations ---------------------

extern tByte In_read_index_G;
extern tByte In_waiting_index_G;

extern tByte Out_written_index_G;
extern tByte Out_waiting_index_G;

/*------------------------------------------------------------------*-

  PC_LINK_IO_Init_T1()

  This (generic) version uses T1 for baud rate generation.

-*------------------------------------------------------------------*/
void PC_LINK_IO_Init_T1(const tWord BAUD_RATE)
   {
   PCON &= 0x7F; // Set SMOD bit to 0 (don't double baud rates)

   // Receiver enabled.
   // 8-bit data, 1 start bit, 1 stop bit,
   // Variable baud rate (asynchronous)
   // Receive flag will only be set if a valid stop bit is received
   // Set TI (transmit buffer is empty)
   SCON = 0x72;

   TMOD |= 0x20; // T1 in mode 2, 8-bit auto reload

   TH1 = (256 - (tByte)((((tLong)OSC_FREQ / 100) * 3125)
            / ((tLong) BAUD_RATE * OSC_PER_INST  * 1000)));

   TL1 = TH1;
   TR1 = 1;    // Run the timer
   TI = 1;     // Send first character (dummy)

   // Set up the buffers for reading and writing
   In_read_index_G = 0;
   In_waiting_index_G = 0;
   Out_written_index_G = 0;
   Out_waiting_index_G = 0;

   // Interrupt *NOT* enabled
   ES = 0;
   }

/*------------------------------------------------------------------*-
  ---- END OF FILE -------------------------------------------------
-*------------------------------------------------------------------*/
```

Listing 9.10 Part of a data-acquisition example

```
/*------------------------------------------------------------------*-

   PC_IO.C (v1.00)

  ------------------------------------------------------------------

  Core files for simple PC link library for 8051 family

  Uses the UART, and Pins 3.1 (Tx) and 3.0 (Rx)

  See text for details (Chapter 9).

-*------------------------------------------------------------------*/

#include "Main.h"
#include "PC_IO.h"

// ------ Public variable definitions ------------------------------

tByte In_read_index_G;     // Data in buffer that has been read
tByte In_waiting_index_G;  // Data in buffer not yet read

tByte Out_written_index_G;  // Data in buffer that has been sent
tByte Out_waiting_index_G;  // Data in buffer not yet sent

// ------ Private function prototypes ------------------------------

static void PC_LINK_IO_Send_Char(const char);

// ------ Private constants ----------------------------------------

// The receive buffer length
#define RECV_BUFFER_LENGTH 8

// The transmit buffer length
#define TRAN_BUFFER_LENGTH 50

#define XON 0x11
#define XOFF 0x13

// ------ Private variables ----------------------------------------

static tByte Recv_buffer[RECV_BUFFER_LENGTH];
static tByte Tran_buffer[TRAN_BUFFER_LENGTH];

/*------------------------------------------------------------------*-
```

```
  PC_LINK_IO_Update()

  Checks for character in the UART (hardware) receive buffer
  Sends next character from the software transmit buffer

-*---------------------------------------------------------------*/
void PC_LINK_IO_Update(void)
   {
   // Deal with transmit bytes here

   // Is there any data ready to send?
   if (Out_written_index_G < Out_waiting_index_G)
      {
      PC_LINK_IO_Send_Char(Tran_buffer[Out_written_index_G]);

      Out_written_index_G++;
      }
   else
      {
      // No data to send - just reset the buffer index
      Out_waiting_index_G = 0;
      Out_written_index_G = 0;
      }

   // Only dealing with received bytes here
   // -> Just check the RI flag
   if (RI == 1)
      {
      // Flag only set when a valid stop bit is received,
      // -> data ready to be read into the received buffer

      // Want to read into index 0, if old data has been read
      // (simple ~circular buffer)
      if (In_waiting_index_G == In_read_index_G)
         {
         In_waiting_index_G = 0;
         In_read_index_G = 0;
         }

      // Read the data from UART buffer
      Recv_buffer[In_waiting_index_G] = SBUF;

      if (In_waiting_index_G < RECV_BUFFER_LENGTH)
         {
```

```
            // Increment without overflowing buffer
            In_waiting_index_G++;
            }

         RI = 0; // Clear RT flag
         }
      }

/*------------------------------------------------------------------*-

   PC_LINK_IO_Write_Char_To_Buffer()
   Stores a character in the 'write' buffer, ready for
   later transmission

-*------------------------------------------------------------------*/
void PC_LINK_IO_Write_Char_To_Buffer(const char CHARACTER)
   {
   // Write to the buffer *only* if there is space
   // - No error reporting in this simple library...
   if (Out_waiting_index_G < TRAN_BUFFER_LENGTH)
      {
      Tran_buffer[Out_waiting_index_G] = CHARACTER;
      Out_waiting_index_G++;
      }
   }

/*------------------------------------------------------------------*-

   PC_LINK_IO_Write_String_To_Buffer()

   Copies a (null terminated) string to the character buffer.
   (The contents of the buffer are then passed over the serial link)

   STR_PTR - Pointer to the NULL-TERMINATED string.

-*------------------------------------------------------------------*/
void PC_LINK_IO_Write_String_To_Buffer(const char* const STR_PTR)
   {
   tByte i = 0;

   while (STR_PTR[i] != '\0')
      {
      PC_LINK_IO_Write_Char_To_Buffer(STR_PTR[i]);
      i++;
```

```
      }
   }
/*--------------------------------------------------------------------*-

   PC_LINK_IO_Get_Char_From_Buffer()

   Retrieves a character from the (software) buffer, if available

   The character from the buffer is returned, or - if no
   data are available - PC_LINK_IO_NO_CHAR is returned.

-*--------------------------------------------------------------------*/
char PC_LINK_IO_Get_Char_From_Buffer(void)
   {
   char Ch = PC_LINK_IO_NO_CHAR;

   // If there is new data in the buffer
   if (In_read_index_G < In_waiting_index_G)
      {
      Ch = Recv_buffer[In_read_index_G];

      if (In_read_index_G < RECV_BUFFER_LENGTH)
         {
         In_read_index_G++;
         }
      }

   return Ch;
   }

/*--------------------------------------------------------------------*-

   PC_LINK_IO_Send_Char()

   Based on Keil sample code, with added (loop) timeouts.
   Implements Xon / Off control.

   Uses on-chip UART hardware.

-*--------------------------------------------------------------------*/
void PC_LINK_IO_Send_Char(const char CHARACTER)
   {
   tLong Timeout1 = 0;
   tLong Timeout2 = 0;

   if (CHARACTER == '\n')
      {
```

```
      if (RI)
         {
         if (SBUF == XOFF)
            {
            Timeout2 = 0;
            do {
            RI = 0;

            // Wait for uart (with simple timeout)
            Timeout1 = 0;
            while ((++Timeout1) && (RI == 0));

             if (Timeout1 == 0)
               {
               // UART did not respond - error
               // No error reporting in this simple library...
               return;
               }

            } while ((++Timeout2) && (SBUF != XON));

         if (Timeout2 == 0)
            {
            // UART did not respond - error
            // No error reporting in this simple library...
            return;
            }

         RI = 0;
         }
      }

   Timeout1 = 0;
   while ((++Timeout1) && (TI == 0));

   if (Timeout1 == 0)
      {
      // UART did not respond - error
      // No error reporting in this simple library...
      return;
      }

   TI = 0;
   SBUF = 0x0D; // Output CR
   }
```

```
   if (RI)
      {
      if (SBUF == XOFF)
         {
         Timeout2 = 0;

         do {
            RI = 0;

            // Wait for UART (with simple timeout)
            Timeout1 = 0;
            while ((++Timeout1) && (RI == 0));

            if (Timeout1 == 0)
               {
               // UART did not respond - error
               // No error reporting in this simple library...
               return;
               }

            } while ((++Timeout2) && (SBUF != XON));

         RI = 0;
         }
      }

   Timeout1 = 0;
   while ((++Timeout1) && (TI == 0));

   if (Timeout1 == 0)
      {
      // UART did not respond - error
      // No error reporting in this simple library...
      return;
      }

   TI = 0;

   SBUF = CHARACTER;
   }

/*------------------------------------------------------------------*-
  ---- END OF FILE -------------------------------------------------
-*------------------------------------------------------------------*/
```

Listing 9.11 Part of a data-acquisition example

```
/*------------------------------------------------------------------*-

   Simple_EOS.C (v1.00)

  ------------------------------------------------------------------

   Main file for Simple Embedded Operating System (sEOS) for 8051.

   - This version for project DATA_ACQ (Chapter 9).

-*------------------------------------------------------------------*/

#include "Main.H"
#include "Simple_EOS.H"

#include "Menu_Data.H"

/*------------------------------------------------------------------*-

  sEOS_ISR()

  Invoked periodically by Timer 2 overflow:
  see sEOS_Init_Timer2() for timing details.

-*------------------------------------------------------------------*/
void sEOS_ISR() interrupt INTERRUPT_Timer_2_Overflow
   {
   // Must manually reset the T2 flag
   TF2 = 0;
   //===== USER CODE - Begin ====================================
   // Call MENU_Command_Processor every 5ms
   MENU_Command_Processor();

   //===== USER CODE - End ======================================
   }

/*------------------------------------------------------------------*-

  sEOS_Init_Timer2()

  Sets up Timer 2 to drive the simple EOS.

  Parameter gives tick interval in MILLISECONDS.

  Max tick interval is ~60ms (12 MHz oscillator).
```

```
   Note: Precise tick intervals are only possible with certain
   oscillator / tick interval combinations. If timing is important,
   you should check the timing calculations manually.
-*------------------------------------------------------------------*/
void sEOS_Init_Timer2(const tByte TICK_MS)
   {
   tLong Inc;
   tWord Reload_16;
   tByte Reload_08H, Reload_08L;

   // Timer 2 is configured as a 16-bit timer,
   // which is automatically reloaded when it overflows
   T2CON   = 0x04;   // Load Timer 2 control register

   // Number of timer increments required (max 65536)
   Inc = ((tLong)TICK_MS *  (OSC_FREQ/1000)) / (tLong)OSC_PER_INST;

   // 16-bit reload value
   Reload_16 = (tWord) (65536UL - Inc);

   // 8-bit reload values (High & Low)
   Reload_08H = (tByte)(Reload_16 / 256);
   Reload_08L = (tByte)(Reload_16 % 256);

   // Used for manually checking timing (in simulator)
   //P2 = Reload_08H;
   //P3 = Reload_08L;

   TH2    = Reload_08H; // Load T2 high byte
   RCAP2H = Reload_08H; // Load T2 reload capt. reg. high byte
   TL2    = Reload_08L; // Load T2 low byte
   RCAP2L = Reload_08L; // Load T2 reload capt. reg. low byte

   // Timer 2 interrupt is enabled, and ISR will be called
   // whenever the timer overflows.
   ET2    = 1;

   // Start Timer 2 running
   TR2 = 1;

   EA = 1;            // Globally enable interrupts
   }

/*------------------------------------------------------------------*-
```

```
  sEOS_Go_To_Sleep()

  This operating system enters 'idle mode' between clock ticks
  to save power. The next clock tick will return the processor
  to the normal operating state.

-*------------------------------------------------------------------*/
void sEOS_Go_To_Sleep(void)
   {
   PCON |= 0x01;    // Enter idle mode (generic 8051 version)
   }

/*------------------------------------------------------------------*-
  ---- END OF FILE -------------------------------------------------
-*------------------------------------------------------------------*/
```

9.13 Example: Remote-control robot

In this example, we will use a Serial Menu architecture to control a remote robot. Such devices are used for inspecting the inside of gas pipes and for landmine detection or bomb disposal.

In our simplified example, the robot is power by two stepper motors (Figure 9.5). Such motors rotate a fixed amount (typically 7.5°) in response to an applied voltage

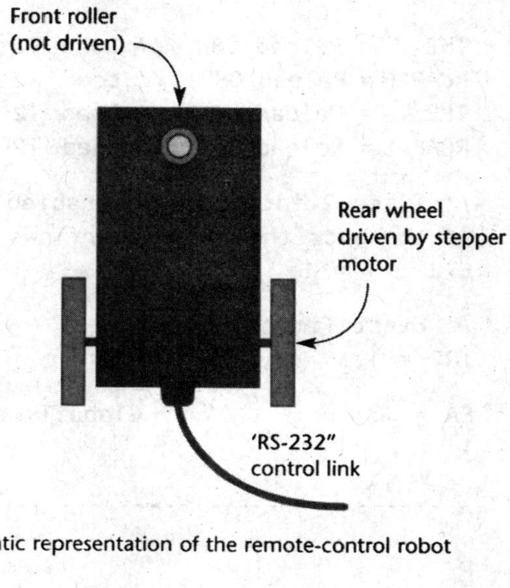

FIGURE 9.5 A schematic representation of the remote-control robot

pulse. In this case, the two motors are driven by pulses from pins on Port 1. By 'stepping' one or both motors, we can control the direction of movement.

Output from the system running in the simulator is shown in Figure 9.6. Complete code for this example is given on the CD.

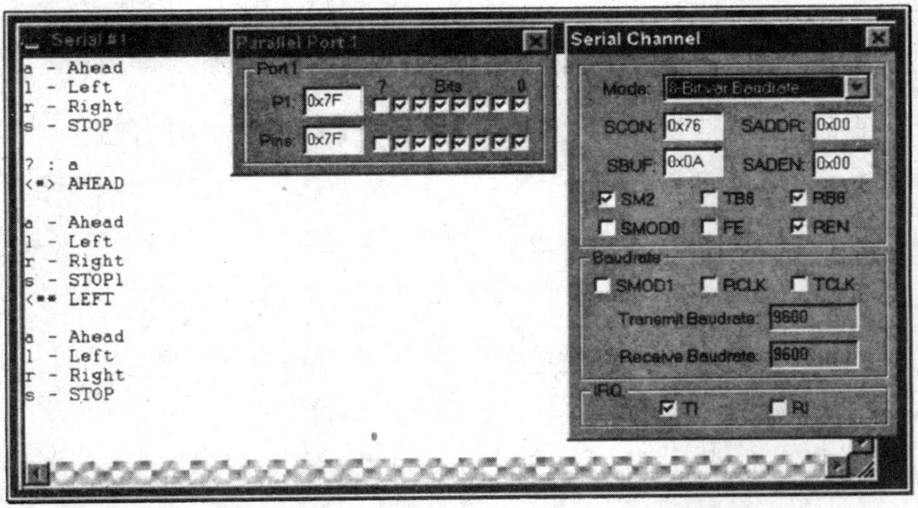

FIGURE 9.6 Interface to a remotely-controlled robot, running in the simulator

9.14 Conclusions

In this chapter, we have examined how the serial interface on the 8051 microcontroller may be used in practical embedded systems involving data transfers to (or from) a desktop PC, or similar device.

In the next chapter a case study is presented. This study illustrates how the key techniques discussed throughout this book may be used, in combination, in order to create substantial and reliable systems.

chapter 10

Case study: Intruder alarm system

10.1 Introduction

In this case study, we will consider the design and implementation of a small intruder alarm system suitable for detecting attempted thefts in a home or business environment.

As an example of a typical application of this type of system, Figure 10.1 shows a small art gallery containing three statues.

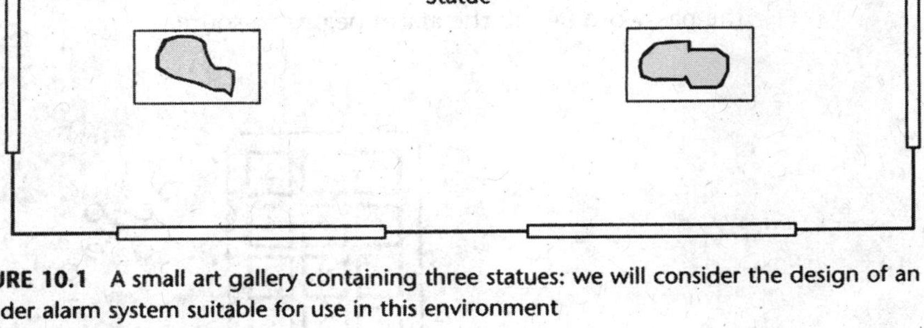

FIGURE 10.1 A small art gallery containing three statues: we will consider the design of an intruder alarm system suitable for use in this environment

Figure 10.2 shows the same gallery with the alarm system installed. In this figure, each of the windows has a sensor to detect class breakage. A magnetic sensor is also attached to the door. In each case, the sensors appear to be simple switches as far as the alarm system is concerned. Figure 10.2 also shows a 'bell box' outside the property: this will sound if an intruder is detected.

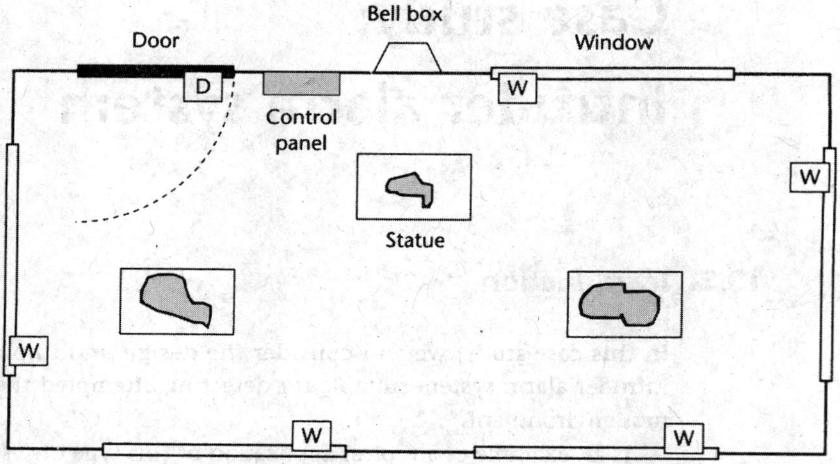

FIGURE 10.2 The art gallery with alarm system installed. See text for details

Inside the door (in Figure 10.2), we have the alarm control panel: this consists mainly of a small keypad, plus an additional 'buzzer' to indicate that the alarm has sounded (Figure 10.3). The alarm system is designed in such a way that the user – having set the alarm by entering a four-digit password – has time to open the door and leave the room before the monitoring process starts. Similarly, if the user opens the door when the system is armed, he or she will have time to enter the password before the alarm begins to sound.

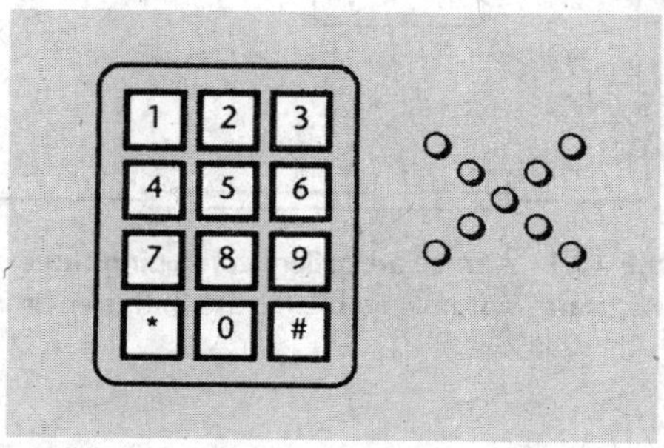

FIGURE 10.3 The main control panel for the alarm system

Overall, the system is to operate as follows:

- When initially activated, the system is in 'Disarmed' state.
- In **Disarmed** state, the sensors are ignored. The alarm does not sound. The system remains in this state until the user enters a valid password via the keypad (in our demonstration system, the password is '1234'). When a valid password is entered, the systems enters 'Arming' state.
- In **Arming** state, the system waits for 60 seconds, to allow the user to leave the area before the monitoring process begins. After 60 seconds, the system enters 'Armed' state.
- In **Armed** state, the status of the various system sensors is monitored. If a window sensor is tripped,[31] the system enters 'Intruder' state. If the door sensor is tripped, the system enters 'Disarming' state. The keypad activity is also monitored: if a correct password is typed in, the system enters 'Disarmed' state.
- In **Disarming** state, we assume that the door has been opened by someone who may be an authorized system user. The system remains in this state for up to 60 seconds, after which – by default – it enters Intruder state. If, during the 60-second period, the user enters the correct password, the system enters 'Disarmed' state.
- In **Intruder** state, an alarm will sound. The alarm will keep sounding (indefinitely), until the correct password is entered.

Overall, our demonstration system is somewhat simplified, but the overall system architecture is correct, and the code may be easily extended to add additional features.

10.2 The software architecture

As the description above makes clear, this system translates naturally into a multi-state task, of the type discussed in Chapter 8.

10.3 Key software components used in this example

This case study uses the following software components:

- Software to control external port pins (to activate the external bell), as introduced in Chapter 3.

31. In our demonstration system, only a single window sensor is mentioned.

- Switch reading, as discussed in Chapter 4, to process the inputs from the door and window sensors. Note that – in this simple example (intended for use in the simulator) – no switch debouncing is carried out. This feature can be added, if required, without difficulty.
- The embedded operating system, sEOS, introduced in Chapter 7.
- A simple 'keypad' library, based on a bank of switches. Note that – to simplify the use of the keypad library in the simulator – we have assumed the presence of only eight keys in the example program (0 – 7). This final system would probably use at least 10 keys (see Figure 10.3): support for additional keys can be easily added if required.
- The RS-232 library (from Chapter 9) is used to illustrate the operation of the program. This library would not be necessary in the final system (but it might be useful to retain it, to support system maintenance).

10.4 Running the program

Figure 10.4 shows this system in operation in the Keil simulator.

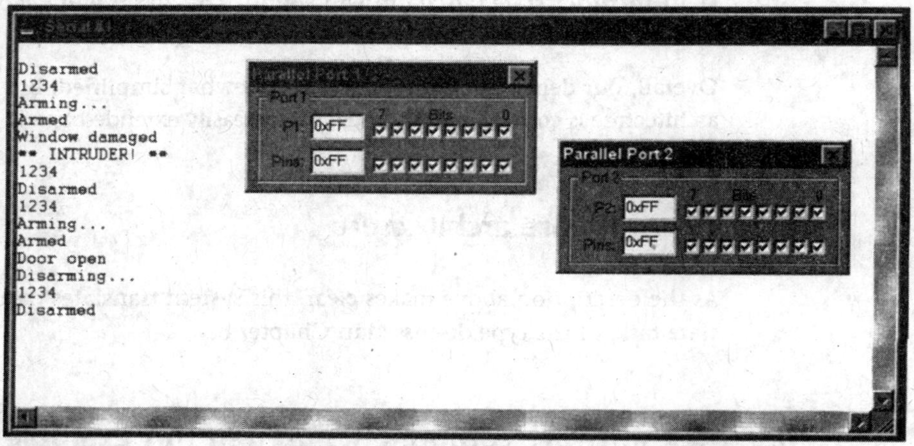

FIGURE 10.4 The intruder alarm running in the simulator

10.5 The software

A full listing of all the files associated with this project are given in this section. These files are also included on the CD.

Listing 10.1 Part of the intruder-alarm code (the Project Header file)

```
/*------------------------------------------------------------------*-

   Main.H (v1.00)

  ------------------------------------------------------------------

   'Project Header' (see Chap 5).

-*------------------------------------------------------------------*/
#ifndef _MAIN_H
#define _MAIN_H

//------------------------------------------------------------------
// WILL NEED TO EDIT THIS SECTION FOR EVERY PROJECT
//------------------------------------------------------------------

// Must include the appropriate microcontroller header file here
#include <reg52.h>

// Oscillator / resonator frequency (in Hz) e.g. (11059200UL)
#define OSC_FREQ (11059200UL)

// Number of oscillations per instruction (12, etc)
// 12 - Original 8051 / 8052 and numerous modern versions
//  6 - Various Infineon and Philips devices, etc.
//  4 - Dallas 320, 520 etc.
//  1 - Dallas 420, etc.
#define OSC_PER_INST (12)

//------------------------------------------------------------------
// SHOULD NOT NEED TO EDIT THE SECTIONS BELOW
//------------------------------------------------------------------

// Typedefs (see Chap 5)
typedef unsigned char tByte;
typedef unsigned int tWord;
typedef unsigned long tLong;

// Interrupts (see Chap 7)
#define INTERRUPT_Timer_0_Overflow 1
#define INTERRUPT_Timer_1_Overflow 3
#define INTERRUPT_Timer_2_Overflow 5
```

```
#endif

/*------------------------------------------------------------------*-
  ---- END OF FILE -------------------------------------------------
-*------------------------------------------------------------------*/
```

Listing 10.2 Part of the intruder-alarm code (the Port Header file)

```
/*------------------------------------------------------------------*-

   Port.H (v1.00)

  ------------------------------------------------------------------

   'Port Header' (see Chap 5) for project INTRUDER (see Chap 10)

-*------------------------------------------------------------------*/

// ------ Keypad.C -----------------------------------------------

#define KEYPAD_PORT P2

sbit K0 = KEYPAD_PORT^0;
sbit K1 = KEYPAD_PORT^1;
sbit K2 = KEYPAD_PORT^2;
sbit K3 = KEYPAD_PORT^3;
sbit K4 = KEYPAD_PORT^4;
sbit K5 = KEYPAD_PORT^5;
sbit K6 = KEYPAD_PORT^6;
sbit K7 = KEYPAD_PORT^7;

// ------ Intruder.C ---------------------------------------------
sbit Sensor_pin = P1^0;
sbit Sounder_pin = P1^7;

// ------ Lnk_0.C ------------------------------------------------

// Pins 3.0 and 3.1 used for RS-232 interface

/*------------------------------------------------------------------*-
  ---- END OF FILE -------------------------------------------------
-*------------------------------------------------------------------*/
```

Listing 10.3 Part of the intruder-alarm code (Main.C)

```
/*------------------------------------------------------------------*-

   Main.c (v1.00)

  ------------------------------------------------------------------

   Simple intruder alarm system.

-*------------------------------------------------------------------*/

#include "Main.H"
#include "Port.H"
#include "Simple_EOS.H"

#include "PC_O_T1.h"
#include "Keypad.h"
#include "Intruder.h"

/* ................................................................ */

void main(void)
   {
   // Set baud rate to 9600
   PC_LINK_O_Init_T1(9600);

   // Prepare the keypad
   KEYPAD_Init();

   // Prepare the intruder alarm
   INTRUDER_Init();

   // Set up simple EOS (5ms tick)
   sEOS_Init_Timer2(5);

   while(1) // Super Loop
      {
      sEOS_Go_To_Sleep();  // Enter idle mode to save power
      }
   }

/*------------------------------------------------------------------*-
  ---- END OF FILE -------------------------------------------------
-*------------------------------------------------------------------*/
```

Listing 10.4 Part of the intruder-alarm code (Intruder.H)

```
/*------------------------------------------------------------------*-

   Intruder.H (v1.00)

  ------------------------------------------------------------------

   - See Intruder.C for details.

-*------------------------------------------------------------------*/

#include "Main.H"

// ------ Public function prototypes -------------------------------

void INTRUDER_Init(void);
void INTRUDER_Update(void);

/*------------------------------------------------------------------*-
  ---- END OF FILE -------------------------------------------------
-*------------------------------------------------------------------*/
```

Listing 10.5 Part of the intruder-alarm code (Intruder.C)

```
/*------------------------------------------------------------------*-

   Intruder.C (v1.00)

  ------------------------------------------------------------------

   Multi-state framework for intruder alarm system.

-*------------------------------------------------------------------*/

#include "Main.H"
#include "Port.H"

#include "Intruder.H"

#include "Keypad.h"
#include "PC_O.h"

// ------ Private data type declarations ---------------------------

// Possible system states
typedef
enum
{DISARMED, ARMING, ARMED, DISARMING, INTRUDER} eSystem_state;
```

```
// ------ Private function prototypes ----------------------

bit INTRUDER_Get_Password_G(void);
bit INTRUDER_Check_Window_Sensors(void);
bit INTRUDER_Check_Door_Sensor(void);
void INTRUDER_Sound_Alarm(void);

// ------ Private variables --------------------------------

static eSystem_state System_state_G;

tWord State_call_count_G;

char Input_G[4] = {'X','X','X','X'};
char Password_G[4] = {'1','2','3','4'};

tByte Position_G;

bit New_state_G = 0;

bit Alarm_bit = 0;

/* ------------------------------------------------------- */
void INTRUDER_Init(void)
   {
   // Set the initial system state (DISARMED)
   System_state_G = DISARMED;

   // Set the 'time in state' variable to 0
   State_call_count_G = 0;

   // Clear the keypad buffer
   KEYPAD_Clear_Buffer();

   // Set the 'New state' flag
   New_state_G = 1;

   // Set the (two) sensor pins to 'read' mode
   Window_sensor_pin = 1;
   Sounder_pin = 1;
   }

/* ------------------------------------------------------- */
void INTRUDER_Update(void)
   {
```

```
   // Incremented every time
   if (State_call_count_G < 65534)
      {
      State_call_count_G++;
      }

   // Call every 50 ms
   switch (System_state_G)
      {
      case DISARMED:
         {
         if (New_state_G)
            {
            PC_LINK_O_Write_String_To_Buffer("\nDisarmed");
            New_state_G = 0;
            }

         // Make sure alarm is switched off
         Sounder_pin = 1;

         // Wait for correct password ...
         if (INTRUDER_Get_Password_G() == 1)
            {
            System_state_G = ARMING;
            New_state_G = 1;
            State_call_count_G = 0;
            break;
            }

         break;
         }

      case ARMING:
         {
         if (New_state_G)
            {
            PC_LINK_O_Write_String_To_Buffer("\nArming...");
            New_state_G = 0;
            }

         // Remain here for 60 seconds (50 ms tick assumed)
         if (++State_call_count_G > 1200)
            {
```

```
         System_state_G = ARMED;
         New_state_G = 1;
         State_call_count_G = 0;
         break;
         }

      break;
      }

   case ARMED:
      {
      if (New_state_G)
         {
         PC_LINK_O_Write_String_To_Buffer("\nArmed");
         New_state_G = 0;
         }

      // First, check the window sensors
      if (INTRUDER_Check_Window_Sensors() == 1)
         {
         // An intruder detected
         System_state_G = INTRUDER;
         New_state_G = 1;
         State_call_count_G = 0;
         break;
         }

      // Next, check the door sensors
      if (INTRUDER_Check_Door_Sensor() == 1)
         {
         // May be authorised user - go to 'Disarming' state
         System_state_G = DISARMING;
         New_state_G = 1;
         State_call_count_G = 0;
         break;
         }

      // Finally, check for correct password
      if (INTRUDER_Get_Password_G() == 1)
         {
         System_state_G = DISARMED;
         New_state_G = 1;
         State_call_count_G = 0;
```

```
         break;
         }

      break;
      }

   case DISARMING:
      {
      if (New_state_G)
         {
         PC_LINK_O_Write_String_To_Buffer("\nDisarming...");
         New_state_G = 0;
         }

      // Remain here for 60 seconds (50 ms tick assumed)
      // to allow user to enter the password
      // - after time up, sound alarm
      if (++State_call_count_G > 1200)
         {
         System_state_G = INTRUDER;
         New_state_G = 1;
         State_call_count_G = 0;
         break;
         }

      // Still need to check the window sensors
      if (INTRUDER_Check_Window_Sensors() == 1)
         {
         // An intruder detected
         System_state_G = INTRUDER;
         New_state_G = 1;
         State_call_count_G = 0;
         break;
         }

      // Finally, check for correct password
      if (INTRUDER_Get_Password_G() == 1)
         {
         System_state_G = DISARMED;
         New_state_G = 1;
         State_call_count_G = 0;
         break;
         }
```

```
         break;
         }

      case INTRUDER:
         {
         if (New_state_G)
            {
            PC_LINK_O_Write_String_To_Buffer("\n** INTRUDER! **");
            New_state_G = 0;
            }

         // Sound the alarm!
         INTRUDER_Sound_Alarm();

         // Keep sounding alarm until we get correct password
         if (INTRUDER_Get_Password_G() == 1)
            {
            System_state_G = DISARMED;
            New_state_G = 1;
            State_call_count_G = 0;
            }

         break;
         }
      }
   }

/* ------------------------------------------------------------------ */

bit INTRUDER_Get_Password_G(void)
   {
   signed char Key;
   tByte Password_G_count = 0;
   tByte i;

   // Update the keypad buffer
   KEYPAD_Update();

   // Are there any new data in the keypad buffer?
   if (KEYPAD_Get_Data_From_Buffer(&Key) == 0)
      {
      // No new data - password can't be correct
      return 0;
      }
```

```
      // If we are here, a key has been pressed

      // How long since last key was pressed?
      // Must be pressed within 50 seconds (assume 50 ms 'tick')
      if (State_call_count_G > 1000)
         {
         // More than 50 seconds since last key
         // - restart the input process
         State_call_count_G = 0;
         Position_G = 0;
         }

      if (Position_G == 0)
         {
         PC_LINK_O_Write_Char_To_Buffer('\n');
         }

      PC_LINK_O_Write_Char_To_Buffer(Key);

      Input_G[Position_G] = Key;

      // Have we got four numbers?
      if ((++Position_G) == 4)
         {
         Position_G = 0;
         Password_G_count = 0;

         // Check the password
         for (i = 0; i < 4; i++)
            {
            if (Input_G[i] == Password_G[i])
               {
               Password_G_count++;
               }
            }
         }

      if (Password_G_count == 4)
         {
         // Password correct
         return 1;
         }
      else
```

```
      {
      // Password NOT correct
      return 0;
      }
   }

/* ------------------------------------------------------------------ */

bit INTRUDER_Check_Window_Sensors(void)
   {
   // Just a single window 'sensor' here
   // - easily extended
   if (Window_sensor_pin == 0)
      {
      // Intruder detected...
      PC_LINK_O_Write_String_To_Buffer("\nWindow damaged");
      return 1;
      }

   // Default
   return 0;
   }

/* ------------------------------------------------------------------ */

bit INTRUDER_Check_Door_Sensor(void)
   {
   // Single door sensor (access route)
   if (Door_sensor_pin == 0)
      {
      // Someone has opened the door...
      PC_LINK_O_Write_String_To_Buffer('\nDoor open');
      return 1;
      }

   // Default
   return 0;
   }

/* ------------------------------------------------------------

void INTRUDER_Sound_Alarm(void)
   {
```

```
    if (Alarm_bit)
       {
       // Alarm connected to this pin
       Sounder_pin = 0;
       Alarm_bit = 0;
       }
    else
       {
       Sounder_pin = 1;
       Alarm_bit = 1;
       }
    }

/*------------------------------------------------------------------*-
  ---- END OF FILE -------------------------------------------------
-*------------------------------------------------------------------*/
```

Listing 10.6 Part of the intruder-alarm code (Keypad.H)

```
/*------------------------------------------------------------------*-

   Keypad.h (v1.00)

-*------------------------------------------------------------------*/

#ifndef _KEY_H
#define _KEY_H

// ------ Public function prototypes ------------------------------
void KEYPAD_Init(void);
void KEYPAD_Update(void);

bit KEYPAD_Get_Data_From_Buffer(char* const);
void KEYPAD_Clear_Buffer(void);

#endif

/*------------------------------------------------------------------*-
  ---- END OF FILE -------------------------------------------------
-*------------------------------------------------------------------*/
```

Listing 10.7 Part of the intruder-alarm code (Keypad.C)

```
/*------------------------------------------------------------------*-

   Keypad.C (v1.00)

   ------------------------------------------------------------------

   Simple library, for a switch-based "keypad".

-*------------------------------------------------------------------*/

#include "Main.h"
#include "Port.h"

#include "Keypad.h"

// ------ Private function prototypes ------------------------------

bit KEYPAD_Scan(char* const);

// ------ Private constants -----------------------------------------

#define KEYPAD_RECV_BUFFER_LENGTH 6

// Any valid character will do - must not match anything on keypad
#define KEYPAD_NO_NEW_DATA (char) '-'

// ------ Private variables -----------------------------------------

static char KEYPAD_recv_buffer[KEYPAD_RECV_BUFFER_LENGTH+1];
// Data in buffer that has been read
static tByte KEYPAD_in_read_index;
// Data in buffer not yet read
static tByte KEYPAD_in_waiting_index;

static char Last_valid_key_G = KEYPAD_NO_NEW_DATA;

static data char Old_key_G;

/*------------------------------------------------------------------

 KEYPAD_Init()

 Init the keypad.

-*------------------------------------------------------------------

void KEYPAD_Init(void)
```

```
   {
   KEYPAD_in_read_index = 0;
   KEYPAD_in_waiting_index = 0;
   }

/*------------------------------------------------------------------*-

  KEYPAD_Update()

  The main 'update' function for the keypad library.

  Must call this function approx every 50 - 200 ms.

-*------------------------------------------------------------------*/
void KEYPAD_Update(void)
   {
   char Key;

   // Scan keypad here...
   if (KEYPAD_Scan(&Key) == 0)
      {
      // No new key data - just return
      return;
      }

   // Want to read into index 0, if old data has been read
   // (simple ~circular buffer)
   if (KEYPAD_in_waiting_index == KEYPAD_in_read_index)
      {
      KEYPAD_in_waiting_index = 0;
      KEYPAD_in_read_index = 0;
      }

   // Load keypad data into buffer
   KEYPAD_recv_buffer[KEYPAD_in_waiting_index] = Key;

   if (KEYPAD_in_waiting_index < KEYPAD_RECV_BUFFER_LENGTH)
      {
      // Increment without overflowing buffer
      KEYPAD_in_waiting_index++;
      }
   }

/*------------------------------------------------------------------*-
```

```
   KEYPAD_Get_Char_From_Buffer()

   The Update function copies data into the keypad buffer.
   This function extracts data from the buffer.

-*------------------------------------------------------------------*/

bit KEYPAD_Get_Data_From_Buffer(char* const pKey)
   {
   // If there are new data in the buffer
   if (KEYPAD_in_read_index < KEYPAD_in_waiting_index)
      {
      *pKey = KEYPAD_recv_buffer[KEYPAD_in_read_index];

      KEYPAD_in_read_index++;

      return 1;
      }

   return 0;
   }

/*------------------------------------------------------------------*-

   KEYPAD_Clear_Buffer()

-*------------------------------------------------------------------*/
void KEYPAD_Clear_Buffer(void)
   {
   KEYPAD_in_waiting_index = 0;
   KEYPAD_in_read_index = 0;
   }

/*------------------------------------------------------------------*-

   KEYPAD_Scan()

   This function is called from scheduled keypad function.

   Must be edited as required to match your key labels.

   Adapt as required!

-*------------------------------------------------------------------*/
bit KEYPAD_Scan(char* const pKey)
   {
```

```
      char Key = KEYPAD_NO_NEW_DATA;

      if (K0 == 0) { Key = '0'; }
      if (K1 == 0) { Key = '1'; }
      if (K2 == 0) { Key = '2'; }
      if (K3 == 0) { Key = '3'; }
      if (K4 == 0) { Key = '4'; }
      if (K5 == 0) { Key = '5'; }
      if (K6 == 0) { Key = '6'; }
      if (K7 == 0) { Key = '7'; }

      if (Key == KEYPAD_NO_NEW_DATA)
         {
         // No key pressed
         Old_key_G = KEYPAD_NO_NEW_DATA;
         Last_valid_key_G = KEYPAD_NO_NEW_DATA;

         return 0; // No new data
         }

      // A key has been pressed: debounce by checking twice
      if (Key == Old_key_G)
         {
         // A valid (debounced) key press has been detected

         // Must be a new key to be valid - no 'auto repeat'
         if (Key != Last_valid_key_G)
            {
            // New key!
            *pKey = Key;
            Last_valid_key_G = Key;

            return 1;
            }
         }

      // No new data
      Old_key_G = Key;
      return 0;
      }

/*------------------------------------------------------------------*-
  ---- END OF FILE -------------------------------------------------
-*------------------------------------------------------------------*/
```

Listing 10.8 Part of the intruder-alarm code (PC_O_T1.H)

```
/*------------------------------------------------------------------*-

   PC_O_T1.h (v1.00)

  ------------------------------------------------------------------

   - see PC_O_T1.c for details.

-*------------------------------------------------------------------*/

#include "PC_O.h"

// ------ Public function prototypes -------------------------------

void PC_LINK_O_Init_T1(const tWord);

/*------------------------------------------------------------------*-
  ---- END OF FILE -------------------------------------------------
-*------------------------------------------------------------------*/
```

Listing 10.9 Part of the intruder-alarm code (PC_O_T1.C)

```
/*------------------------------------------------------------------*-

   PC_O_T1.C (v1.00)

  ------------------------------------------------------------------

   Simple write-only PC link library Version A (generic)
   [Sends data to PC - cannot receive data from PC]

   Uses the UART, and Pin 3.1 (Tx)

   See text for details (Chapter 9).

-*------------------------------------------------------------------*/

#include "Main.h"
#include "PC_O_T1.h"

// ------ Public variable declarations -----------------------------

extern tByte Out_written_index_G;
extern tByte Out_waiting_index_G;

/*------------------------------------------------------------------*-
```

```
   PC_LINK_O_Init_T1()

   This version uses T1 for baud rate generation.

   Uses 8051 (internal) UART hardware

-*------------------------------------------------------------------*/
void PC_LINK_O_Init_T1(const tWord BAUD_RATE)
   {
   PCON &= 0x7F;   //  Set SMOD bit to 0 (don't double baud
                       rates)

   // Receiver disabled
   // 8-bit data, 1 start bit, 1 stop bit, variable baud rate
   (asynchronous)
   SCON = 0x42;

   TMOD |= 0x20; // T1 in mode 2, 8-bit auto reload

   TH1 = (256 - (tByte)((((tLong)OSC_FREQ / 100) * 3125)
   / ((tLong) BAUD_RATE * OSC_PER_INST * 1000)));

   TL1 = TH1;
   TR1 = 1;    // Run the timer
   TI = 1;     // Send first character (dummy)

   // Set up the buffers for reading and writing
   Out_written_index_G = 0;
   Out_waiting_index_G = 0;

   // Interrupt *NOT* enabled
   ES = 0;
   }

/*------------------------------------------------------------------*-
  ---- END OF FILE -------------------------------------------------
-*------------------------------------------------------------------*/
```

Listing 10.10 Part of the intruder-alarm code (PC_O.H)

```
/*------------------------------------------------------------------*-

   PC_O.h (v1.00)

  ------------------------------------------------------------------

   - see PC_O.h for details.
```

```
-*------------------------------------------------------------------*/

// ------ Public function prototypes ---------------------------------

void PC_LINK_O_Write_String_To_Buffer(const char* const);
void PC_LINK_O_Write_Char_To_Buffer(const char);
void PC_LINK_O_Send_Char(const char);
void PC_LINK_O_Update(void);

/*------------------------------------------------------------------*-
  ---- END OF FILE -------------------------------------------------
-*------------------------------------------------------------------*/
```

Listing 10.11 Part of the intruder-alarm code (PC_O.C)

```
/*------------------------------------------------------------------*-

   PC_O.C (v1.00)

  ------------------------------------------------------------------

   Core files for simple write-only PC link library for 8051 family
   [Sends data to PC - cannot receive data from PC]

   Uses the UART, and Pin 3.1 (Tx)

   See text for details (Chapter 9).

-*------------------------------------------------------------------*/

#include "Main.h"
#include "PC_O.h"
#include "Elap_232.h"

// ------ Public variable definitions --------------------------------

tByte Out_written_index_G; // Data in buffer that has been written
tByte Out_waiting_index_G; // Data in buffer not yet written

// ------ Private function prototypes --------------------------------

static void PC_LINK_O_Send_Char(const char);

// ------ Private constants ------------------------------------------

// The transmit buffer length
#define TRAN_BUFFER_LENGTH 20
```

```
// ------ Private variables ----------------------------------------

static tByte Tran_buffer[TRAN_BUFFER_LENGTH];

static tByte Time_count_G = 0;

/*------------------------------------------------------------------*-

  PC_LINK_O_Update()

  Sends next character from the software transmit buffer

  NOTE: Output-only library (Cannot receive chars)

  Uses on-chip UART hardware.

-*------------------------------------------------------------------*/
void PC_LINK_O_Update(void)
   {
   // Deal with transmit bytes here
   //
   // Are there any data ready to send?
   if (Out_written_index_G < Out_waiting_index_G)
      {
      PC_LINK_O_Send_Char(Tran_buffer[Out_written_index_G]);

      Out_written_index_G++;
      }
   else
      {
      // No data to send - just reset the buffer index
      Out_waiting_index_G = 0;
      Out_written_index_G = 0;
      }
   }

/*------------------------------------------------------------------*-

  PC_LINK_O_Write_String_To_Buffer()

  Copies a (null terminated) string to the character buffer.
  (The contents of the buffer are then passed over the serial link)

-*------------------------------------------------------------------*/
```

```
void PC_LINK_O_Write_String_To_Buffer(const char* const STR_PTR)
   {
   tByte i = 0;

   while (STR_PTR[i] != '\0')
      {
      PC_LINK_O_Write_Char_To_Buffer(STR_PTR[i]);
      i++;
      }
   }

/*------------------------------------------------------------------*-

  PC_LINK_O_Write_Char_To_Buffer()

  Stores a character in the 'write' buffer, ready for
  later transmission

-*------------------------------------------------------------------*/
void PC_LINK_O_Write_Char_To_Buffer(const char CHARACTER)
   {
   // Write to the buffer *only* if there is space
   // (No error reporting in this simple library...)
   if (Out_waiting_index_G < TRAN_BUFFER_LENGTH)
      {
      Tran_buffer[Out_waiting_index_G] = CHARACTER;
      Out_waiting_index_G++;
      }
   }

/*------------------------------------------------------------------*-

  PC_LINK_O_Send_Char()

  Based on Keil sample code, with added (loop) timeouts.
  Implements Xon / Off control.

  Uses on-chip UART hardware.

-*------------------------------------------------------------------*/
void PC_LINK_O_Send_Char(const char CHARACTER)
   {
   tLong Timeout1 = 0;

   if (CHARACTER == '\n')
```

```
      {
      Timeout1 = 0;
      while ((++Timeout1) && (TI == 0));

      if (Timeout1 == 0)
         {
         // UART did not respond - error
         // No error reporting in this simple library...
         return;
         }

      TI = 0;
      SBUF = 0x0D; // Output CR
      }

   Timeout1 = 0;
   while ((++Timeout1) && (TI == 0));

   if (Timeout1 == 0)
      {
      // UART did not respond - error
      // No error reporting in this simple library...
      return;
      }

   TI = 0;

   SBUF = CHARACTER;
   }

/*------------------------------------------------------------------*-
  ---- END OF FILE -------------------------------------------------
-*------------------------------------------------------------------*/
```

Listing 10.12 Part of the intruder-alarm code (Simple_EOS.H)

```
/*------------------------------------------------------------------*-

   Simple_EOS.H (v1.00)

  ------------------------------------------------------------------

   - see Simple_EOS.C for details.

-*------------------------------------------------------------------*/
```

```
void sEOS_Init_Timer2(const tByte TICK_MS);
void sEOS_Go_To_Sleep(void);

/*------------------------------------------------------------------*-
  ---- END OF FILE -------------------------------------------------
-*------------------------------------------------------------------*/
```

Listing 10.13 Part of the intruder-alarm code (Simple_EOS.C)

```
/*------------------------------------------------------------------*-

   Simple_EOS.C (v1.00)

   ------------------------------------------------------------------

   Main file for Simple Embedded Operating System (sEOS) for 8051.

   Part of intruder alarm case study (Chapter 10).

-*------------------------------------------------------------------*/

#include "Main.H"
#include "Simple_EOS.H"

#include "PC_O.H"
#include "Intruder.H"

// ------ Private variable definitions ------------------------------
static tByte Call_count_G;


/*------------------------------------------------------------------*-

  sEOS_ISR()

  Invoked periodically by Timer 2 overflow:
  see sEOS_Init_Timer2() for timing details.

-*------------------------------------------------------------------*/
void sEOS_ISR() interrupt INTERRUPT_Timer_2_Overflow
   {
   // Must manually reset the T2 flag
   TF2 = 0;
   //===== USER CODE - Begin ==================================
   // Call RS-232 update function every 5ms
   PC_LINK_O_Update();
```

```
   // This ISR is called every 5 ms
   // - only want to update intruder every 50 ms
   if (++Call_count_G == 10)
      {
      // Time to update intruder alarm
      Call_count_G = 0;

      // Call intruder update function
      INTRUDER_Update();
      }
   //===== USER CODE - End =====================================
   }

/*------------------------------------------------------------------*-

  sEOS_Init_Timer2()

  Sets up Timer 2 to drive the simple EOS.

  Parameter gives tick interval in MILLISECONDS.

  Max tick interval is ~60ms (12 MHz oscillator).

  Note: Precise tick intervals are only possible with certain
  oscillator / tick interval combinations. If timing is important,
  you should check the timing calculations manually.

-*------------------------------------------------------------------*/
void sEOS_Init_Timer2(const tByte TICK_MS)
   {
   tLong Inc;
   tWord Reload_16;
   tByte Reload_08H, Reload_08L;

   // Timer 2 is configured as a 16-bit timer,
   // which is automatically reloaded when it overflows
   T2CON = 0x04; // Load Timer 2 control register

   // Number of timer increments required (max 65536)
   Inc = ((tLong)TICK_MS * (OSC_FREQ/1000)) / (tLong)OSC_PER_INST;

   // 16-bit reload value
   Reload_16 = (tWord) (65536UL - Inc);

   // 8-bit reload values (High & Low)
```

```
   Reload_08H = (tByte)(Reload_16 / 256);
   Reload_08L = (tByte)(Reload_16 % 256);

   // Used for manually checking timing (in simulator)
   //P2 = Reload_08H;
   //P3 = Reload_08L;

   TH2    = Reload_08H; // Load T2 high byte
   RCAP2H = Reload_08H; // Load T2 reload capt. reg. high byte
   TL2    = Reload_08L; // Load T2 low byte
   RCAP2L = Reload_08L; // Load T2 reload capt. reg. low byte

   // Timer 2 interrupt is enabled, and ISR will be called
   // whenever the timer overflows.
   ET2 = 1;

   // Start Timer 2 running
   TR2 = 1;

   EA = 1;          // Globally enable interrupts
   }

/*------------------------------------------------------------------*-

  sEOS_Go_To_Sleep()

  This operating system enters 'idle mode' between clock ticks
  to save power. The next clock tick will return the processor
  to the normal operating state.

-*------------------------------------------------------------------*/
void sEOS_Go_To_Sleep(void)
   {
   PCON |= 0x01;      // Enter idle mode (generic 8051 version)
   }

/*------------------------------------------------------------------*-
  ---- END OF FILE -------------------------------------------------
-*------------------------------------------------------------------*/
```

10.6 Conclusions

This case study has illustrated most of the key features of embedded C, as discussed throughout the earlier chapters in this book.

chapter 11

Where do we go from here?

11.1 Introduction

In this closing chapter, we review the material that has been presented throughout this introductory book, and consider some further topics that you will need to consider if you want to learn more about embedded systems.

11.2 Have we achieved our aims?

As we stated in the preface, this book was intended to provide an introduction to embedded software for people who:

- Already knew how to write software for 'desktop' computer systems.
- Were familiar with a C-based language (Java, C++ or C).
- Wanted to learn how C is used in practical embedded systems.

In previous chapters, we have covered a lot of essential material. To summarize:

- We have considered the choice of processor and programming language for embedded systems.
- We have shown how to exploit key object-oriented design and programming features in embedded C programs, with the aim of making it easier to re-use code in subsequent projects.
- We have described the Super Loop software architecture used in many simple embedded applications.

- We have described a simple embedded operating system, suitable for use in a wide range of embedded applications. This operating system, driven by timer interrupts, provides very accurate control over system timing but uses less than 1% of the available processor power.
- We have explored techniques for controlling the state of individual port pins.
- We have examined the reading of port pins and mechanical switches.
- We have described how to use the 8051's serial port.
- We have presented a case study, to illustrate how all of the above material comes together in a real application.

11.3 Suggestions for further study

If you are still keen to learn more about embedded systems, then some suggestions for further study are made in this section.

a) Hardware issues

This introductory book has used a hardware simulator to introduce key aspects of embedded software. This is a good way to begin work in this area, not least because it allows you to concentrate on getting the software right without having to worry about possible wiring errors.

However, we have gone as far as we can with a simulator. Some aspects of hardware cannot be ignored if you want to progress further in this area. Some key areas that you need to address are:

- Designs for oscillator and reset circuits.
- Techniques for connecting external ROM and RAM memory.
- Interface circuits suitable for controlling low- and high-voltage DC and AC loads.

b) LCD and LED displays

Many embedded applications make use of LCD or LED displays. These require particular programming techniques that we have not been able to consider in this introductory book.

c) Monitoring and control

Many embedded applications serve monitoring or control functions. This requires – for example – the use of analog-to-digital converters, digital-to-analog converters, pulse-width modulation, and suitable control algorithms (such as the ubiquitous PID algorithm).

d) Operating systems

The simple operating system (OS) presented in this book is able to control a single periodic task. We have not been able to consider OSs suitable for use with more than one task.

In addition, a drawback with the simple OS presented in this book was that – in response to a task longer than the tick interval – the system would 'lose ticks' (Figure 11.1).

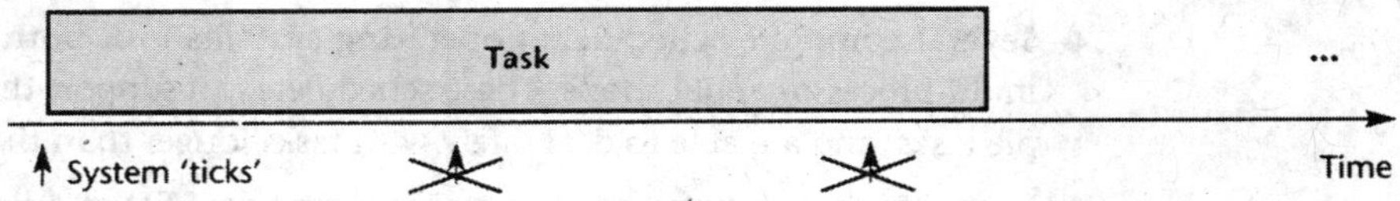

FIGURE 11.1 Losing ticks as a result of executing a 22 ms task using an OS with a 10 ms tick interval

This type of OS is not suitable for use in high-reliability applications.

e) Multi-processor systems

All of the applications we have considered in this book have contained only one embedded processor. However, in practice, an intruder alarm system (of the type considered in Chapter 10) might well contain 6 processors, distributed in the various sensors and the control panel, while a modern car will typically contain 50 embedded processors. Overall, multi-processor applications are becoming increasingly common. Such processors may be linked together by means of a popular serial standard such as RS-485 or the CAN bus.

11.4 *Patterns for Time-Triggered Embedded Systems*

If you are looking for a more advanced book on embedded systems after you finish this book, then *Patterns for Time-Triggered Embedded Systems* (*PTTES*) may be of interest.[32]

PTTES is a large (1000-page) book that covers all of the topics highlighted in the previous section. The overall approach is the same as this introductory book, but *PTTES* covers this material at a more advanced level, and in more depth than was appropriate here. *PTTES* also discusses hardware design for microcontroller-based systems. In total, more than 70 patterns are described, complete with guidelines to help you apply these techniques in your own projects: full source code for all of the patterns is included on the *PTTES* CD.

The patterns described in *PTTES* include:

- Hardware patterns describing reset, oscillator and memory circuits. Numerous complete hardware schematics for 8051-based designs are included.
- Several complete schedulers ('operating systems') for both single-processor and multi-processor applications. These schedulers can support the scheduling of multiple tasks, and are able to deal safely with tasks longer than the system tick interval.
- User-interface designs using switches, keypads, LED and liquid-crystal displays.
- Patterns for RS-232, RS-485, CAN, SPI and I^2C serial communications.
- Patterns for analog-to-digital and digital-to-analog conversion using both on-chip and external hardware.
- Patterns for pulse-width modulation (PWM).
- Patterns for control-system design (including implementations of industry-standard 'PID' algorithms).

11.5 *Embedded Operating Systems*

Like the present book, *PTTES* focuses on the use of the 8051 microcontroller. As we discussed in Chapter 7 (Section 7.5), the co-operative, time-triggered operating systems introduced in this book are used with a very wide range of embedded systems.

If you would like to learn more about the design and implementation of operating systems for embedded environments, then a forthcoming book – *Embedded Operating Systems* (*EOS*) – may be of interest.[33]

32. Pont, M.J. (2001) *Patterns for Time-Triggered Embedded Systems: Building reliable applications with the 8051 family of microcontroller*, ACM Press, New York. [ISBN 0-201-33138-1].
33. Pont, M.J. (in preparation) *Embedded Operating Systems*, Addison-Wesley, UK. Due for publication January, 2004.

EOS will describe the design and implementation of co-operative, time-triggered, operating systems for a broad range of 8-, 16- and 32-bit processors.

11.6 Conclusions

In this closing chapter we have reviewed the material that has been presented throughout this introductory book, and considered some further topics that you will need to consider if you want to learn more about embedded systems. This brings us to the end of 'Embedded C'.

Index

Installing the Keil software on a Windows PC

To make full use of the material in this book, you will need to install the Keil C51 development tools: these are included on the CD-ROM.

To install this software, please proceed as follows:

- Insert the CD-ROM in your computer's CD drive.
- On most computers, the CD will "auto run", and you will see the Keil installation menu. If the mènu does not appear, manually "double click" on the Setup icon, in the root directory: you will then see the Keil menu.
- On the Keil menu, please select **"Install Evaluation Software"**. (You will not require a licence number to install this software.)
- Follow the installation instructions as they appear.

Please note: these instructions assume that you are using a "Windows" PC (that is, a machine running Windows 95 or later). Some guidance on the use of the example projects in this book with the Linux operating system is given on p. 303.

Loading the projects

The example projects for this book are **NOT** loaded automatically when you install the Keil compiler.

These files are stored on the CD in a directory "/Pont". The files are arranged by chapter: for example, the project discussed in Chapter 3 is in the directory "/Pont/Ch03_00-Hello".

Rather than using the projects on the CD (where changes cannot be saved), please copy the files from the CD onto an appropriate directory on your hard disk. Note: you will need to change the file properties after copying: files transferred from the CD will be 'read only'.

Working with Linux

The Keil compiler will not operate under the Linux operating system.

If you require a compiler for Linux, you may like to consider the SDCC compiler. Details are included on this WWW site:

`http://sdcc.sourceforge.net/`

Please note that neither the publisher nor the author can provide support for this compiler.

Licensing Agreement